Reviewers recommend

DYING DIGNIFIED

I hope everyone who cares f⸱   families will read
and inwardly digest this f⸱

Format makes it easy to   ⸱nce. . . .

Well-written and insightful   value to all who affect the
care of the dying, professiona⸱   y persons alike.

Virginia Major Thomas, RN, MA
Geriatric Nursing, September/October 1984
©American Journal of Nursing Company
Reprinted with permission

This book has so much to commend it that most physicians will find
many areas that will broaden their knowledge and clinical skills. . . .

Provides many illustrations of clinical care that help [in discussing]
painful subjects with patients and their families. . . .

The authors define and illustrate with sensitivity the complex personal
and ethical issues that arise. . . .

Thoroughness of this book permits it to be used both as a resource
volume and relevant to everyday clinical practice.

Gerald Alder, MD
Massachusetts General Hospital, Boston
Annals of Internal Medicine, Vol. 101, September 1984

DYING DIGNIFIED
The Health Professional's Guide to Care

Thomas Andrew Gonda, M.D.

John Edward Ruark, M.D.

Photographs by Mark Tuschman

ADDISON-WESLEY PUBLISHING COMPANY
Medical Division • Menlo Park, California
Reading, Massachusetts • London • Amsterdam
Don Mills, Ontario • Sydney

From TAG   to my wife Elizabeth,
my children Paul, Bill, and Lynn,
and their families;

from JER   to my wife Terry Stein,
and our family to come.

Sponsoring editor: Richard W. Mixter
Production coordinator: Pat Franklin Waldo
Book designer: Leigh McLellan
Manuscript editor: Lyn Dupré
Photographer: Mark Tuschman

Library of Congress Cataloging in Publication Data

Gonda, Thomas Andrew, 1921–
    Dying Dignified: The Health
    Professional's Guide to Care
    Bibliography: p.
    Includes index.
    1. Terminal care.   I. Ruark, John Edward, 1951–
II. Title. [DNLM: 1. Attitude to death. 2. Death.
3. Hospices. 4. Terminal care—Psychology. BF 789.D4
G636g]
R726.8.G66   1984   362.1'75   83–11877
ISBN 0-201-10603-5

  CDEFGHIJ–MA– 8987

Addison-Wesley Publishing Company
Medical Division
2725 Sand Hill Road, Menlo Park, California 94025

Foreword

Most of us share the memory of a golden age, when the community was a world of extended families and shared values. From birth to death, our forebears (in this dream) passed their lives in the midst of family and friends. Familiar processes gave meaning and completeness to the critical events of life. This was especially true when it came time to die.

She saw at once in her father's face that now death was very near. About his nostrils the skin was snow-white, his lips and the circles around his great eyes were bluish, the hair had fallen apart, and lay in damp strands over the broad dewy forehead. But he was in his full senses now, and spoke clearly though slowly and in a weak voice.

The house-folk went forward to his bed, one by one, and Lavrans took each of them by the hand, thanked them for their service, bade them farewell, and prayed them to forgive him if he had ever wronged them in any wise; he prayed them too, to think of him with a prayer for his soul. Then he said farewell to his kindred. He bade his daughters bend down so that he might kiss them, and he called down the blessing of God and of all the saints upon them. . . .

Last of all, Lavrans bade farewell to his wife. They whispered some words to each other that none could hear, and exchanged a kiss in the sight of all, as was fitting and seemly, since death was in the room.

Kristin Lavransdatter*

The contemporary Western world provides us with a very different reality. Our families are broken and scattered across the land. We

*Undset, S. 1929. Kristin Lavransdatter. Nobel Prize Edition. New York: Alfred A. Knopf Inc., p. 246.

are people of diverse beliefs and customs. When we complicate the process of dying with complex technology, and when eighty percent of deaths now take place in hospitals or nursing homes, we encounter a setting in which death is often lonely and bitter. Many of the tasks that should be finished become difficult to accomplish.

My good friends Drs. Gonda and Ruark have written a most helpful book for clinicians who must often substitute in many of the roles that previously had been performed exclusively by family and friends. Their book grew out of their daily experiences in a large academic medical center, as well as their thoughtful observations of the acquaintance with death of close friends. Health care professionals have received little guidance in the roles society expects them to play with dying persons. From this exposition they stand to gain the self-assurance to deal sensitively and positively with patients and families.

Many important ethical issues related to death and dying are currently debated. The authors of this book have wisely focussed their concerns on more practical psychologic, institutional, cultural, and demographic facets of dying, leaving some controversial ethical problems such as abortion and euthanasia to be analyzed in other fora. I only wish I had had this book before I began my internship nearly forty years ago. But regardless of the stage of our careers, we can all benefit from this wise treatise.

Count D. Gibson, Jr., M.D.
Chairman and Professor, Department of Family,
Community, and Preventive Medicine
Stanford University School of Medicine
Stanford, California

Preface

Our Approach

When we were first asked to write a book on the care of dying persons, our publishers intended it to be part of a series directed mainly toward primary care physicians. However, as the work evolved, it became increasingly clear that other professionals had equal, if not greater, influence on the quality of the experiences of patients and families faced with life-threatening illnesses. Because we regard a team-oriented approach to be central to optimal management of difficult health care situations, we have shifted our target audience accordingly. This book is now intended to help the wide range of professionals and laypersons who deeply affect the care of dying patients. We hope that this brief history will allow readers to understand any remaining artifacts of our original orientation.

But, why write a practical guide directed toward those who care for persons who are confronted with death? Our answer to this query springs primarily from our own experiences with people who are dying or grieving. What we have found is a health care system that, in spite of its own best intentions, too often fails to provide optimal humane care for these most vulnerable clients. Such failures have their roots in a variety of causes that we shall explore at length. It is our conviction, however, that those working with the dying and grieving are fully capable of recognizing and changing behaviors and attitudes that contribute to problems in terminal care. In this book we develop some practical guidelines for correcting these difficulties, as well as a framework for understanding the complex factors that contribute to them.

Our design is to acquaint readers, professional and lay alike, with a complete but down-to-earth structure intended to promote common awareness, understanding, and ultimately a more dignified experience for everyone involved with a death. Then, for those who are interested in the concepts underlying this approach, the second half of the book reviews relevant information and principles central to a balanced understanding of dying in America. We feel that this organization is particularly suited to the study of a topic whose essence is both psychosocial and diagnostic or technical.

Scope and Sequence

To emphasize the strongly clinical orientation of this book, we begin in Part 1 by presenting four actual case scenarios involving terminal illness. Each of them is written by an individual who was on the receiving end of the health care system, either as a patient or a family member. Throughout this work we will refer back to these cases for examples. In our minds, these poignant statements provide the clinical thread that ties the remainder of our approach together.

Parts 2, 3, and 4 contain chapters addressing specific areas of practical concern. Part 2 is devoted to psychological and interpersonal considerations. These include defining problems in communication that commonly arise in terminal care settings, and proposing some solutions. In Part 3 we present a detailed chronologic survey of a generalized terminal illness. This is followed in Part 4 by special clinical topics, including Death and Children, Suicide, and the Hospice.

In Parts 5 and 6 we review a number of issues that form the basis for our way of thinking about death in the United States. This is ushered in by an exploration of the nature and origin of problems in terminal care, followed by a survey of relevant demographic data. Finally, we address the sociocultural foundations for our approach.

Our Intent

We do not presume to lecture experienced clinicians on how to conduct themselves with their patients. After all, the particular personalities of individual professionals are a precious part of the gift they bring to those whom they serve. We are also aware, however, that many of our colleagues feel uncomfortable and ill-prepared to deal with this difficult area. If our outline of some sensible ways of thinking about problems involving death can lessen this uneasiness to any significant degree, then our goals will be met.

Once individual personalities and emotions come strongly into play, as is likely when death is confronted, management suggestions may apply only loosely to any given situation. At the outset, we advise readers to look over the various ideas and techniques presented, and to try them on for size. Some of our suggestions may not fit the personal style of any particular clinician, without there being a lack on anyone's part. Clearly, any attempt to use an approach that creates uneasiness or that is poorly understood will more likely cause problems than solve them.

Our hope is that this volume may be used as a practical guide to issues arising in the daily course of terminal care management. In addition, we attempt to provide the beginnings of a more scholarly survey of the entire field, with a guide to relevant literature for those desiring to delve further.

We add one further note regarding style. Throughout this book, the word "family" should be taken to include any person whose intimate involvement affects, or is affected by, the patient's illness. Also, the term "professional" should be understood as shorthand for "health care professional."

Acknowledgments

We are grateful to the Levison-Brittan fund for financial support during the writing and revision of this work, and to the following individuals for invaluable help and criticism:

Louis Baer, M.D.
Phil Broughton
Count Gibson, M.D.
Ellen Gottheil, M.D.
Dave Kaplan, Ph.D., L.C.S.W.
Steve Katz, Ph.D.
Peggy Keeler, R.N., M.S.

Barbara McCoard, M.D.
Dave Spiegel, M.D.
Terry Stein, M.D.
Liza Taft, R.N., M.S.
Marion Tanous
Ernle Young, Ph.D.

Thomas Andrew Gonda
John Edward Ruark

Contents

DYING DIGNIFIED
The Health Professional's Guide to Care

PART 1

Case Studies

We begin our practical approach to terminal care with four personal statements. Each of them is written by an individual who was on the receiving end of the health care system, either as a patient or a family member. One is a former director of health education for the United States Public Health Service, and the secretary of an important philanthropic foundation. The second is a lawyer and sculptor. The third is an undergraduate premedical student. The last contributor was a physician, as well as an important pioneer in this very field of thanatology. Throughout this work, we will reexamine these cases by referring the reader back to specific page numbers in our marginal notes. Through this vehicle we provide a clinical thread that ties our observations directly to the experiences of patients and their families.

Case A: Ann O'Toole Broughton's Last Illness

These are excerpts of notes dictated by Philip Broughton shortly after the death of his wife Ann in the spring of 1974 following an illness of less than a year with cancer. Three close friends suggested that he attempt this project. They hoped that it would be a catharsis, a sorting out of the complex emotions of grief. In his words, "It began as a tribute, a memorial essay to Ann. It developed as a record of the vagaries and successes of our system of medical care. It persisted in the hope that its observations might do a service to the medical profession."

The authors are indebted to Mr. Philip Broughton for his permission to publish these notes.

Foreword

As I dictate this, specific items may be subjective, somewhat accidental in their impingement on my mind. This essay is reconstructed in part from doctor and hospital bills, in part from memory. One makes no notes at the time, because one does not expect that such a record will be needed. The reader should allow for the coloring of feelings, even of misunderstanding.

I was the husband of a patient, and that overrides any small claim I might have to professional objectivity. I have, however, adequate competence to describe the hangups of this husband of this particular patient. I can report intimately—perhaps even more intimately than the doctors themselves—what the patient was saying and thinking throughout her illness.

Coping with dying. (34)

Depression. (125)

If I had made a daily record, it would have had a rather manic-depressive pattern. There were days when I was grasping at some straw of hope, days when I plunged into despair, a number of times when I was depressed. I would write something only to discover somewhat later that my whole concern was one which resulted from a complete misunderstanding as to what was going on.

About Ann

Ann and I were together for 47 years, and I doubt if two people ever were closer—intellectually, emotionally, or physically. Any reference to our sex life may seem a diversion in this context, but it is relevant; our ongoing romance symbolized the vibrancy of our relationship. I could hardly think of us as two people; we were as one.

Interpersonal death. (30)

Ann was an active person. She swam 20 lengths of the pool every day. During World War II she was a member of a team that taught safety swimming to nonswimming soldiers who would be carried on transports. She taught horseback riding as well. When in her thirties, a former Czarist Cavalry Officer taught her to mount and dismount a horse in full motion. Diet, exercise, swimming, hiking—she took care of herself in every way.

On the day of her first admission to the hospital on July 30, 1973, she went over to the pool; she admitted that she did not quite feel like it, but did not know when she would get another swim. She did her twenty lengths at twelve noon. It was to be the last swim of her life. By chance, in the adjoining lane was her admitting physician, a neurologist. At about two-thirty she entered the hospital. When she was discharged on August 8, she could not walk a hundred yards without feeling utterly exhausted, and could only walk safely with someone at her arm at all times.

As for her interests, in Pennsylvania she had been active in civic affairs, vice president of the League of Women Voters, and State Public

Health Chairman. She was the sort of person that organizations seemed to tag as their president when they were in a state of turmoil. Somehow or other the tensions would soon disappear, and the organization would be clicking again.

Denial of aging. (286)

I give Ann's background simply to indicate what kind of person she was. It gives dimension to her internist's advice to her early in June of 1973: "Never tell anyone your age. Say you are over fifty. Few of my patients of that age are in as fine health as you are." This is the little lady who began rubbing her left cheek in June, wondering if she had an abscessed tooth, and went to her dentist to check on it. All through the following months, while the physicians were going inside her head—including four arteriograms, and two pneumoencephalograms—all the while she rubbed her left cheek, saying "It's right there."

Diagnosis at Last

"Diagnostic enigma" was the most common phrase I heard for four months. Finally, there was the X-ray film of November 2, the "foggy" reading of November 5, the physical findings of November 7 by an otolaryngologist, and the operation of November 9. There it was, half an inch from where she had been rubbing all these months, a primary cancer in the area of the nasal pharynx.

You can hardly blame a layman for wondering, no matter how logical the explanations, about squamous cell cancer not showing up on the X-ray films. Way back in June, Ann thought she had an infected tooth on the left side, and had gone to the dentist on her own initiative. Over and over again, both in the Community Hospital and the University Hospital, she had rubbed her left cheek and said "It's right here." To use a metaphor, it was like a pilot who looked so hard at his instruments that he forgot to look out the window and see that there was another plane passing in front of him. And who, furthermore, ignored the warning of a mere passenger who urged him to look.

Blaming the doctor. (164)

What greater peace of mind for me if someone had had the courtesy to look in July.

The success of the radiation to Ann's left pharynx showed that the primary cancer in that area yielded readily to the radiation. I can only assume that had anyone only heeded Ann a little earlier, the cancer might never have had a chance to travel to her thyroid and kidneys.

Quality of Life and the Process of Dying

I think I knew, deep in my heart, that the odds were very much against us. I imposed a few rules, a few disciplines, on myself. I would never utter to her any word which carried a negative connotation. I would

Loving communications. (142)

try to give her confidence. Above all, I would make her feel that, if she pulled through, she would know that love had helped her to make it. If she did not survive, she would go right through to the end knowing that she was the best loved person in the world.

Family helplessness. (51, 105)

Yet, as I did this, I sometimes felt a certain selfishness. She was in such pain, but she seemed to realize what I was doing. I can remember her once saying, "You are trying awfully hard, aren't you?" But from September on she would sometimes say, "This is too hard. Can't you just let me slip away?" I could not do that, and yet I had a guilty realization that I would want someone to do just that if something like her disease ever hits me. I hope I will be allowed to slip away very promptly. Consider this an order to all friends and family: no medical heroics.

Sensing emotions. (54)

A lump appeared at Ann's thyroid and another in her inguinal area, and there were signs that a lump was appearing above her kidney. When the first biopsy showed the spread of malignancy, I knew. My own physician said in the most kindly and understanding way that I really should pray that my little lady would not last too long.

Minor medical heroics. (101)

The catheter for her hyperalimentation broke and an attempt was made to replace it. The surgeon failed to execute this properly, and confessed to me that he felt a special guilt about the procedure because of the improbability that it would do Ann any great service. In other words, there were incidents where physicians recognized that their interventions simply prolonged Ann's agony.

Prolonging dying. (112)

The oncologist into whose hands the case finally fell was trying to bring Ann's weight up to the point where she could stand the necessary chemotherapy. Having dropped from 138 to 105, and finally to 90 pounds, she was a pretty fragile person, and the antimetabolic character of the anticancer chemicals would have been devastating.

Better communication. (62)

On the Saturday before Ann's death, he came out to evaluate the care she was getting at home to be sure there was nothing lacking. He was pleased with our arrangements. He stayed for nearly two hours, discussing the whole nature of Ann's case. It was a good discussion—in depth, rather than simply crisp, professional decision making.

Nutritional support. (122)

Ann, he said, was hypermetabolic. Every attempt to build her normal cells also fed the spreading cancer cells. No chemotherapy was to take place. We could not avoid the feeling that somehow this treatment would sentence Ann to a long, long torture, and that our love would be somehow transmuted into a kind of selfishness. But it was not always so. At times, Ann would say in her wonderful trusting way, "Doctor, you'll make me well, won't you?" What light does one follow?

Denial. (52)

Preterminal phase. (35, 115, 122)

As the final two months approached, Ann had lost control of her voice and many of her bodily functions (for example, she had to be diapered). She used a little gadget to amplify sound, because she could not speak above a whisper. The gadget consisted of a small microphone which could be held either to her lips or against her throat. But the radiation had apparently so altered the power of her vocal cords to articulate that even with this she found communication difficult.

Autopsy. (157)

As the autopsy confirmed, her brain was never affected. I could tell by the expression in her eyes that she understood the things going on about her, had ideas about them. Her complete inability to communicate, either in writing or by voice, must have been a terrifying frustration. All her food had to be blenderized; she got no satisfaction from eating.

Institutional death. (245, 290)

Death at home. (208)

Shortly before Ann's death, her oncologist proposed sending her to the convalescent home next door to the hospital. She had a terrible sense out of such places, where people were sent to be warehoused to die. "You would not," she said, "send me to a place like that, would you?" Plainly, I would not. Moreover, our home was so organized that I thought we could do just as well or better there. At home I could surround her with her flowers and her birds, and give her a sense of this place which she had so enjoyed, tucked away as it is in a forest. Quail were mating. Somewhere in the neighborhood pairs of both downy and acorn woodpeckers were raising families and came daily to the suet. The varied thrush were still there in large numbers, later than usual—waiting for Ann, I said. She had planned to attract them and had worked to make the little area around her a nature sanctuary.

Fortunately, I was retired and could make Ann my sole business. There was nothing else that I would have found any satisfaction in doing. I read aloud to her. We re-read Aldo Leopold's *Sand County Almanac* completely. As the months went on, I read news less and less. Things that required no reaction were best to read, especially after we got to the point where she could no longer respond. Anything that required response, of course, produced frustration. War and Watergate are not restful. We had often said that Nixon's was a lovely Administration from which to be three thousand miles away.

Emotional swings. (99, 113)

Still, for some months before the end, she would say to one of her doctors, pleadingly, "You will take care of me, won't you? You will make me well?" She placed herself in their hands, a supplicant reaching out for life. Yet in other moods she would say, "This is just too hard. Just let me slip away."

Lifetime coping patterns. (219)

She was so concerned with not causing any extra trouble for the nurses or attendants that she would attempt things herself which she could not do. Once she even tried to clean the floor of food that she had spilled. One of the doctors kidded her, saying, "Ann, if you had your way you'd make your own bed so as not to put the nurses to any trouble." But that was Ann. She was an independent spirit who simply was not going to put people out or be dependent if she could help it.

Christmas was trying for Ann. Our house was so arranged that

Humanization of dying.
(207, 218)

Family conflicts in letting
go. (138)

Neonatal death. (187)

Emotional shockwave. (228)

Alternatives to burial. (158,
269)

she could have a great deal of privacy. But the mere sense of having so many people around whom she loved and with whom she wanted to communicate, given that she could not do so effectively, was a trial. I hope that love and flowers and birds and the sense that she was home and not in an institution helped. Yet I think that my little lady was rather truly robbed of any sense of personal dignity during those last months as she lost her ability to communicate and her control of bodily functions. One cannot avoid the sense that we have a system of medicine which may encourage torture through unsatisfactory and undignified extensions of dying. What of the ethics? Should the patient be given the choice? Should the patient be subject to the decisions of loved ones who cannot bear to let her or him go? What do we do about those cases where, under current law, the patient's own choice is facilitated by someone close to him or her, when that person does it only at the personal risk of criminal prosecution or suicide?

Ann and I had a confrontation with such questions years ago: a defective, absolutely nonviable baby. It never reached the point where we were forced to make a choice. We have always believed in and inwardly thanked the obstetrician, who practiced no heroics. Yet, I can recall that Ann cried out in the night years later, remembering even after two decades: "Today would have been his birthday. He would have been twenty-one."

Ann wished to be cremated, and wanted her ashes sprinkled at sea out beyond her beloved Point Lobos. That is what we did. There is no headstone, save that most wonderful piece of natural statuary in the world, pointing into the sunset sea.

Impact of the Health System

Nowhere along the line did either of us have any professional criticism of any of the physicians with whom we dealt. Whatever their mistakes, they were of the variety only hindsight can identify. Every person was someone you would be delighted to know socially and intellectually outside his or her professional sphere.

Medical teaching. (103)

Need to feel useful. (103)

Lateral pass. (91, 243)

The nurses, technologists, and attendants were superb. The University Hospital situation reminded Ann of our teaching days when she always had a houseful of students around. Most of her doctors were about the age of our son, who is a law professor, and this held for her a hope and a pride; her hope that she had made some contribution that might help somebody else. That was always Ann.

An aspect of Ann's care that vastly confused her has to do with the organization of medicine. There seemed to be such a succession of doctors, such a lateral passing from one to another—from internist to neurologist, from local hospital to University Medical Center. Each physician would emphasize to her that she was his or her patient now. This was to reassure and to establish our confidence, but it also connoted a break in continuity, a feeling that nobody was in charge. Although her own physician conscientiously kept daily tabs on her through daily reading of her chart, he told me he did not want to run up her bill by looking in frequently. I suppose that in the days before computers and insurance, things could be done humanly; a greeting, a smile, a pat on the cheek, any morale booster, did not have to be accounted for on the same monetary basis as a medical procedure.

I was happy that I went the 90 miles in the ambulance with her and could hold her hand. She was sedated and very ill. This was the period when carcinomatosis seemed the probable diagnosis. When in her vague consciousness she would frown or her mouth would hang open, I would pat her hand or squeeze it. I held it all the way, and at these little acts of endearment her mouth would close again and the wrinkles would go away. I think if she had just been taken there with attendants, no matter how well trained, she would have been deeply traumatized. She would have felt that she was simply being shipped out of town. Yet, strangely, someone at Community Hospital had told me I would not be allowed to go with her. When she was in the vehicle I was told by the attendants that I would be welcome. I am very glad that I found this out in time.

The only incident of friction in the hospital occurred when one of the attendants at Community Hospital was adamant about strapping her down so she would not fall out of bed. Her sense of confinement was more than she could bear. At University Hospital one night, she crawled out of a very complicated arrangement. Then they put up a cot for me in her room. For three or four nights I slept beside her bed so that if she did attempt to get out I would be there to help her.

Her sense of a kaleidoscope, that nobody was really the quarterback or captain of the team, would not go away. Sometimes each doctor made it quite clear that, for this phase, he or she was the boss. Surgeons were quickly swept aside after they had performed their technical services. Anesthesiologists and blood people passed in a shadowy haze. This feeling was much more acute at Community than it was at University Hospital. There, in the medical school pattern, the doctors operated in a team, and they would visit in a group. Ann comprehended and accepted the team from professor to student. There was a sense of discussion about the case—we felt in on it. Participation reassured her.

We also happened to have had for eighteen years a team of physicians in Pittsburgh that were a genuine group practice. Though Harry had been our original doctor, the way they worked any one of them might say, "You know, Bert (or Carl, or Jim) has seen a case like this very recently; I'd like him to take a look at you too." We might easily

Supporting via touch. (67)

Family support. (108)

Fear of abandonment. (91)

Incorrect information. (225)

No quarterback. (91, 242)

Participation in decision-making. (48)

end up seeing two or three of them, even if briefly, in the same visit. We got to the point where we would not even ask with whom we were having an appointment. The group was a group.

Meeting family needs. (165, 211, 225)

We thought that the individual doctors in our current group were among the best in town, and we both had strong personal good feelings for all of them. Nevertheless, one was my physician, another was Ann's physician. We never felt that my doctor knew much about Ann, or hers about me. My physician only became aware of my schedule of caring for Ann after a couple of months. At that point he told me that, with my heart condition, I simply could not go on being a 24-hour nurse and housekeeper. Had we shared the same physician, or had the group had better internal communication, this problem might have been spotted earlier.

Need to inquire about feelings. (86)

It seems that when people who are close are approaching their seventies, as we were, they develop a mutuality to the maintenance of health. Two people who were as close as we were provide a lot of mutual support and understanding. Any medical group might find it wise to initiate a frank discussion of whether each couple wants to be cared for separately or together. A chance to choose without affront should be offered, as such discussions may be embarrassing for patients to initiate. Medically, we had respect for all of them, but we felt they were somewhat divided and without a common dimension of communication.

Expectations toward doctors. (238)

My criticisms have to do with the system: the lateral pass between specialists, the patient's loss of a sense of continuity of physician relationship, the possible proliferation of cost in that kind of passing, the sense of solo practice versus group cooperation, and the lack of real give-and-take participation in debate and inquiry. There is a need for continuity, for personal contact and conversation and challenge. Perhaps the family doctor of the past was usually (like the democracy of the New England town meeting) a myth. Even so, it is a missing ingredient of current complex systems.

The Influence of the Insurance System

Misconceptions. (84)

A few days after Ann died, I received a simple inquiry: "What services did Community Hospital perform on February 1?" I answered in violent language, "How should I know? Ask the hospital." I was an emotional frazzle. The incident coincided closely with my discovery of the autopsy report and the sudden reversal of my initial understanding of Ann's situation. As it turned out, the tumor had not originated in the kidney, but in the sinus. My feelings were raw. About the same time came news that $350 of prescription drug claims had never been received. Fortunately, I had xeroxes of the claims plus signed certified mail receipts. It had been received; Blue Shield had just lost it.

Cost of dying. (266)

Acute grief. (37)

Since then, it has hit me that these episodes ought to be in my document. Everything else in this manuscript deals with doctor–patient, doctor–spouse, hospital service. This deals with insurance carrier–spouse relationships. They too had an impact on my ability to weather the storm, that mortal storm, that engulfed me. Every damn receipt, every damn request, every haggle caused me to relive some episode, some tragic transition that I was trying to control. All too often it turned me back into a blubbering child. The money be damned. How can one forget, close the door, be clear? Unlike the travail of income tax, I could not turn it over to an accountant. I, for one, did not care anymore what happened, who paid what. My explosions, my incoherence, were relevant testimony.

Did I say, "The money be damned"? Sometime in July came a receipt, notice of payment for the service rendered on February 1. I still do not know what the service was, but the mountain had labored and brought it forth. It was a two dollar item.

None of this, as I have indicated, is intended to be personally critical of anybody's skill or good intentions. Much of it may by implication criticize the structure of modern medicine and its financing system. Perhaps it merely reflects the rage of a frustrated husband.

Readjustment

Engagement in grief. (163)

What about the psychological adjustment of the person who is left? It is always easy to say, "Only time takes care of that." One gets a lot of conflicting advice: rest, keep busy, go away, stay put. During the first weeks after Ann's death, many events were traumatic. As I started to dictate one night, I realized that it was April 11, and that Ann had died on March 11. It had been one month. I broke up like a child. I simply wish to indicate that this is also a part of how survivors feel.

Need to talk it through. (167, 168)

I was frequently driven by a sense of doubt—I guess you would call it guilt—as to whether there was something different that might have been done, other choices that might have been made. That, I suspect, is bad mental health. My outlet was to bother wise friends in the health care professions. I sometimes think this was less for information than for therapy for me.

After a month had passed, I limited myself to three ounces of vodka before my light evening meal. Previously I had anesthetized myself with nearly three times that amount.

Mourning begins. (38)

It may be that I have nothing more here than a catharsis for me, a confession, a sorting out of my feelings, my half knowledge, and my responses. Ann's death was such a painful experience—the most painful of my life. But how much more painful it was to the wonderful little lady who in the end not only lived in pain—masked by codeine and dilaudid—but lost control of her bodily functions. In her last days, she was denied even the dignity of being able to respond at all, and showed by the pain in her eyes her absolute frustration. Not even the dignity of response.

When I look back at trickling Sustacal down her throat with a hospital syringe even in that last hour, I tend to feel guilty about the whole process, the process that did this to her. It seems worse because in the process and the philosophy all along there was kindness and commitment and consideration on everybody's part. She appreciated it all even when she sought to escape.

Mourning continues. (38)

Within a few months I seemed to come out onto a new psychological plateau, the nature of which I do not fully understand. I suppose you could call it a kind of acceptance, though it really is not that. But my anger is gone. Perhaps more accurately, I should say that my anger is gone most of the time. It flares up occasionally. It is a strange kind of anger. I am not angry at anyone in the sense that I blame them.

Anger. (36)

I am angry at the incomprehensible fact that it happened to Ann; my anger arises out of frustration. Anger, one very wise lady said to me, is a part of mourning. But it is a strange anger that flares up and subsides and is all the more difficult because it is not directed at any person or thing, but at the shape of events, the world itself.

Another aspect of this new mood of acceptance of the fact that Ann is indeed gone is that I begin to remember new things. One of these is that repeatedly I was given advice and suggestions, which at first I resented, and then began much later to recognize were true. The fact that I recognized them as true did not mean that I could accept them.

I find myself also reverting to longer memories. One earlier resurgence occurred when I went up to Berkeley and was on the campus for two days. Ann and I had met at Cal in 1926 and were married before commencement in 1927. I found those two days on campus unspeakably traumatic—Ann was everywhere, in every path and hallway and grove of trees, on every street where we had walked. I fled the place a day earlier than I had planned.

Another flood of positive memories were evoked by a new projector I bought during Ann's illness. Ann was beyond the point of being able to read. The movements of and continuous attention required for television were difficult for her. But the large, brightly colored image of a slide on the screen would hold still until she was ready to move it. The fact that it dealt with established memories, evoked familiar things, proved to be very pleasant. We could revisit Greece and Northern Italy and Ireland. We could see our old houses and gardens. These directed attention to the happier and more beautiful episodes of our life.

This, in due course, led to a kind of therapy for me. There were scores of photographs to choose from, and I perused Ann's scrapbooks and her writings and finally began to understand how lucky I was to live with such a lady for 47 years. And perhaps how terrible it would have been for her to live any longer as helpless as she was in her last weeks.

I can also see why my physician was so concerned about my actions. I am certain that if, in the first days after Ann was gone, any moderately serious illness had hit me, I would not have been able to cope with it. I would not have wanted to get well. I can see that this would be a most dangerous period for those surviving a death. Ann's death was certainly the most devastating thing that has ever hit me personally.

Putting it all down has been good for me. I was afraid it might rub salt on my sore psyche. One ends up, I think, with the conclusion that what helps one through grief is an individual matter. Right now, I intend to stay living here. I will make no moves that cannot be undone, pass no points of no return. My first project is to complete some of the plans Ann and I had for the house. If I stay, we will want them. There is that "we" again; it will always be so.

Physical illness in the bereaved. (162,165)

Need to be we. (38)

Case B: A Daughter's Retrospective

The following is the response of Ann Broughton's daughter, Elizabeth Brisell, to the authors' request for her views on her father's essay. It is of note that her words were written in April of 1981—some seven years after both Ann's death and the writing of Mr. Broughton's essay in memory of her.

The authors are grateful to Elizabeth Brisell for her permission to publish these memoirs.

Some of the experiences I will discuss I have never mentioned to my father. He does not know that I slipped extra pills to my mother. Nor does he know that I asked the doctor to come and tell him of my mother's death. These revelations might have bothered him at the time, but I do not think they would now. I always hesitated to burden him with my own emotional pain; he had enough of his own.

Both of us have resentment for the lack of proper diagnosis, and the feeling that "someone should have found this." We all resent death when it takes away someone who is loved. My mother was dearly loved.

I came to California just as my mother fell ill. I had looked forward to spending time with her, walking on the beach, talking, seeing the great Western vistas with her. It was not to be.

It is impossible to pinpoint the exact time when I realized that my mother's illness was terminal. I was aware that she knew. My sons knew, but it was unspoken knowledge. She was taking the kinds of drugs seldom prescribed for patients with hope. We had shared a

Blaming the doctor. (89, 164)

Mutual pretense. (184)

weight problem for years. Now she commented that it would be easy simply to starve. Having raised dogs, I knew that starvation is the natural escape of animals when pain becomes too great and illness too overwhelming. Modern medicine will not allow this for human beings.

How many things we learn of ourselves and our families from such traumas. My youngest son, John, accompanied his grandparents to the beach one day and a hurried woman became impatient with my mother's slow pace and obvious infirmity. John was incensed and leapt to her defense. I was pleased at his empathy, found so young.

Small things appalled me. Mother's cancer caused sagging on one side of her face. She did not want friends to see her lest they find her grotesque. (She was never severely disfigured, except in her own mind.) In our society we grasp at pride, wanting to look well even though dying.

Clinical detachment. (237)

I once accompanied her to an examination where the doctor was dictating to his nurse. He used such phrases as "breasts flaccid," "loss of muscle tone," "sagging of the face," "pallid." Small comments, but hurtful ones. In sickness, one's entire life is centered around a decaying body. Professionals tend to discuss a patient as a *thing* rather than a *human being.* Mother was at no time deaf or mentally retarded.

Guilt. (221)

Occasionally mother would tell me that she must have done something terrible that God would punish her like this. What a terrible God to believe in—yet how many others must have felt this way.

Increasing debility. (115, 138, 218)

I was embarrassed by her gratitude for tiny services. When I cut her toenails and fingernails, one would have thought from her reaction that I had done some truly fine act of kindness. There was a reversal of parent–child roles that I found distressing.

Need for control. (218)

We are incredibly ambivalent under this kind of stress. Mother, aware that she was dying, resented overmanagement. We all want to picture ourselves as masters of our own fate. Yet she needed and welcomed help, and wanted relief from pain.

Effects of denial. (35, 42, 114)

My father, knowing intellectually that mother was dying, could not accept the fact in his heart. He seemed to cling to following the exact orders of doctors in vain hope that precise action could perform a miracle. He, too, was a patient, and at times I felt as sorry for him as for her. When her Dilaudid was due every four hours, and she was in excruciating pain after three, he would give speeches on the directions the doctor had given, the danger of the drug, and the possibility of addiction. Perhaps his concern for the possibility of addiction could be interpreted as a denial that she was dying. The speeches may have comforted him, I do not know. They had little effect on my mother, through her wall of pain. They infuriated me. I slipped my mother extra pills on occasion. The danger worried me, but it seemed the only humane thing to do. She was terribly grateful.

Pain control. (117)

Concern about addiction. (119, 120)

I remember well the incident in which the physician told my father "I hope your little lady will not last too long." I hoped my father would note and accept it as a verdict of death. Reading his essay I find he "knew," but at the time it seemed to me that he did not. If he had accepted, I believe she might have received a better program of pain relief, such as hospices provide. To accept such a therapy program, one must perceive death as a non-negotiable fact. Never did my father appear to surrender to that inevitability. Often I berated myself for not being able to take the reins and insist on more complete pain therapy. Yet my mother's death seemed a private thing between my parents, and I feared intruding. My parents were exceptionally close, almost to the point that my brother and I felt excluded. This is not a criticism, just a fact.

When the hospital could do no more, they suggested that she go to a nursing home. I did not think that dad could care for her and was in favor of following their advice. When we spoke to her about this, one large tear rolled down her cheek. What could we do? I told him that he must find help, and he found a warm and caring woman named Elizabeth, not a nurse, but a fine human being.

Once I lost my temper. We went to the hospital to take my mother home, and she was receiving whole blood. I was furious! I felt they were merely trying to keep her alive till she was well away from their care. I took the doctor aside and let him have it. He was well versed at fending off aggrieved relatives, and deflected my anger expertly. But I kept my resentment.

Initially Elizabeth wasn't aware that mother was dying, but she liked her and cared for her like a baby. With mother at home, my father clung to every crumb of hope. His denial was intense, and he insisted she was getting better.

The day of my mother's death I went to work. I felt she was near the end, but no longer trusted my feelings for I had been fooled before. I asked my son, Bill, to go over to his Grandad's, fearing death could come at any time.

At eleven o'clock he called. "Grandmom just breathed a deep sigh, and now Elizabeth and I can't get a pulse." I went to them instantly. One look and I knew she was gone. I hugged my son and Elizabeth. We all knew. My father didn't.

The doctor was to come over that morning. Shortly I heard my father on the phone explaining that there was no rush for the appointment because Ann was "looking much better." I took the phone and told him to take the extension in the bedroom. As soon as he was out of earshot I told the doctor that she was dead and that he had better come to tell my father. I knew there would be no way for my father to accept our diagnosis. At this point I honestly do not think he knew she had died.

The physician came and went to the bedroom alone. He quickly returned and broke the news. Dad has several times since expressed surprise that the doctor "seemed to know she was gone."

Hospice care. (209)

Shift from curing *to* caring. *(108)*

Lack of open communication. (98)

Institutional death. (290)

Questionable therapy. (132, 246)

Anger reflecting frustration. (220)

Denial. (163)

Breaking the news. (147, 155, 156)

My reaction to grief was suppression. I felt a responsibility to stand apart, to *be strong*. I was fearful of indulging in my own histrionics lest everyone else fall apart, and lest I could not get on course again. I was torn between relief, that she was beyond pain and humiliation, and guilt that I felt that way. I felt guilty for smoking (she had asked me to stop on her deathbed). I felt guilty that I had not done more to help relieve her pain.

My father gave in to his grief. My brother went to Point Lobos for a day to commune with a God of his understanding, and came to terms with his grief. I was annoyed that he should so indulge himself—in reality jealous because I feared letting go. Drinking was my method of noncoping, and I indulged at home—alone.

For months, even years, my father would call when in his cups, crying. None of us had expected that she would go first. She was the strong, athletic one. I feared he was becoming an alcoholic.

Years later, when my brother died in a mountain climbing accident in Pakistan, I was half glad that he was well out of the reach of the medical profession. His wife told me that he feared a death like mother's. So do I! People have been dying for eons without doctors, and doing a better job of it. Yet relatives are mesmerized by modern miracles, and we all pray for cure to the great God science.

I am not convinced that doctors can help in the grieving process. The medical profession today is immersed in the physical side of illness—the emotional side is too time consuming. The time that they must invest in mastering techniques may of necessity involve the diminution of their intuitive skills.

No two grief experiences are alike, just as no two people are alike. A clinician's handling of the emotional needs of one family might be perfection itself, but applied to another family might be a total disaster. Professionals, like other people, can give only that help which is within their experience. They should not berate themselves for feeling clumsy when on unfamiliar ground.

I am a great believer in group therapy involving people undergoing similar experiences. My particular prejudice in this regard comes from my experience with a well known fellowship for alcoholics. No therapist ever helped my particular ailment, alcoholism. Yet the aid and support of others with the same problem freed me.

No unafflicted clinician, or layperson, can say to a cancer victim, "I know how you feel." For all their sympathy or expertise, such a statement is patently untrue. But a group of patients can give aid and support to one another. The authority of the expert cannot possibly help as much as the sympathy of someone who has *been there*. Shared pain is eased, shared grief is eased.

I would like to see health care people encourage the formation of support groups, and encourage patients and their families to attend such meetings. It is not an admission of defeat or lack of knowledge to allow patients to help patients. It would not be a diminution of authority to acknowledge that our expertise ends when death is imminent. Mortals can perform only certain miracles.

I have been profoundly disturbed by the ethics and morality of modern medicine. I have come to feel that I would not want to fall into the clutches of a profession which worships physical life above functional life. I hope that someday a distinction can be found between prolonging life and prolonging dying, and that medicine will limit its practice to the former.

Let patients decide. (113)

Trajectory of dying. (112)

Case C: Reflections on a Mother's Death

Tanya Bednarski wrote a term paper entitled The Physician, Death, and Dying *to fulfill a requirement for a freshman seminar on "Problems Surrounding Death." About 18 months previously her mother had died of cancer. It is of note that during the course of completing her paper, Tanya and her father were able to discuss her mother's illness and death for the first time. The following is excerpted from her paper.*

The authors are indebted to Natanya Bednarski for her permission to publish the following essay.

Deception is impractical. (51)

Mom knew she was dying. Before the cancer was diagnosed, she wrote a letter to a friend, telling her that her health was "rapidly deteriorating." I remember laughing and telling Mom she was exaggerating.

Referral by family physician. (97)

Breaking the news. (82)

In August of 1977, she went to her family physician because of a swollen abdomen and phlebitis. He referred her to Dr. A, an oncologist, who performed a liver biopsy and diagnosed liver cancer. He informed Mom of the diagnosis, but by this time she intuitively knew she was dying. He wanted to start chemotherapy, but first Mom was referred to Dr. B for a second opinion. He confirmed the diagnosis and located the primary tumor in her pancreas.

Limitations of medical care. (206)

By this time, her liver was too enlarged to operate on the pancreas. Dr. B admitted her to the hospital, where she began chemotherapy. After two weeks of treatment, Dr. B told Dad that the liver was not shrinking as he had hoped. He would finish up with the chemotherapy and then release Mom. He admitted to Dad that there was not much else that he could do.

At the end of September, we brought Mom home. She grew weaker and continued to lose weight. Dr. B recommended a high protein, quick weight gain diet. When Mom next saw Dr B, he could not understand why she was so weak and unresponsive. He thought that perhaps she had some brain damage or more blood clotting. He told Dad that we could admit Mom to the hospital, where she would receive "sympathetic treatment." We wanted her to be at home where we could be with her all the time.

The last week, Mom deteriorated rapidly as we stood by, not knowing what to do or how to care for her. Dad knew a nurse, and she came by the house and told us how to make things comfortable for Mom. A doctor friend also came by and told us that Mom hadn't much time left, and that pneumonia probably would be the cause of death. The afternoon before Mom died, Dad called Dr. B for help; he gave Dad the phone number of the coroner. The day after Mom died, Dr. B's nurse called to see how Mom was. My sister told her that Mom had died the night before. When Dr. B called a couple of hours later, Dad said that we were very upset that he had not offered his support and care when we needed it. Dr. B said he had not realized that we needed any help.

After Mom's death, my recovery was difficult. I felt a lot of resentment and anger toward Dr. B. At the time, I felt that he had let Mom die. Now I realize that she would have died no matter who the doctor was, but that all of us, including Mom, could have had a less painful experience with a different physician.

In the process of writing this paper I interviewed four physicians. Dr. P is a psychiatrist who conducts weekly seminars for the oncology fellows at a University Hospital. Feelings of depression and failure are common among the fellows. Dr. P helps them to work through these problems so they can deal with their patients better. Dependency and attachments to patients are other problems that Dr. P discusses with the fellows. He told me that one of the most difficult decisions a physician makes is deciding when to stop trying to cure a patient. At this point, the physician lets go medically, but this does not mean that he or she should abandon the patient emotionally.

Dr. C is a young, easygoing oncologist who has just started his own practice. I was impressed by his honesty, warmth, and helpfulness. After graduation from medical school, Dr. C originally had been in training to be a psychiatrist. During that time, his wife developed cancer, and was ill for over a year before she died. Dr. C was deeply affected by the whole experience, and decided to change his specialty to oncology. He reports that he finds much satisfaction in working with terminally ill patients, although it can be depressing. He stresses a policy of total honesty with his patients, and tries to build close relationships with them. One thing he finds less satisfying is his rela-

No time for families. (237)

Maintaining hope. (35, 90)

Time for family. (167)

Interpersonal death. (30)

Impersonal death. (30)

Physical avoidance. (224)

Clinical detachment. (237)

Awareness of feelings. (65, 220)

Suboptimal care result. (229)

tionship with families after patient deaths. He finds he does not have time to spend with the family to help them adjust to their loss.

Dr. A is also a young oncologist. He trained at a denominational university, where he received an extensive education in theology. He thinks this was a good background for his work with terminally ill patients. Dr. A believes in informing the patient of the diagnosis, but sugar coating it to give the patient hope. He tells them of all the treatment possibilities and of the research that is being done. He feels that hope is essential, and tries to keep it alive in the patient. He also tries to see the family after the death to help them adjust to their new situation. Dr. A remembers Mom as an incredible person. He was saddened by her death because she was still a young woman and had already given so much of her life to others.

Finally, I talked to Dr. B. He is middle aged, and has a professional manner. He started the interview by telling me he remembers little of Mom's case except what is in his files. He read through her case history with me, explaining the treatment procedures and hospital practices. As he couldn't remember his thoughts during Mom's illness, I asked about his personal and professional policies. He said he had no formal training in medical school that dealt with death and dying. When treating terminally ill patients, he develops close relationships with those who have no supporting family. If they do, as Mom had, he does not get involved, but rather leaves it to the family members to work through the experience together. After the patient dies, Dr. B has little or no contact with the family. He thinks it is too painful for them to see him, as it reminds them of their loss. He related incidents where family members had gone out of their way to avoid passing by his office. Dr. B talks with his patients about their concerns regarding death only when they express a need for his help.

I got different impressions of the personalities and attitudes of each of the doctors with whom I talked. Dr. C has had both personal experience with and medical training in death. These have generated positive attitudes and thoughts that he can communicate to his patients, and use to develop good relationships with them. Dr. A also seems to have the ability to develop satisfying relationships with his patients. However, although I believe that Dr. B is a competent medical professional, I suspect that sometimes he is out of touch with people and their feelings. He may not spend enough time developing relationships with them, and as a result his patients may suffer. This brings up the question of the doctor's role with terminally ill patients. I believe that when a cure is no longer possible, the doctor must continue to care.

This role is vital, and if the doctor can fill it, everyone involved benefits. We needed someone with whom to talk who had had personal experience with the dying process. Dr. B did not share with us his own thoughts and suggestions, or offer his support. I know Mom would not have lived if she had a different physician, but our experience during her illness could have been different.

When the dying process has been satisfactory for the health care professional and the family, bereavement and recovery will be easier for them all. Positive memories of the experience are important for the continuance of life of the survivors. I hope that all clinicians can be people first, and technicians second.

Case D: Erich Lindemann, M.D., Talks About His Own Terminal Illness

On February 17, 1972, Erich Lindemann, M.D., participated in a session of a University undergraduate freshman seminar entitled "Homotransplantation and Death." The following is an edited transcript of a tape recording of that session. During the first part of the afternoon, Dr. Lindemann discussed his vast professional experience related to "mutilating surgery" and skin transplantation. He placed particular emphasis on his early studies of the psychological effects of hysterectomy and of the Cocoanut Grove fire, the source of his seminal 1944 article on acute grief reactions. His focus during this discussion was on the relationship of these events to loss and bereavement. After well over an hour of fascinating historical reminiscence by Dr. Lindemann, a student asked this question: "You have been studying the process of death and bereavement for a long time. How does this help or hinder you to accept your own death?" What follows is Dr. Lindemann's response.

The authors are indebted to Mrs. Lindemann for her permission to publish these excerpts.

I was wondering whether someone would ask that. No, no, don't apologize. As a matter of fact, when I came here I was thinking that to write about this sort of thing is very difficult, but to talk about it to friendly listeners is easier. I think the sort of things I might talk a bit about now are terribly important for people to know. Namely, what in detail goes on in a person who has been suddenly confronted with, "Yes, you are going to live, maybe you have three years." The neurosurgeon to whom you went is a good friend of yours. He thought he would find a very benign thing as the basis of your back pain, and instead he finds a malignant tumor. Then he is very embarrassed about it. He practically weeps to your wife, "Why didn't we find it when Erich came three years ago—he might still have . . ." But then he thought it was sort of infectious, or something like that. And so, now you have a sudden confrontation with the fact that life is not infinite.

Breaking the news. (82)

Clinicians' guilt. (221)

Existential plight. (34)

That is a very interesting thing. Usually we live with the notion that our life is infinite, and that we really don't see an end to it except abstractly, not emotionally. And so there comes some time in one's personal life (I was almost 70 at the time) when the dream of immortality suddenly snaps and you have to come to terms with having only so little time left.

Preciousness of life. (43)

You think, "Well, I really thought I was immortal. This is a mean thing of the Lord, or somebody like that, to do. This really cannot be true." And then, when you see it can possibly be true, there comes a very intense preoccupation; not with the disease, but with yourself as a deceased [sic] person. And it is practically impossible to picture yourself dead, or how it would feel to be dead. You pull out some memory similar to that you had of anesthesia. It was sort of like sleeping. Do you think death is like sleeping? Well, now, that can't be—it can't be that when you are dead you are just sleeping. You must still be there, and you must still be able to communicate with people. And then the whole host of religious imagery comes in, of resurrection and of being in heaven perhaps, or of going on in some other way. For me, that turned out to be the most appealing thing; I am so glad that I have been to India.

Intrapersonal death. (31)

Existential concerns. (41)

I talked a lot with the wise people in India, and with friends in psychiatry (a lot of them were wise people, too). We discussed the matter of transmigration of souls, or, in my terms, identities. An identity will get into another form, perhaps in another appearance, and perhaps with another set of functions, and that item of identity could remain in the cosmos in which you were lucky or unlucky enough to be created. And the whole problem of creation brings on new questions. Creation in your mother's body? Creation by God? Why created just this way? Was it just an accident, or was it a miracle? In my case, it seems it's been a damn nice thing—see, you tell yourself that. And then you come to terms with this self. It is something remarkable, isn't it? It was created, wasn't it? And it has a destiny, hasn't it?

Out of this then I came (I don't know how it is in other people) to an intense preoccupation with all the poetry of the past. I noticed an astounding fact: I had many more parents than I had realized. I grew up in Germany, so there was Goethe and people like that. When I started to recite all these poems, my wife learned German as fast as she could to help me. Then came a very interesting Hans Zinsser syndrome [Dr. Lindemann refers to Zinsser's autobiographical book: *As I Remember Him*]. Going back and creating the old Erich Lindemann. How he was as a boy, how as a young person, and then gradually coming to the realization that you were not a single entity. Rather, you were a sequence of different identities following each other, evolving throughout life. You were somebody who becomes someone else as he goes on, grows bigger, changes his mind, has experiences, gets increments, gets altered.

Quality of life decisions. (99, 218)

Desire to participate. (48, 87)

Styles of dying. (99)

Anticipatory grief. (36)

Medical heroics. (243)

Life expectancy. (258)

Open communication. (52, 53, 58, 191)

Empathic listening. (70)

Tolerate emotions. (53, 149)

Of course, there is the problem of what to do with the remaining time. I had an extraordinary urge to be active, and to be doing something, and I pestered the surgeons to make sure I had a functioning apparatus left. They couldn't operate—it was too big, so I began . . . what do you call it? I can't even say it. It's a lousy experience. *Radiation.* Make sure that you don't get burned so much that you can't function afterward! Rather have a little less of radiation, and a shorter life, but a functional life.

I felt a terribly great need to be a responsible decision-maker, a participant with the doctors in this deal from now on. I needed to be not just the receiver of friendly ministrations which were not explained but were given because they were the best things in terms of science. And out of that developed a really fine friendship with my caregivers, and I still have an extremely active life. Since then I've been in Europe a number of times and have given innumerable talks, not about this stuff, but about other things, and have enjoyed things immensely. I've had a very, very happy life. It's a . . . well, it is fine. I can't say about it.

Just to finish with this, I want to tell about a talk we had at Massachusetts General Hospital. The pathologists came and spoke about death and about some people dying early and some later. "It's a sad thing, but it's really just a premature burial. We must not forget that they are going to die sometime anyway, and this is just a little early." Perhaps there might be something favorable about dying now and not when you are ninety, and in a state where you are kept alive only with utmost heroic efforts. When you have a terribly miserable life, you are miserable and you make other people miserable. But there is a time at which it is meaningful to die. In my family most people die in their mid-seventies. It seems that maybe that's when our genes are up. That is an incredibly long life when you compare it to that of those dying in Vietnam.

I would like to speak to those of you who are training to be caregivers, who someday will have patients who are dying. Summing it up very briefly, rely on open communication. Don't fib. The family or the patient always will know if you do, just as children always know. That's number one, and for me it is the basis of helping.

The second important skill is to be able to take the patient's position. Even if what is said seems silly to you, take enough time to hear the patient out, because he may have a very good reason for an attitude which sounds very nonsensical to you at first. So don't brush him aside.

The third skill is not to assume that for the patient to be sad and miserable and crying for a while is bad for him. Don't assume that you have to have a smooth surface and that the patient must smile. He may smile just to keep you happy. I would think that these skills are the most important: open, empathic communication, honesty, and tolerance of emotional expression.

Followup by the physician as well as the other professionals is important, as is their interplay with each other and the family. All this, you understand, is a technical problem.

Given how much I have written about grieving, people sometimes ask me whether reading about death and grieving will better prepare them to assist someone who is dying. Does it help? Tremendously! There is a body of information obtained largely from patients, such as grieving people. This can be communicated to counselors to help them to deal with people who are in life crises. Out of such studies came a new branch of psychological helping work which is called crisis intervention, in contrast to the treatment of emotional illness.

Crisis intervention. (124)

There is a whole set of studies going on now concerning coping mechanisms. Grieving is only one form of coping—coping with a loss. There are many, many other issues, such as coping with marriage, coping with a new child, coping with losing your job, coping with a great many things. Are there some common factors? Can persons who are poor copers either because they are always in doubt, or because they have not learned to cope very well, learn to become better copers? I think yes, even though our skills to help are still very crude and certainly not the best.

Now, I suspect that this is more than you expected about this business from the horse's mouth. Actually, this was life. You have been such stimulating faces, and this was very nice for me. Well, I'm tired now, so if you excuse me, I wish you the best. It was grand to talk with you.

Dr. Lindemann died in 1974.

References

Barton, D. ed. 1977. *Dying and Death: A Clinical Guide for Caregivers.* Baltimore: Williams & Wilkins Co.
Barton authors the first eight chapters of this work, in which he outlines some current approaches to terminal care. This is a useful starter for the clinician. The multi-authored* second part consists of nine chapters, and, although uneven in quality, deals well with death issues relating to children and the elderly. For those seeking articles in special areas, the volume abounds with cogent references.

*Multiple authorship and multidisciplinary participation are very prevalent in the thanatologic literature. A significant proportion of contributions comes from a relatively small cadre of authors whose works appear as chapters in many different books.

Shneidman, E. S. ed. 2nd ed. 1980. *Death: Current Perspectives.* Palo Alto, California: Mayfield Publishing Co.

The editor is a distinguished professor of thanatology who brings together a potpourri of published works by nearly four dozen scholars in areas related to death. These selections are skillfully organized into groups dealing chiefly with cultural, societal, interpersonal, and personal perspectives on death. The authors of the second (and improved) edition read as a veritable *Who's Who* in their respective fields. This work makes valuable reading for the educated layperson as well as for professionals who deal with the dying.

Simpson, M. A. 1979. *The Facts of Death.* Englewood Cliffs, New Jersey: Prentice-Hall, Inc.

In his preface, Simpson laments the "boom in doom literature," and outlines some reasons for his discontent. Then with sensitivity and humor he presents "a complete guide for being prepared" that is useful for both general and professional readers. This is an excellent practical overview right down to the most basic details of planning for a death. It is available in a reasonably priced paperback edition, and we strongly recommend it to any literate person.

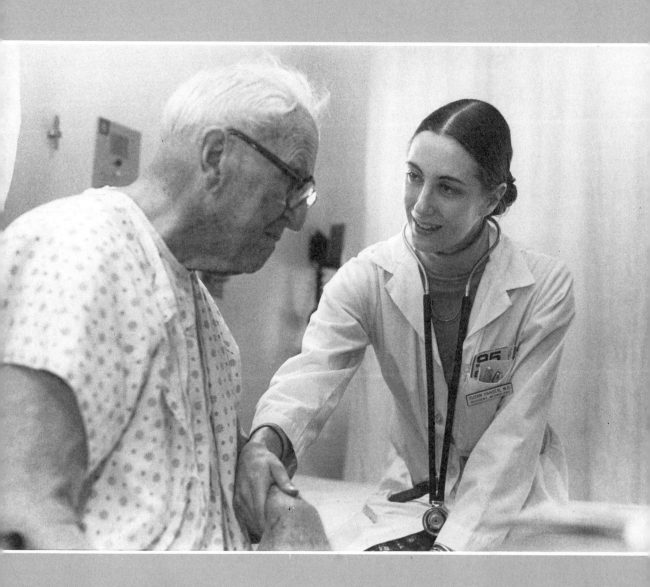

PART 2

Psychological and Interpersonal Foundations for Terminal Care

Knowledge of the psychology of death and grief combined with a sensitivity to existential concerns are important components in a balanced approach to terminal care. Additionally, sound communication among care providers, their patients, and significant loved ones is vital to optimal management. Accurate and timely exchange of relevant information is the primary means by which practitioners obtain adequate data for appropriate decision-making. Therefore, before we embark on our detailed survey of issues arising during a terminal illness, some germane aspects of theories about death and grief, as well as of interpersonal communication, will be reviewed. This will include presentation of some techniques to optimize the therapeutic effect of interpersonal communication in the medical setting.

1 Psychological Considerations

Overview

Understanding psychological issues is of considerable importance in the clinical assessment of problems encountered during dying and grieving. Such knowledge is also of value in preventing and treating pathological responses. In this chapter, we will look at psychological theories related to the care of the dying and their loved ones. We will also express some more philosophical thoughts regarding terminal care.

The Psychology of Death

Historical Perspective

Given the universality of death and the extent to which it has preoccupied humankind over the ages, the paucity of attention granted it by psychological theorists is surprising. Between Durkheim's (1951) penetrating work concerning suicide in the last century and the current revival, important psychological thinkers generally have avoided coming to grips with issues surrounding death.

Despite the lack of attention paid it by earlier theorists, thanatology has become a firmly established discipline.

Freud himself may have contributed to this hiatus in systematic efforts to understand the psychology of death. He believed that the earliest years of life were the most important in the formation of human personality. Freud also contended that young children were unable to grasp the concept of death. It therefore followed that any psychology of death was merely derivative from more fundamental psychological structures. One effect of this line of reasoning probably was a lack of work in a field that has held an enormous intrinsic fascination throughout history. This may stand as one testimony to the degree to which the thoughts of this single man have loomed over Western culture in this century.

Beginning with the pioneering work of Lindemann in the late 1940's and Herman Feifel in the 1950's, as well as that of Norman Farberow, Edwin Shneidman, and Richard Kalish, the long silence was broken. The discipline of thanatology is now firmly established, with a burgeoning literature that has gone from a trickle of articles four decades ago to a flood of current writings. With this frame of reference, we will explore specific aspects of the psychology of death that relate to the care of the dying and their loved ones.

Developmental Issues

Loss and separation are universal factors in child development and key components in the psychology of death. For example, as the growing infant develops the physical and sensory capacities necessary for autonomous behavior, issues of definition of self from nonself come sharply into question. The first step on this pathway generally is recognized to be the awareness of mother as a separate entity with the potential to grant or withhold nurturance in ways often beyond the control of the infant. While this process is taking place, the child may exhibit exquisite sensitivity to the presence and absence of its mother.

Early experiences with loss and separation strongly influence the individual's reaction to death.

The relevance of this concept to the psychology of death arises in the success or failure of the resolution of the emotional tensions created within each child as this stage progresses. Many children learn that mother eventually will return, and that nurturance (both physical and emotional) will be provided before harm befalls. For them, issues surrounding loss and separation are likely to be resolved successfully.

For others, a less satisfactory transition toward increasing independence from key caretakers is made. These individuals may experience problems coping with loss and separation in many contexts throughout life. We emphasize that death is perhaps the most disturbing encounter with loss that most of us experience. The nature of the resolution of these developmental tensions colors later attitudes and responses toward death and dying.

CASE ILLUSTRATION

A 40-year-old woman was found wandering in the rain in an acutely psychotic state with her 3-year-old son clutched in her arms. She was hospitalized, and after her acute agitated depression was treated she began long-term psychotherapy. Over the course of a year of intensive treatment, it emerged that her own mother had died when she was two-and-one-half years old, and that her childish expressions of grief had been strongly suppressed by her distraught father. She did well as a child, but experienced her first clinical depression at age 20 when her brother was killed in Vietnam. Her most recent decline began when her husband left her about 6 months prior to her hospitalization. As she began to work through her childhood grief, her depression resolved and she was able to resume working and caring for her son. In retrospect, the failure of her caretakers to support adequate resolution of her devastating early loss probably figured strongly in her compulsive reversion to a very infantile state when faced with significant losses in later life.

Persons with early unresolved losses require special support when facing death.

The above reasoning represents a vast oversimplification of some concepts fundamental to object relations theory. This construct has proven valuable in connecting a variety of developmental issues with adult behavior and psychopathology. We refer those who are interested in more satisfying discussions to the works of Otto Kernberg and Gertrude and Rubin Blank. The *take home message* for professionals dealing with the dying and grieving is as follows: unresolved losses or separations in early childhood may cause more problems when death is later confronted than might be expected on the basis of the individual's coping skills in other areas. Thus, if clinicians know that a patient or family member has such a history, they are wise to be especially clear and supportive.

Ways of Thinking About Death

People have an ability to think about death in a number of ways depending upon the context. Kastenbaum and Aisenberg (1972) ably elucidate this concept. They suggest that three principle ways in which we view death are *impersonally,* *interpersonally,* and *intrapersonally.*

The *impersonal* approach to death is characterized by the sense of distance with which most of us received, for example, the daily body counts reported during the Vietnam war. It is the death of the stranger, the death of the other, and we seem disinclined to associate it with the possibility of our own demise. In fact, we may even experience a perverse sense of our own fantasied invulnerability on hearing of the death of the other.

Impersonal views of death are not associated with any personal sense of loss. (17)

An impersonal attitude toward death has been ascribed by many observers to a large proportion of health care professionals. For many of the latter, this distance may serve as an important defense against the strain of constant encounter with mortality. Problems arise when this way of thinking about death predominates regardless of its appropriateness in any given setting.

Another way of viewing death is *interpersonal.* In this process, death touches us on more than just an informational level. In his famous declaration that "No man is an island," John Donne spoke an important truth in asserting that none of us ultimately is detached from any other. Practically, however, it is the death of someone close that affects us on a more personal level. Many individuals are woven into the fabric of our lives to various degrees. The loss of any one of them therefore constitutes the death of some part of our own selves. For each individual and each relationship at any particular moment, the degree to which he or she is touched by a given death will vary.

Interpersonal deaths touch us because we were somehow emotionally engaged with the deceased. (2, 16, 17)

As far as health care professionals in terminal care settings are concerned, an interpersonal viewpoint about death may be particularly relevant. Those involved in the care of the dying often care very deeply for patients and family members. Particularly in smaller communities, they may even have been lifelong friends. Given this, it is hardly possible to imagine abiding with someone through a terminal illness without becoming humanly engaged with that individual. Those professionals who maintain a facade of dealing with death as an impersonal matter may be defending against their own troublesome emotional reactions. Finally, virtually every death is likely to be viewed interpersonally by someone. It should be treated with appropriate respect on that basis alone.

A third way of thinking about death might be termed *intrapersonal.* Because this involves the individual's confrontation with the death of the self, in many ways it constitutes an ultimate unthinkable thought. How can one imagine that one's own consciousness, which is instinctively (and correctly, in a phenomenologic sense) felt to define the entire universe, possibly could cease to be? Tolstoy (1886) put it most poignantly in his *Death of Ivan Ilyich,* in the following passage:

Intrapersonal *thoughts of death touch one's own sense of mortality. (19)*

> In the depth of his heart he knew he was dying, but not only was he not accustomed to the thought, he simply did not and could not grasp it. The syllogism he had learned from Kiezewetter's Logic: "Caius is a man, men are mortal, therefore Caius is mortal," had always seemed to him correct as applied to Caius, but certainly not as applied to himself. . . . Caius really was mortal, and it was right for him to die; but for me, little Vanya, Ivan Ilyich, with all my thoughts and emotions, it's altogether a different matter. It cannot be that I ought to die. That would be too terrible.

By observing patients during "little deaths," professionals gain clues as to the patients' reaction to terminal illness.

The intrapersonal thought of death is indeed a difficult one even to ponder. How can a consciousness truly comprehend its own nonexistence? And yet, we actually encounter all manner of "little deaths" during daily living. They include minor losses of self-esteem over failed expectations or loss of physical objects to which we have become attached. The range extends to major traumas such as the loss of health (temporarily or permanently), the loss of organs or limbs, the loss of jobs or homes, and especially the loss of loved ones. The manner in which an individual copes with these lesser deaths can provide some hints as to how real death is likely to be handled. Thus, observant health care professionals may find clues in an individual's past behavior or coping histories as to what may be expected in an encounter with death.

Fears Surrounding Death

The philosopher Jacques Choron (1964) has a particularly apt analysis of the fear of death. He distinguishes three separate foci for this fear. These include *the process of dying, nonexistence,* and *what comes after death.*

Fear of death can be resolved into fears of the dying process, of nonexistence, and of what follows death.

Given the pain and indignity often associated with the graceless death so common in our culture, it is not surprising that a rational person would experience fear when contemplating that prospect. The process of dying can be viewed as an ultimate test of one's ability to maintain some sense of self-esteem in the face of experiences that can be incredibly extreme. One interesting finding with regard to the many specific fears associated with the process of dying is that indignity and pain are reported as only second and third among the fears of those who confront death; their primary fear is of abandonment. Apparently it is more important to most of the dying to feel at one with their fellow humans than to accomplish any other final objective.

The second focus for fear of death concerns extinction or nonexistence. This particular reaction relates again to the difficulty of comprehending fully the existence of the world in the absence of the consciousness with which it has been encountered. If it is true that mankind experiences an innate terror of *the unknown*, what could be more frightening than to contemplate the cessation of knowing? In fact, this may be basic to the fear of abandonment so characteristic of those confronting the reality of death. For some, the loss of human relationships can constitute a particularly poignant paradigm for the loss of the world.

Third, there are fears focused on what may come after death. Many of those who fear what follows their deaths admit they have thoughts of religiously motivated torment. These fears often center around anticipated judgment and punishment for their thoughts and behavior. Thus, feelings of guilt and anticipation of rejection may underlie this reaction. One could regard such fears as less existentially fundamental than fears of dying and of nonexistence. They are, however, nonetheless real and paralyzing for those who experience them.

For those frightened about the anticipated death of another person, two sources of fear are prominent. The first is the fantasy of retaliation for past behaviors toward the deceased person. Obviously, this fear centers around guilt and the sense of unfulfilled expectations (either from oneself or others). It may constitute an important psychological basis for our transcultural fascination with ghost stories.

The second fear may be considerably more reality oriented. It often appears while imagining oneself trying to survive in the absence of a significant figure in one's life. This basic fear of the loss of a relationship is usually quite realistic as well as exceedingly painful. Often, it can best be addressed by assurance that clinicians will stand by the bereaved person even in the face of overwhelming loss.

A Model of Coping with the Dying Process

Kubler-Ross' stages are common reactions that occur in highly individual manners and sequences during the course of terminal illnesses. (Table 1-1)

Since the publication of Kubler-Ross' (1968) popular book, much attention has been given to the concept of stages in the process of dying. As Kubler-Ross herself states, they may or may not characterize any given individual at any point in the course of dying. They may recur a number of times and in varying order during the course of a final illness, and any one of them may be totally absent without implying pathology of any sort. Despite Kubler-Ross' own disclaimers, a surprising number of lay and professional people involved with the dying seem to interpret her stages as ordered passages through which patients *should* progress. Where misused, such concepts can be a yoke laid upon the dying.

Stage one: *denial and isolation.*

The *first stage* (see Table 1-1) described by Kubler-Ross is characterized by *denial and isolation.* This can be so pronounced that patients or family members simply do not recall important statements that have been made to them. Further, there is often a sense of sudden alienation from the remainder of the human race who are not acutely dying. Most patients seem to experience these responses fairly often during their terminal illnesses. They may periodically revert to an almost childlike refusal to confront reality, or be overwhelmed at times with the sense of isolation and disengagement from their fellow creatures.

Stage two: *anger.*

The *second stage* of Kubler-Ross is marked by *anger.* Depending on the personality of a given individual, anger may constitute a rather overt and primary expression throughout the process of dying ("Rage, rage against the dying of the light . . ."). Alternatively, it may be expressed fleetingly and in very subtle or passive ways. Recall that the roots of the word "anger" include an anguish in the face of humankind's limitations and helplessness when confronted with the existential insult of death. Such reactions on the part of the dying are not hard to understand. Anger is almost constantly present on some level in both the dying and their loved ones, and may show itself in many contexts and in unexpected ways.

Stage three: *bargaining.*

Bargaining is the distinctive reaction in the *third stage* described by Kubler-Ross. This is not as ubiquitous among our patients as denial and anger. There are, however, striking instances in which individuals considered acutely moribund have maintained life against all seeming odds in order to achieve a certain goal. When bargaining does occur, it often constitutes an understandable attempt by those who feel overwhelmed and helpless to establish some sense of control over their own destiny.

Table 1-1   Coping with Dying

Stages of Dying (Kubler-Ross)	Phases of Dying (Weisman)
Denial and isolation	Existential plight
Anger	
Bargaining	Mitigation and accomodation
Depression	Decline and deterioration
Acceptance of death	Preterminality and terminality

Stage four: *depression.*

Kubler-Ross' *fourth stage* is characterized by *depression*. This emotion is as universal among our patients as denial and anger. In part, this is because the physiological sequelae of advancing illness and debilitating treatments often contribute to a depressed affect. Also, depression is an appropriate reaction to the existential traumas inflicted by a terminal illness. Clinicians should anticipate its appearance in various contexts during the process of dying.

Stage five: *acceptance.*

The final and *fifth stage* presented by Kubler-Ross is distinguished by *acceptance* of death. We believe that individuals are endowed with the potential to navigate any of the expectable traumas of life with some degree of vitality and grace. Thus, hope exists that any given person can attain a state of serenity and acceptance even in the face of death. Unfortunately, modern American society inadequately prepares its members to cope with dying, and is not well organized to support a dignified dying. Therefore, attainment of a state of acceptance as characterized by Kubler-Ross is far more the exception than the rule.

Often, what we suspect to be a primarily physiological waning of struggle and discord occurs as a person nears death. The satisfying conclusion to life so dearly sought by the authors of the *Ars Moriendi* texts of the Middle Ages (see Aries, 1974), however, is relatively rare. Acceptance of death may be one goal to be sought in terminal care. However, it must not be an expectation that patients, family, and staff must meet in order to feel that their roles have been performed properly.

Phases of the Dying Process

Weisman describes common reactions during the process of dying which are closely tied to the course of a terminal illness. (2, Table 1-1)

Weisman (1980) has also addressed the issue of coping with dying (see Table 1-1). He characterizes the various reactions of the dying as phases which tend to occur primarily in a particular order. Weisman holds, however, that they also may recur and persist in some individuals throughout the course of their illness. The phases he describes are more likely to take place sequentially than the stages of Kubler-Ross in that they are more closely tied to the course of the disease itself. We must repeat our caution that such concepts are useful only insofar as they enlighten professionals regarding the experiences of their patients. They do not constitute guidelines for the behavior of patients or family members.

Phase one: *existential plight. (18)*

Weisman's *first phase* is *existential plight*. It refers to the initial shock of an abrupt confrontation with incontrovertible evidence of one's own vulnerability and mortality. During this early period, patients and family members are likely to exhibit signs of numbness and shock, as well as a sense of being overwhelmed. Weisman's term for this reaction is "impact vulnerability."

Phase two: *mitigation and accommodation.*

Weisman's *second phase* is *mitigation and accommodation.* These reactions often follow initial treatment, when the possibility of relapse or recurrence remains very real. Focus among patients and families tends to shift toward achieving a satisfactory balance between new roles as potentially dying patients and old identities with their associated skills and coping techniques. In this way, the acute threat of demise is mitigated. An accommodation often is made between the daunting reality of disease and the requirements of customary occupations and concerns.

The main emphasis during this period seems to be directed toward achievement of premorbid levels of function. The battle against invalidism becomes primary, and the maintenance of even the most trivial of abilities can become critical to psychological well-being. The role of denial in this dynamic is apparent, although not necessarily problematic.

Phase three: *decline and deterioration.*

The *third phase* characterized by Weisman is *decline and deterioration.* This occurs as illness advances, as recurrences accumulate and treatments result in shorter periods of relative freedom from symptoms, and as energy for living begins to wane. This period of a terminal illness may be the most difficult for many patients and families faced with a seemingly inexorable progress of disease and disability. This is when the signs of advancing illness become unavoidable even to the most denying of observers. The prospect of death assumes a new concreteness.

To be sure, the struggle to maintain function in the face of diminishing capacity and reserves often continues. But the distasteful realities of terminal disease inevitably reassert themselves. Further, they often do so with a regularity that makes denial increasingly difficult to maintain. The period of decline also may be increasingly taxing to the support systems of the patient and family. Everyone involved may have to struggle to maintain hope and a positive attitude. Judicious support from health care professionals may prove particularly vital during this phase. However, it must be carefully negotiated so as to maintain as much autonomy and control for patients as possible.

Everyone involved with the reality of death may have to struggle to maintain hope. (17)

Phase four: *preterminality and terminality. (4)*

Finally, the *fourth phase* of *preterminality and terminality* is entered. Responses to treatment become minimal and everyone involved begins to realize that the focus must shift to palliation of symptoms and assurance of as much comfort as possible. Patients and family may become acutely aware of the limitations of the time they have left together. Consequently, they may appropriately alter their goals to be much more limited than those which were previously sought.

Denial that is not causing problems for patients or families need not be challenged. (12)

We have a few final words regarding staging of the emotional process of dying. In most patients, the downhill course is characterized by a fluid alternation between acceptance and denial of their diseases. Sometimes these variations seem to be correlated with specific events such as remissions or relapses. In other instances, there are few clues as to the motivating factors involved. Our clinical

Anger may cause more problems than any other feeling. (10)

guidepost regarding denial is based on the assessment of its effect on patients and families. If there are no obvious negative sequelae arising from a given period of denial, then we see little sense in challenging it.

Anger is poorly tolerated in our culture. It therefore seems to cause more problems for patients, families, and clinicians in terminal care settings than perhaps any other feeling. It probably requires more concentrated effort toward creative coping by health care professionals than do most of the other reactions encountered among the dying. Some depression seems equally inevitable in the context of terminal illness. From our perspective, the task of clinicians is to support patients and families through these appropriate reactions to the prospect of death, and to intervene when more pronounced pathology becomes evident.

The course of a terminal illness and the anticipatory grief process may proceed at disparate rates.

Some of the conceptual difficulties as to the value of *stages* of dying stem from the complexity of the processes involved. At least two sets of interdependent emotional reactions act simultaneously. First, there are responses primarily related to the nature and course of the terminal disease process. A different set of reactions involving the anticipatory grief process is equally important. Each of these may proceed at a different rate and prompt disparate, sometimes incongruous, behaviors. Professionals should evaluate the actions of patients, families, and staff with this in mind.

Psychological Aspects of Grief and Mourning

Differentiating Grief and Mourning

Grief and mourning are clinically differentiable facets of uncomplicated bereavement.

Many people use the terms *"grief"* and *"mourning"* interchangeably. We have found it convenient to differentiate clinically between them as separate facets of uncomplicated bereavement. From our perspective, *grief* may be thought of as the ordinarily self-limited complex of symptoms and processes that constitute the acute reaction to a significant loss. *Mourning* signifies the longer-range resolution of the acute grief toward a resumption of satisfying function in living. When complications arise in the course of bereavement, the mourning process may fail to resolve the loss. The term "melancholia" is generally employed to designate such pathological mourning (see Chapter 9).

Anticipatory Grief

Grief is a reaction of the dying as well as the bereaved. (20)

We emphasize at the outset that the division between reactions to one's own death and reactions to the loss of a loved one is somewhat artificial. This is because in either case one is coping with a loss. For dying persons, that loss is not only of the self-esteem and satisfactions connected with activities that are increasingly impossible; it is also an anticipatory separation from the entire world. Thus, grief may be thought of as a reaction of terminal patients as well as a response of those who are left behind.

The mechanisms for the resolution of loss seem to allow us to cope more gracefully if there is opportunity for anticipation. As soon as patients, families, and clinicians learn of a terminal illness, they are likely to begin a process of *letting go*. This often occurs even if the afflicted person remains relatively intact. It happens in many instances to both the dying and those who will remain. Given individual variations in the trajectory of anticipatory grief, the pace of letting go may be quite disparate among different persons. At times, premature withdrawal causes problems, especially when an illness is characterized by dramatic reversals in course.

Thus, while anticipatory grieving can be helpful in cushioning the shock of eventual loss, difficulties arise if withdrawal proceeds too far in advance of the actual loss. We address this and other related clinical concerns surrounding anticipatory grief at length in Chapter 7.

Acute Grief

Lindemann's description of the acute grief syndrome remains a classic. (9)

A landmark systematic examination of the nature and parameters of acute grief was undertaken by Lindemann (1944) in his studies of the survivors of the Cocoanut Grove disaster in Boston. His description of the specific symptom complex associated with the grief syndrome remains classic. Reactions include the following: sensations of somatic distress coming in waves at intervals of somewhat less than an hour; feelings of tightness in the throat; choking; shortness of breath; sighing; a sensation of emptiness in the abdomen; lack of muscular strength; and intense feelings of distress best characterized as psychic pain. Also included in the syndrome as he described it were a sense of unreality, gastrointestinal complaints, emotional distance from others, and intense preoccupation with the image of the deceased. Finally, guilt, a loss of warmth in other relationships, and irritability or anger were prominent among the people he observed. He concluded that there were five pathognomonic symptoms of grief. These included somatic distress, preoccupation with the image of the deceased, guilt, hostility, and the loss of habitual patterns of conduct.

Optimally, acute grief reactions can be worked through in about six weeks.

Lindemann thought that the duration of any individual's grief reaction was dependent on the success of the "grief work." He observed that in optimal circumstances and with understanding support, it was possible to settle the acute grief reaction within four to six weeks.

The nature of this grief work is difficult to define precisely. From the psychoanalytic perspective, the work of grieving resides in the

Need to be we. *(10)*

resolution of a specific conflict; although reality testing confirms that the loved person is lost and that attachments should be withdrawn, the bereaved individual seldom is willing to let go of the departed loved one. The exact manner in which this detachment is accomplished has remained mysterious to many observers, including Freud. He noted only that it apparently needed to be slow and gradual. He also observed that this process was lengthened and more prone to pathology when strongly ambivalent feelings existed toward the deceased.

Mourning

Successful mourning is a prerequisite for resolution of a loss.

In his classic paper *On Mourning and Melancholy,* Freud (1917) characterized mourning as ". . . the reaction to the loss of a loved person, or to the loss of some abstraction which has taken the place of one, such as one's country, liberty, an ideal, and so on." He believed that the distinguishing features of this state included ". . . a profoundly painful dejection, cessation of interest in the outside world, loss of capacity to love, [and] inhibition of all activity." Both Freud and later thinkers recognized the process of mourning as an intensely painful one that needed to be seen through were any major loss to be resolved. Given the fundamental human tendency to avoid unpleasant sensations, it is understandable that mourning readily can go astray in cultures which do not actively support it.

Mourning can be divided into three clusters of reactions following acute grief: protest, despair, *and* detachment. *(9, 10)*

Bowlby (1961) and his colleague Parkes (1964) have each addressed the issue of the mourning process insightfully. Their studies divide mourning into three phases following the acute grief reaction. The first phase is one of *protest,* characterized by spontaneous responses focused on the lost person. During this period, bereaved individuals may cling tenaciously to thoughts or images of the deceased. They may display strong expressions of despair and rage directed toward both the deceased and other persons. Particular antagonism may arise toward those who encourage the bereaved person to let go of the lost loved one and resume normal living. The consequence of the expression of this displaced anger may be the disruption of important supportive relationships. This can be far-reaching and unfortunate, particularly given that the mourning period may be the time when the bereaved is most in need of intimate friends.

Bowlby (1961) contends that once the stage of protest is completed, the next phase in the mourning process is one of *despair.* This period usually is precipitated by the acceptance that the deceased is indeed lost. The frenetic activity that may have characterized the first phase now tends to lapse into a sense of disorganization, with free-floating anxiety and depression. It may be that this period of disintegration constitutes a necessary prelude to the final stage of mourning, paving the way for eventual resolution of the loss.

The final phase is characterized by Bowlby as one of *detachment*, in which a reorganization of the personality of the bereaved takes place. Behaviors and emotions that previously centered around the deceased begin to reorient toward other individuals or activities. This process eventually leads to the healthy resolution of a serious loss, and enables the bereaved to resume a satisfying life.

One revealing look at the impact of the loss of a loved one comes from Parkes (1964) in his study of 22 British widows during the year following the loss of their husbands. His observations add a time dimension, and indicate the existence of some fairly characteristic and predictable reactions. After some expression of great distress, most women found themselves in a state of numbness and mindless activity alternating with brief outbursts of panic characteristic of acute grief.

This acute grief reaction ordinarily was followed by the initial *protest* phase of mourning. This is marked by a state of intense yearning and pining for the deceased, characterized by preoccupation with possessions and memories associated with the lost husband. Further, there was a tendency to respond with more pronounced weeping to stimuli evoking memories of the deceased. During this period, roughly one-half of the bereaved experienced actual hallucinations of their lost loved one, ranging from a vague sense of presence to visual, auditory, and tactile phenomena.

The next phase observed by Parkes continued beyond the first year. In this period of despair, disorganization was increasingly apparent. Many of the widows became aimless and apathetic, and found difficulty in looking toward a future or in resuming satisfying life.

Parkes concluded that if the feelings associated with grief and mourning were suppressed or inhibited, they tended to be more intense and difficult to manage when they finally surfaced. In his view, the resistance to the change required to accept a difficult loss forms the basis for grief and mourning. Loneliness, sadness, despair, and reactive depression constitute natural and appropriate responses to a serious loss. Those who refuse to experience these emotions may be ignoring a vital imperative. The sequelae of refusal to engage in the work of grief and mourning, in spite of its painful nature, may be far-reaching and potentially devastating.

Rates of mourning are variable, but the process often persists at least one year.

Hallucinations of the dead are experienced by about one-half of the bereaved.

Pathologic Variants

Each individual possesses at least vestigial mechanisms to heal the psychological wounds caused by a major loss. These processes, however, require a critical level of environmental support in order to enable us to negotiate successfully the painful process of grief and mourning. Unfortunately, many of the bereaved encounter active opposition or discouragement from those around them if they try to enter fully into mourning. It is thus not surprising that grief pathology is relatively common in American culture.

In Chapter 9 we discuss four major manifestations of grief pathology: *massive denial, manic escape, dysfunctional hostility,* and *clinical depression.* Here we examine another parameter of grief pathology: the *time* dimension. At one extreme is failure to enter the grieving process, and at the other extreme is abnormal prolongation of grieving. These two phenomena are inextricably related.

Absence of grief and its extreme prolongation are two major pathologic variants.

The source of the failure to enter fully into the grieving process is not difficult to conjecture. Bereavement is by its very nature among the most painful of human experiences. Even the most stable of persons may resist full participation. Without appropriate personal and cultural support, the usual tendency to avoid immediate pain and the unconscious opposition to the necessary *letting go* of the deceased often impedes mourning. Both Lindemann's investigations of the Coconut Grove disaster and Kaplan and Mason's (1960) studies of mothers with critically ill neonates clearly demonstrate the negative sequelae of the failure to become emotionally involved. Parkes also concluded from his studies that if grief and mourning were inhibited, feelings tended to be more intense and difficult to manage when they emerged. One prominent result of the failure to grieve is that for a prolonged period the bereaved remains incapable of reestablishing a satisfying way of living.

Failure to re-enter some daily routines after about two months of grieving should prompt concern.

It is difficult to know exactly when professionals should become alerted to the possibility of pathological extension of the mourning period. For one thing, variations in emotional expression between different cultures, families, and individuals figure strongly into the limits beyond which there is reason for concern. Examination of different cultures reveals that a shift in primary focus from one's loss to the process of living generally occurs within about a year. If the bereaved is unable to re-enter some daily routine of living within a couple of months after a major loss, however, professional concern is appropriate.

Interminable mourning: when to refer.

Although failure to enter fully into the mourning process is a common source of pathological extension of grief, there are other factors that may come into play. Most prominent among these is the existence of strongly ambivalent feelings toward the deceased. Individuals with such feelings may harbor, without awareness, a sense of responsibility for the death or suffering of their lost loved one. There may be an illegitimate sense of victory, prompting substantial guilt. In such cases, mourning may be prolonged indefinitely in the absence of professional intervention even if the mourner is fully involved in experiencing the process. Such situations frequently require sensitive and careful intervention by a trained professional to reach a satisfactory resolution.

Existential Concerns

Introduction

Existential concerns. (19)   It is impossible to work intimately on a day-to-day basis with the dying without confronting existential issues to some degree. Thus, we will set down some ideas that we have found helpful in coping with fundamental concerns arising from our own work in this setting. By necessity, this brief survey gives the barest glimpse into this realm of human thought. Those whose interests are provoked are referred to the more comprehensive and intellectually satisfying works cited in the bibliography of this chapter.

Interdependence of Life and Death

Philosophers since the ancient Greeks and Romans have recognized that death and life are inextricably related. In many ways, it is only in the context of its counterpart that sense can be made of either. Further, it is often in the awareness of the finitude of our lives on earth that we begin to comprehend the preciousness of each moment. Frequently, we may arrogantly assign cosmic importance to our day-to-day concerns. When this occurs, the ultimate fact of death is always there to restore us to a more appropriate sense of proportion. As Yalom (1980) so aptly puts it, "Although the physicality of death destroys man, the idea of death saves him."

Death as a Source of Primordial Anxiety

Death is probably the most fundamental source of primordial anxiety for the vast majority of humankind. The philosophical basis for this fear is apparent when we realize, as discussed earlier, that our consciousness is the primary tool whereby we are aware of experiencing the world. Each of us might be thought of as *creating* a highly personal reality as sensory data are integrated into a constantly shifting mental picture. No two persons share the same sensory apparatus or fund of experiences, let alone the same internal means of processing them. Thus, on a very basic level, it is difficult to contemplate the world (which has been experienced solely through consciousness) as persisting once consciousness ceases. The thought of one's own death can come to equal (once again, on a very primitive level) the end of the entire world.

Denial-Based Defensive Responses

Denial. (12)

It is not surprising that much of our relationship with death is characterized by denial. In the process of daily work with the dying and grieving, and many hours of reading and thinking about death, we have often encountered our own need to deny the whole damned thing. Surely, if anyone is going to be exempt from dying on the basis of intimate acquaintance alone, it should be us! This is a rather concrete illustration of one of the types of denial we shall address.

Denial may be founded on illusions of control and permanence.

There are a number of denial-based defensive responses to death anxiety that occur among Americans. The one just alluded to is founded primarily on the illusion of control. If knowledge is power, then who is more likely to have power even over death than one who has devoted a great deal of time to studying it? There are much less overt manifestations of the use of a sense of mastery as the means whereby one can maintain denial of death. Some patients, for example, lead lives characterized by an overriding need to control every aspect of their environments. These individuals often encounter severe emotional problems in dealing with a situation wherein even the illusion of control cannot be maintained.

Another subtle denial of death may be found in the materialistic values characteristic of our culture. Possessions seem to enable some of us to maintain an illusion of permanence and inviolability that provides reassurance against the reality of eventual decline and demise. Perhaps the most extreme example of this can be found in the vast tombs erected by the rulers of Egypt and other prominent citizens throughout history. A more contemporary example lies in the current Western passion for maintenance of at least the appearance of youth despite natural deterioration of form and function that occurs with advancing age. But, as Huxley (1939) so pointedly expressed, even the extremes of wealth ultimately are inadequate to stave off the reality of death.

Death Awareness as Life-Giving Insight

One of the ways in which human beings cope with the most extreme and agonizing situations is by trying to make sense of them. We all tend to seek the silver lining even in that darkest of clouds, death.

Patients and families often attempt to reconcile themselves to the indignity and pain associated with terminal illness by looking for a potential benefit for someone in their own suffering. Clearly, it would be presumptuous for health care professionals to offer such ideas to the dying and the grieving as a *band-aid* to cover a gaping emotional wound. However, it is crucial that caretakers find some way of reconciling the seemingly pointless agonies often seen in patients and their families. In some instances, sharing of more philosophical ideas among clinicians, patients, and family members can revitalize everyone.

The insight that the thought of death inspires us to appreciate the preciousness of each moment is not limited to European culture. In Castaneda's (1968) descriptions of the teachings of a Yaqui Indian shaman, a central concept is that of "taking Death as one's advisor" in daily living. This idea is based on a belief that a personified Death resides always at one's side, ready at any moment to reach out and take one's life. The Yaqui warrior is counseled to keep this thought ever near his mind. He is thereby guided through life's decisions by the reminder that each choice or each instant may well be his last. It is therefore incumbent on the warrior to order his life so thoughtfully that he would be content to have any given moment be his final one.

Thoughts of death can remind us of the preciousness of each moment. (19)

A similar wisdom may be found in cultures all around the planet, and in great books ranging from Martin Heidegger's *Being and Time* to the *Tao Teh Ching* of Lao Tzu. In truth, this thought, verified by our own experience, has proven invaluable as we have worked in this field over the years. There can be no denying the emotional toll exacted by the charged atmosphere of terminal care settings. However, we have discovered that daily involvement with death and dying has imbued us with an increased appreciation for our lives that more than compensates us for the negative sides of this work.

In particular, perhaps the greatest gift to emerge is a sense of proportion. We are more acutely aware of what is worth the emotional toll of an argument, or the expenditure on petty conflicts of the mental energy that most professionals already find in such short supply. We find ourselves much less likely to quarrel with our spouses over trivialities, or to leave issues unresolved for long periods. At times, this altered sense of proportion has even allowed us the saving grace of humor and laughter when reality began to assume a particularly grim visage.

Further, we have often marveled at the courage and dignity with which certain patients and families manage to face the most horrifying situations. In many cases, we are profoundly uplifted by the essential nobility of the human spirit that we have been privileged to witness. It is thoughts such as these which sustain us through the moments of depression and despair that are inevitable for those involved in the care of the terminally ill.

References

Aries, P. 1974. *Western Attitudes Toward Death.* Baltimore: Johns Hopkins University Press.

Bowlby, J. 1961. Process of mourning. *Int. J. Psychoanal.* 42:317–340.

Bynner, W. (translator). 1962. *The Way of Life According to Lao Tzu.* New York: Capricorn Books.

Castaneda, C. 1968. *The Teachings of Don Juan.* New York: Simon & Schuster.

Choron, J. 1964. *Modern Man and Mortality.* New York: MacMillan Publishing Company, Inc.

Durkheim, E. 1951. *Suicide.* New York: The Free Press.

Freud, S. 1917. Mourning and melancholia. In Freud, S. 1953. *Complete Works, Vol XIV.* London: Hogarth.

This is Freud's historical contribution to the understanding of the grief process. It presents an early classical psychoanalytic viewpoint on mourning.

Heidigger, M. 1962. *Being and Time.* New York: Harper and Row.

Huxley, A. 1939. *After Many a Summer Dies the Swan.* New York: Harper and Row, Publishers, Inc.

Kaplan, D. and Mason, E. July 1960. Maternal reactions to premature birth. *Amer. J. Orthopsych.* 30:539–547.

Kastenbaum, R. and Aisenberg, R. 1972. *The Psychology of Death.* New York: Springer Publishing Company, Inc.

This superb volume is a 498 page compendium of the psychology of death. The major parameters of the topic are objectively and critically summarized. There is scholarly documentation in each chapter, plus serviceable author and subject indices at the end of the book. The prose at times borders on impenetrable, but is nevertheless worth the effort. A must for those seeking an in-depth perspective on the psychology of death.

Kubler-Ross, E. 1969. *On Death and Dying.* New York: Macmillan Publishing Company, Inc.

This best seller represents a dominant force in bringing dying patients to public attention. Although the theoretical model is admittedly oversimplified, there are sensitive descriptions and credible examples. If only because of its seminal role in demystifying terminal care, this book should be read by most educated persons.

Lindemann, E. 1944. Symptoms and management of acute grief. *Am. J. Psychiat.* 101:141.

Parkes, C. 1964. Effects of bereavement on physical and mental health. *Brit. Med. J.* 2:274–279.

Pattison, E. M., ed. 1977. *The Experience of Dying.* Englewood Cliffs, New Jersey: Prentice-Hall, Inc.

Tolstoy, L. 1886. *The Death of Ivan Ilych.* 1960 ed. New York: New American Library.

Weisman, A. D. 1980. Thanatology. In Kaplan et al, eds. 1980. *Comprehensive Textbook of Psychiatry.* Baltimore: Williams & Wilkins Co.

Yalom, I. 1980. *Existential Psychotherapy.* New York: Basic Books, Inc.
The author focuses on the four ultimate concerns of life: death, freedom, isolation, and meaninglessness. Within an existential framework he shows how these concerns are manifested in individual thoughts, feelings, and actions. He develops an approach to psychotherapy with which all counselors who deal with the dying or critically ill should be familiar. The case examples are valuable illustrations of practical approaches to interpersonal aspects of management of serious illness. Lots of nourishing mental food to last for many meals.

Barriers to
Effective
2 Communication

Overview

In this chapter, we explore first some circumstances under which communication problems between the seriously ill and others in their environment are most likely to arise. Three particular areas of interpersonal concern are assumption of authority, disclosure of information, *and* expression of strong emotions.

Later in the chapter we look at several negative results of ineffective communication *in the setting of life-threatening illness. Failures to communicate effectively may lead to mistrust, powerlessness, resentment, isolation, and inability to attend to important concerns.*

Circumstances Under Which Communications Tend to be Disrupted

Assumption and Divestment of Authority

Patients comply more readily when collaborating with an authoritative physician than when obeying an authoritarian one. (20)

Traditional attitudes of deference and unquestioning respect toward doctors are giving way to a more assertively consumer-oriented approach on the part of those receiving care. Many physicians may feel uncomfortable with more militant expressions of this attitude. There can be some clear advantages in this, however, for all concerned. These have to do with the authority-related issues of power and control. It is important to recognize that many patients are more likely to influence their health and quality of life positively when acting in collaboration with, rather than under orders of, caregivers.

Current epidemiologic evidence suggests that people can alter their life-styles to reduce their risks of getting many common catastrophic diseases. A sense of partnership between patients and professionals is more likely to evolve when patients assume responsibility for the way they live their lives. This becomes more feasible when patients know that by so doing they may reduce the likelihood of many cancers, vascular and lung diseases, hypertension, diabetes, and gastrointestinal ailments. Such a relationship creates a climate allowing easier interchange of thoughts and feelings among all parties involved. This, in turn, can prove to be an invaluable foundation when more catastrophic medical problems arise.

Patient participation in decision-making is particularly important in the context of life-threatening illness. (7, 20)

The cornerstone of the relationship between health care professionals and their patients is *mutual trust.* Individuals generally need to believe that those on whom they rely to guide them through the confusing maze of modern medical care are acting as true patient advocates. Consequently, professionals should make as few assumptions as possible as to what constitute the best interests of those whom they serve. This is particularly true in cases of terminal illness, because of the heavy emotional charge and feeling of helplessness inherent in most confrontations with death. Such strong reactions are too likely to cloud accurate judgment for clinicians to presume that they know what is best for their patients.

Where, then, does ultimate responsibility most appropriately belong in the patient–professional relationship? Ideally, professionals should operate in the framework of an open consensus as to the manner in which the interests of patients are being served. Most professionals find their work to be more satisfying and more effective when this is the case. In this way, the awesome responsibility of decision-making surrounding such vital issues as quantity and quality of life is shared among those most likely to make appropriate choices.

Professionals should work to counteract patients' feelings of inferiority.

All too often, patients and families see themselves as subordinate to health care professionals. When this is the case, they may be reluctant to participate to the extent necessary to insure that their own viewpoints are adequately presented. If professionals always were accurate in assessing and responding optimally to the needs of patients and families, then few problems would ensue. However, at least in fields primarily involving patient contact, a strong case can be made that such confidence in one's personal judgment constitutes unwarranted arrogance. Given the enormity of the possible consequences of decisions made in the setting of life-threatening illness, the appropriate sharing of responsibility with those most affected by such choices seems in order.

Opinions will differ sometimes as to the best course to follow. It may at times behoove professionals to yield to their patients' desires even when these are not entirely in line with medical judgment. This depends on each clinician's ability to reconcile personal ethics and self-esteem to such a course. If flexibility is possible, patients are provided with concrete evidence of their ability to influence the course of their treatment. There may be times when the result of capitulating to patients' desires is objectively negative as perceived by the professional. Even in such cases, there may be emotional benefits to patients and families in preserving their sense of control.

Further, the positive effect that such an exchange can have on patient–professional relationships in the long run may counterbalance any acute ill effects for patients. Clearly, barring mental incompetence, the ultimate power of decision should reside with the patient. At times, this precept may involve professionals in treatment programs that they cannot reconcile with their own judgment. When this is the case, they should reserve the right to withdraw from the case; this move should be made with respect, gentleness, and understanding. Further, it should include sincere efforts to provide an acceptable alternative caretaker.

Reaching Agreement on Disclosure of Information

Disclosure of information by professionals to patients is an important parameter of care.

Our minds constitute the primary tool whereby we order our world, and for most of us, *knowledge is power.* Hence, clinicians should attempt to provide their patients with as much information about their health care as can be usefully processed to guide informed and independent decision-making. In this way, professionals may assist patients to retain some sense of potency even in the face of death. Many people feel powerless when important decisions about their lives are made in ways that are mysterious to them. This may cause patients to withdraw or to become passively or overtly hostile. If this occurs, the patient may not only be an ineffective ally, but can evolve into an active opponent to optimal care.

Certain patients have no desire to maintain a sense of control regardless of their medical situations. Many of them may in fact expect those whom they place in authority to assume an overtly parental role. This regressive response is understandable in the face of life situations that are totally overwhelming. In fact, such behavior is often effective in eliciting the most attentive care in a traditional setting in which the *good patient* model tends to approximate that of an obedient child.

Such parent–child authority relationships between professional and patient tend to be even more prominent in the presence of terminal illness. In this context, problems of disclosure of information require special consideration. First, clinicians usually do not have the pervasive knowledge of the inner workings and value systems of their patients that parents generally possess concerning their children. Second, they are not granted the power to influence the lives of their patients that parents ordinarily have over offspring. Indeed, health care professionals may find that they have responsibilities akin to those of parenthood. They can feel rather uncomfortable when they realize they have neither the knowledge nor the prerogative to exercise such duties appropriately. At the very least, those who take on this *in loco parentis* (sometimes translated as *crazy parent*) role stand on shaky foundations while bearing a very heavy responsibility for correctly assessing the best interests of their assumed charges. For this reason alone, many clinicians find it necessary to insist on certain minimal levels of disclosure even in the face of direct requests to the contrary.

Strategies regarding disclosure should be developed early in the physician–patient relationship.

The degree and timing of disclosure should be discussed early in the formation of the patient–professional relationship, and as directly as possible. This involves an early open inquiry as to how much the patient and family wish to know, as well as how often. Such an exchange can identify and may well circumvent many potential problems related to disclosure. In addition, it clearly demonstrates to patients and families that their thoughts and feelings are likely to be heard.

Differences between the wishes of patients and families and those of professionals often cause conflicts in terminal care settings. A good rule in dealing with such conflicts at their outset applies as well to many other therapeutic circumstances. Briefly, it is often useful to begin with nonjudgmental inquiry into the emotions and fantasies underlying the content of expressions of conflict. In a surprising number of cases, the opportunity to voice ordinarily unexpressed feelings surrounding highly charged issues may considerably reduce the intensity of emotion. This often suffices to allow more reasoned and appropriate communications. Additionally, professionals may be provided with further information about the intrapersonal and interpersonal psychodynamics of patients and their families. The resultant insights can prove invaluable in guiding clinicians toward more effective management of future interactions.

In some instances, however, simple ventilation will not suffice to enable patients, families, and professionals to agree about the most reasonable solution of disclosure conflicts. An alternative is a compromise between the disparate viewpoints. This is often difficult to obtain in such emotionally charged settings. In some situations, particularly when the professional is one of the parties at odds, an experienced consultant serving as an outside mediator can be of great value. In other instances, it may be necessary either to accede to the wishes of patients and families, or even to refer to another professional who might be willing to do so.

When to refer.

Health care professionals must clearly and explicitly retain the right to reevaluate any agreements made with patients and families about limitations on disclosure. There may be times when clinicians are pressed into tacit or overt collaboration in restricting information. In such cases, it is important that all parties be aware that situations may arise where clinical judgment dictates breaking the silence. This often happens as the course of a disease progresses to a point where the truth becomes obvious even to the most opaque of those not in confidence. It also may be precipitated by some psychological crisis arising from the high stress inherent in such situations.

Clinical judgment may dictate violation of disclosure restrictions in some instances.

When the need to break the silence arises, the professional should discuss it openly with the other parties involved in the conspiracy, if feasible. The professional should describe in simple terms the specific factors involved in the assessment that the silence must be broken. If resistance persists, an attempt to focus on underlying feelings is again in order. Sometimes this technique will not suffice, and appropriate intervention by outside mediators may prove ineffective or be unavailable. Then, an alternative is to suggest disclosure as a precondition for continuing care. These measures usually obviate the need for referral, but if such becomes indicated the transfer should be made in as supportive a manner as possible.

When to refer.

Adverse Effects of Withholding Information

It is usually impractical even to attempt deception. (4, 15)

Much communication of feelings ordinarily takes place nonverbally. In the setting of terminal illness, an intense emotional atmosphere often is present. Therefore, it is naive to assume that loved ones confronted with the patient's imminent mortality could conceal that something important is occurring. Even if they were skilled enough actors to maintain such a deception to the world in general, the persons least likely to be taken in would be those with whom they are most intimate.

Furthermore, these same people are the cast around whom the greatest conflicts arise concerning disclosure of information in the setting of life-threatening disease. Any effort to deceive the persons to whom one is closest is most likely doomed to failure, and generally serves only to complicate an already confusing situation.

Families who wish to conceal the nature or prognoses of diseases from a member who is suffering from them operate under a peculiar assumption. They imagine that the terminally ill will be more likely to believe what they are told than to heed signals from their own bodies. As most of us are well aware, persons with life-threatening illnesses generally reach a point of instinctive awareness that something major is amiss.

Patients often deny the gravity of their illnesses. (4)

Patients often deny the gravity of their status in spite of subliminal awareness. There are often painful and poignant moments when they ask directly for reassurance that their situation is not critical. However, such statements should not be interpreted simply as indications that patients do not wish to be told the seriousness of their situations. Rather, these requests for reassurance generally constitute examples of common coping reactions to the overwhelming reality to be faced. One way of reacting to such comments is to address openly the underlying feelings of powerlessness and hopelessness without attempting to deal with the manifest content of the statement unless the patient pursues it.

The unknown seems to summon a much larger and more frightening collection of hobgoblins for most of us than does the known. When fear of death arises, no matter how certain we may profess to be about what may follow this life, we generally have no direct corroborative experience to which to appeal. When people sense that they or a loved one are seriously ill, legions of negative fantasies often emerge. However, if they are not told that death is imminent, the usual coping mechanisms that assist in contending with negative realities often cannot come into play. Too often we forget that humankind has been dealing with devastating truths since the beginning of human awareness. We firmly believe that mechanisms for healing terrible emotional wounds are present in most people. Hence, insulating any competent person from reality concerning issues of utmost personal and existential concern is more likely to do harm than good.

Some guidelines about professional collaboration in deception. (20)

As we have noted, pressure not to disclose information about the situation is commonly encountered by staff members in settings of terminal illness. This can derive from the patient or from the family; ironically, in a large number of cases, it is simultaneously present in both. Fortunately, this situation has been illuminated to some extent by systematic outcome studies which examined the effect of communication on families faced with terrible realities. Work described by

Kaplan (1976) supports the view that open communication of information about life-threatening disease is a reliable predictor of better adjustment for the family system in question. There are equally good data to support the contention that patients with intact mental status rarely are deceived successfully about the nature and seriousness of their condition.

Disclosure should be limited as little as is practicable. (20)

Clearly, in most cases the interests of all involved are served best by reducing limitations on disclosure to as low a level as is practicable. Ideally, all key members of the patient's support community should be aware of significant information regarding the patient's illness. In order to achieve this end, however, it usually is not appropriate for professionals simply to defy the expressed wishes of the family or patient when the latter disagree with such a standard of disclosure. Professionals, however, should not partake in any restrictions of disclosure with which they experience moral or ethical discomfort.

When families request that patients not be informed of their prognosis, the situation usually is less conflicted for the professional. Many believe that such a prohibition is a serious denial of the fundamental right of individuals to have the opportunity to confront that most enormous of realities—their own death. It thus would seem particularly reasonable, when circumstances permit, to make disclosure of such information to the patient a precondition of participation in the care of that person.

Situations in which patients request that professionals withhold information from family members are not so well-defined, and often present a greater problem. Clinicians should begin by exploring the feelings and thoughts underlying such a request. They should do so without any effort to dissuade, but rather in the hope that further clarity resulting from unpressured discussion might permit a more reasoned approach. This can be followed by clear and simple explanations of the probable advantages for all concerned of an open climate of disclosure. When patients remain adamant even in the face of such measures, the responsibility of maintaining deceptions can be placed squarely on the patient by a clear statement that professionals are not willing to lie if directly confronted on the issue.

Expression of Strong Emotions

The common unease of physicians dealing with strong emotions arises from sources in both the general culture and their specific training. (20)

Few of us who grew up in the cultural mainstream with exposure to the popular media can claim total exemption from the widespread American taboo against public demonstration of vulnerability. Societal admiration of coolness under pressure serves us well in many respects; maintenance of a stoic front in situations calling for emotional expression is not one of them. If any life event requires the ability to express and resolve difficult feelings in order to be successfully negotiated, it is an encounter with death.

Many health care professionals have an additional and more specific barrier to comfort with direct experience and expression of strong feelings (see Chapter 14). They often learn, chiefly by example, behavior referred to as *"clinical detachment."* Even in popular usage, the adjective "clinical" generally is considered to be antithetical to "warm" or "emotionally involved." We do not mean that a dispassionate stance is not useful or vital in many settings, such as for the surgeon or anesthesiologist during a highly technical operation. However, the level of detachment required to wield a scalpel optimally is likely to be anathema in dealing with strong feelings surrounding loss and grief. It is incumbent on health care professionals to recognize that personal styles of dealing with strong emotions constitute an important part of what they can offer to patients. They should strive to be aware of the nature of these styles in general and of their own emotional interaction with each patient in particular. If they are not, it is as though they blindly prescribe treatments whose properties are unfamiliar.

The one area in most of our lives about which even the most taciturn of us is likely to harbor and express strong emotions is that of death. This may apply even more to health care professionals than to the general public (see Chapter 14). In any event, those who are involved with patients in the setting of life-threatening illness are bound to encounter frequent expression, either overt or indirect, of strong feelings. Outpourings of anguish or despair are bound to strike responsive chords within attendant professionals. The exact nature of the reaction varies widely among clinicians, depending on their own degree of comfort with the issues and emotions in question. At one end of the range of response there is profound participation in the grief of patients and families. At the opposite extreme clinicians may feel a sense of discomfort or intrusion, and even rage at being forced to confront that with which one is existentially uncomfortable.

Patients are likely to sense the emotions of their caretakers. (4)

There is one aspect of this situation, however, about which we can be relatively certain. This is that patients and families are likely to sense professionals' reactions, regardless of how indirectly the latter express themselves, or how adept they may be at verbal concealment of inner experience. The sheer intensity of feelings evoked by death and dying enhances the strength of nonverbal expressions to the point where they are unlikely to be missed. This probability may be further increased by an augmented sensitivity of patients and families to the emotional atmosphere surrounding this most intense of life situations. Hence, like it or not, it is safe to assume that those for whom professionals care probably will be aware of their caretakers' reactions.

Mixed Messages

Mixed messages are a particular problem in terminal care settings.

Given the likelihood that the feelings of professionals involved in the care of the dying will be sensed by patients and families, a question arises concerning agreement of overt and covert communications. In general, most of us are more comfortable with situations and relationships wherein a sense of ambiguity is kept at a minimum. The psychological origins of this phenomenon in the course of personality development are more discussed than agreed upon, but its truth is not in great dispute. Of course, living presents us with many ambiguous situations, and each of us develops methods of coping with them. The extent of inconsistency that most of us find comfortable is related to the emotionality of a situation. Generally, the more intense the feelings elicited, the less equivocation is easily tolerated.

Clinicians involved with the terminally ill may be particularly likely to encounter problems surrounding ambiguity both within themselves and within their patients. Trust in caregivers becomes even more crucial in the face of the overwhelming realities of death. Dying patients and their families are likely to exhibit exquisite sensitivity to double messages from professionals. If such confusion does occur, the reactions are likely to be mistrust, withdrawal, and anger.

Professionals also need to be aware of their own reactions, and sensitive to the appropriateness of the expression of their feelings. Some resolution concerning the existential issues surrounding death and dying is vital if clinicians' reactions are not to shift the focus of therapeutic interaction from distress of the patient to that of the professional.

Mixed messages can result in resentment, mistrust, guilt, and a sense of abandonment, as well as causing inappropriate role reversals. (16)

When health care personnel are ill at ease either with their own emotional responses or with the communication of such reactions, a number of possible untoward sequelae may arise. As discussed, patients and families are unlikely to remain in the dark about the fact that something adverse is going on, although they may or may not sense the specific problem. Given the gravity of the situation, they will tend to fear the worst or to attribute the professional's response to some shortcoming on their own part.

One common reaction of patients is to assume a caretaking stance toward professionals whom they sense to be uncomfortable. At times, such a role reversal can be a welcome relief for patients who are constantly confronted with their powerlessness and need to be taken care of. However, in most such instances the resultant additional confusion and perpetuation (or even escalation) of mixed messages are detrimental for all concerned. Feelings of resentment, mistrust, guilt, and abandonment are likely results when patients feel obliged to take on the care of professionals.

A related complication is that patients and families may be encouraged to ignore or deny important clinical signs because of possible dire implications. Professionals may tacitly support this denial by the nonverbal communication that such news is unwelcome, and hence better left unsaid. When this happens, patients may unconsciously or even willfully withhold important information in order to "help" clinicians to deal with their own unwanted feelings. The resulting failure of timely communication, as well as the negative emotional climate, work against the provision of optimal care. Both are preventable, as discussed in Chapter 3. But first, we will examine more closely some direct results of poor communication in terminal care settings.

Results of Poor Communication

Mistrust

Reactions of mistrust naturally arise in situations where people receive conflicting messages about very important matters. Conflicting messages may arise either from other people or from one's own body. For example, when a conspiracy of silence exists, no matter how well it is orchestrated, there are likely to be inconsistencies on both verbal and nonverbal levels. Even if everyone involved could coordinate their stories precisely, few nonprofessional actors could carry on such a deception on an emotional level as well. This is particularly true when the unwitting audience is intimately familiar with the key players.

Mistrust can arise when mixed messages are received.

Overt conflicts almost inevitably arise on an informational level as well. This generally happens as the conspirators are forced to improvise in the face of a very complex reality and a very worried patient. The dying persons who are the focus of such deceptions are likely to come to doubt the trustworthiness of those on whom they are most dependent. This mistrust occurs at a time when a sense of solidarity and mutuality are more critical than at any other period. We emphasize that this principle applies as much to their family and friends as it does to the dying patients themselves.

Powerlessness

Issues of power and control become glaringly prominent in the context of terminal disease. There is probably no phenomenon other than death that forces us to confront so starkly the difficult reality of our own limitations in life. This encounter with finitude serves more than any other single fact of our lives to remind us of our limited ability to influence what happens to ourselves and our loved ones. Thus, in order to have active partners in creating an optimal experience for all involved, caregivers should reinforce whenever possible a sense of mastery and control in patients and families. This encourages those receiving care to be effective allies operating to serve their own best interests.

Issues of communication often become intimately linked with those of power and control. Frequently, in the setting of terminal care, patients, caregivers, or significant members of the support system may be excluded from important knowledge. When this occurs, they are likely to experience an amplification of their feelings of powerlessness. This probably derives from the observation that it is largely through knowledge that we are enabled to order our existence. In popular language, the attempt to plot one's course without adequate information is indeed "stumbling in the dark." The ability to act as effectively as possible can become painfully precious when one is harshly forced to confront one's limitations. Clearly, appropriate communication is vital to the quality of the experience of anyone involved with life-threatening disease.

Feelings of powerlessness are amplified when patients are excluded from important information.

Resentment and Uncooperativeness

One of the consequences of the mistrust and powerlessness that frequently ensues from poor communication in settings of terminal illness is the development of anger. This emotion tends to arise from loss of a sense of control, and may be accentuated when feelings of impotence seem to be reinforced by the actions of others. This is especially true in situations involving those upon whom the dying already feel dependent for support. Anger may be expressed in a number of ways. Family members may encounter it in the patient's ill-temper, sullenness, or complaining and demanding behavior. Professionals more often observe withdrawal and unwillingness to cooperate in treatment as a manifestation of anger. This passively expressed animosity can make the already frustrated caregiver even more exasperated. As a result, matters can escalate in a frenetic spiral of indirectly expressed anger on everyone's part.

Anger resulting from poor communication often manifests as lack of cooperation.

Isolation and Abandonment

Another outcome of communication failures with life-threatening disease is that those excluded from significant knowledge are likely to feel isolated and abandoned. This is particularly poignant because, more than in any other situation, dying brings up the need to feel nurtured and supported. Solidarity and a sense of mutual connection with those who are most important is vital. It is sadly ironic to see

Exclusion caused by poor communication results in feelings of isolation and abandonment.

patients or family members so often assaulted with precisely the opposite feeling.

This sense of exclusion is further heightened by the tendency of those involved in a deception to avoid (either physically or emotionally) the deceived person. This often occurs precisely because of the tension involved in maintaining such a fiction. Such abandonment occurs not only within families, but has been experimentally observed and quantified on hospital wards as well (see Glaser and Strauss, 1968).

Failure to Attend to Important Business

Poor communication may result in failure to attend to important material, emotional, and spiritual business.

Foreknowledge of an impending death offers all those involved an opportunity to prevent a number of problems. On a purely mundane level, those who die with their worldly affairs in order free their loved ones to attend to the important emotional business of grieving. Otherwise, the bereaved are likely to find themselves spending a critical period of their lives trying to sort through unfamiliar business affairs while in a state of shock.

Even more critical, however, is an opportunity for the dying and their loved ones to finish up some of the unresolved emotional business that inevitably exists even in the most blissful of relationships. The amount of guilt and self-recrimination that can be prevented by the successful outcome of such exchanges is enormous. Needless to say, it is often difficult to take care of any of these matters when everyone is struggling to maintain the fiction that death is not actually imminent. Further, if a deception is being played out on a family member, that person may well act out many of these negative emotions toward the dying patient. This can result eventually in greatly increased guilt and self-recrimination, with a high potential for grief pathology.

Open communication serves everyone's best interests. (20)

In summary, the best interests of everyone involved in a terminal illness generally are served by as open a climate of communication as possible. Health care professionals should evolve a personally comfortable set of approaches whereby they can promote an atmosphere of openness. Some strategies for accomplishing these ends constitute the bulk of Chapter 3.

References

Bok, S. 1978. *Lying: Moral Choice in Public and Private Life*. New York: Pantheon Books, Inc.

This is an excellent comprehensive philosophical study of one of the most pervasive potential barriers to effective communication. The entire book is worthwhile; the chapters on the nature of lying, how lying affects human choice, paternalistic lies, and lies to the sick and dying are particularly cogent.

Garfield, C. A. ed. 1978. *Psychosocial Care of the Dying Patient.* San Francisco: McGraw-Hill Books, Inc.

Despite redundancy of content and variability of quality in 39 chapters by at least as many authors, the book's overall rating is quite good. There are several outstanding contributions in the area of therapeutic communication with the dying. The chapters by Cicely Saunders and Edwin Shneidman warrant particular attention.

Glaser, B.G. and Strauss, A. L. 1968. *Time for Dying.* Chicago: Aldine Publishing Company.

Kaplan, D. M, Grobstein, R. and Smith, A. 1976. Predicting the impact of severe illness in families. *Health and Social Work* 1:72–82.

Kaplan, D. M. 1982. Interventions for disorders of change. *Social Work* 27:404–410.

Senescu, R. 1969. The problem of establishing communication with the seriously ill patient. *Annals of the New York Academy of Science* 164:696–706.

3 Attaining Effective Communication

Overview

In Chapter 2, we presented some major negative consequences of ineffective communication on the care of the dying. In addition, we explored aspects of interpersonal relationships in which communication problems are most likely to arise. We shall now focus more closely on some guidelines that may promote more effective communication between the seriously ill and others in their environment.

We begin by examining strategies intended to reduce anxiety in both health care professionals and their patients. Then we present a set of specific techniques to enhance the effectiveness of communication in terminal care.

Elements of a Strategy for Better Communication

Creation of a Relaxed and Unhurried Environment

Most medical settings seem to be pervaded by an atmosphere of chronic hurry and overwork. This constant sense of rush imparts a strained and unnatural quality to encounters between health care personnel and their patients. Therefore, professionals should aim for as relaxed and unhurried an atmosphere as is practical when they are interacting with their patients. This becomes particularly important in settings surrounding life-threatening illness. Once again, we must recall that in such situations assistance with coping on an emotional level may be the most concrete help professionals can offer.

Before discussing difficult issues, clinicians should (1) take stock of the level of tension, (2) assess time limitations, and (3) tailor communication to the degree of upset. (4)

Before initiating a discussion that is likely to involve difficult issues, clinicians should take stock of their own state of tension. They should also assess the realistic limits on the amount of time immediately available for the encounter at hand. If they do not have the necessary time, or if they are unable to enter the room in a calm and focused state of mind, then they should leave emotionally charged issues for another interaction. In a similar vein, if clinicians assess their patients to be in a state of emotional turmoil, then they should tailor the amount of information to be presented or sought to the degree of upset. Heightened tensions, particularly in the context of life-threatening illness, often reduce the quantity of data that individuals usefully can absorb; regardless of the importance of what is being communicated. Patience and willingness to repeat explanations until patients clearly understand key points will pay great dividends.

Asking patients to recapitulate key points can aid communication.

Most professionals have learned to recognize patients' glassy-eyed look when they lose the thread of an interaction. There will be times when caregivers detect such signals, or, more generally, when the emotional tension during an interview is high. At such moments, professionals can interrupt the flow of conversation periodically to ask patients to recapitulate what they consider to be the key points of the communication.

If the patient's interpretations are obviously in error, attempts to correct them can be made at once. If the patient's statements are correct, it may be deemed appropriate to proceed further. In the presence of an anxiety-laden emotional climate, professionals may conclude that further information would serve only to cloud the issue. At times, however, it may be considered vital that a particular agenda of communication be met at a given encounter regardless of the emotional climate. In such instances, clinicians should be willing to adjust the mode of the interaction or to take additional time if required, rather than simply reducing the scope of the interview.

Finally, the moment of disclosure of a life-threatening illness cannot always be orchestrated or even anticipated. As one oncology nursing coordinator put it, "Many people have hit me with The Big Question while I was performing the most innocuous of tasks." In such instances, a frank statement that the clinician who happens to be on the spot is not yet sufficiently informed to be certain often suffices to divert important disclosures until a more opportune moment. If patients or family members persist, they can be reminded that important issues are best discussed when everyone involved is as fully prepared as possible. Although such a statement is undeniably ominous, it is honest and may even allow the patient and family some time for advance emotional preparation.

Demystification of Medical Issues

The language of medicine alone easily can serve to render medical concepts inaccessible to patients and families in any setting. Current estimates approximate the number of new words encountered in the process of standard medical education to be somewhere around ten times the speaking vocabulary of the average American. Hence, health care personnel can have entire conversations with laypersons in which few words and even fewer concepts are understood. This can happen even without any attempt to be obscure.

The use of appropriate vocabulary is a first step in demystifying medical issues.

In the face of the existential abyss presented by life-threatening illness, it is natural for professionals to feel nonplussed. Therefore, it is not uncommon to react to personal feelings of discomfort by taxing patients with extensive technical explanations. This can serve the purpose of falsely reassuring caregivers that maybe they do have some power over the disease in question. At least they certainly can demonstrate a great deal of knowledge about it! Such behavior may also convince patients that their attendant professionals are apparently in control of the situation. Unfortunately, it can equally persuade the dying and their loved ones that they are totally helpless and dependent even in the understanding of their own situations. Such an attitude is unlikely to result in the enlistment of patients as active and effective allies in coping with their situations. Behavior that might produce these feelings is therefore to be avoided whenever possible.

If communication rather than intimidation is the goal of professionals, they should use language that is likely to be comprehensible to their patients. One guide for this is to use the patient's own vocabulary for key phrases in an interaction. However, special caution is necessary when patients use medical terminology, which frequently is ill-understood by them. Problems arising in this context often can be avoided by asking patients to define key terms that they employ. This can be done while explaining that clear communication is critical to provision of health care.

Problems with authority and the medical mystique are addressed by minimizing the hierarchical distance between professionals and patients.

A related consideration concerns the magnitude of hierarchical superiority held by health care professionals. This may derive in part from the aura of mystery surrounding this arcane and vital realm of human endeavor. The mystique surrounding medicine is supported by clinicians' daily contact with such awesome realities as birth, pain, disease, and death. In addition, it is assiduously cultivated in the popular media. Even those who make no conscious or unconscious efforts to encourage such a mystique may routinely encounter deification by their patients. Unfortunately, this hierarchical ordering encourages the mystique and magnifies authority problems. These, in turn, severely limit professional effectiveness by closing avenues of communication.

Open channels for the transfer of information are even more central in the setting of terminal disease than in routine medical care. This is because the burden of providing optimal care for the dying rests so heavily on the family and support community. Professionals serve their patients best by dealing sensitively with authority problems arising from these hierarchical attitudes. In so doing, they can enable crucial supporting persons to feel that they are important peers involved in a cooperative effort.

Temporization with Prognostic Statements

Consider timing, content, and mode of presentation when making prognoses.

One of the most difficult issues confronting professionals in the setting of life-threatening illness is an expectation that they will be able to predict the course of the disease. In reality, few, if any, can do this with certainty for any given patient. Nonetheless, statistical information about outcomes for patients in similar stages of similar diseases can be of great use to patients and families. It gives them some clues, albeit tentative, about their probable future.

However, professionals should always surround prognostic statements with clear disclaimers as to the ability of statistics to describe or predict the course of any individual's disease. Similar reasoning applies to prognoses derived from clinical judgment, because these too are based on experience with some referent population. In brief, prognostic information can and should be sensitively communicated when it is deemed of use to patients and families, or when it is sought by them. Such communications should be tentative, general, and made when there is time to help the recipients to cope with their reactions. We will address this issue in more detail in Chapter 4.

Modulation of Personal Involvement

Those who are involved in the care of persons confronting life-threatening illness are bound to encounter strong emotions both in their patients and themselves. Sadness, fear, and anger are the most common emotions encountered in these settings. Cultivation of an awareness of these feelings in themselves and in their patients and colleagues is the initial task professionals face in approaching this issue. Failing this, there can be little successful facilitation of emotional processes, because the necessary emotional data will not have been collected. This can be particularly distressing in situations in which technological interventions no longer are useful. At that point, assisting patients and families with the resolution of emotional issues may constitute the most concrete help that professionals have to offer.

Awareness of feelings is the first step in effective modulation of personal involvement. (17)

Once awareness of feelings is established, clinicians should work toward an optimal experience for patients, their families, and other caregivers. Particular pathways toward that end may be difficult to anticipate, but we can offer some guidelines regarding communication of feelings.

First, if there is emotional tension between staff members, the whole sense of mutual collaboration toward coping with this trying situation is jeopardized. This is only partly due to the atmosphere generated by interpersonal uneasiness. In addition, colleagues may be the best support system available for help in clarifying and resolving emotional issues surrounding patient care. Thus, a vital foundation for dealing with such issues among caregivers in high stress settings is the establishment of a relatively free climate for expression and resolution of strong emotions within the health care team. Even in the best of circumstances, situations may become too highly charged to be worked out among colleagues in isolation. In such cases, the availability of skilled outside mediators often can be of great value for all concerned.

Professionals should differentiate between (1) communication of feelings among colleagues, and (2) communication of feelings to patients and families.

When to consult.

Another issue involves expression of feelings by health care professionals to patients and their families. The important questions to keep in mind are: *Who is the patient?* and *Who is the caretaker?* The expression of strong emotions often can be a supportive and nurturing experience for persons receiving them, particularly for those facing terminal disease. Hearing about such feelings from those upon whom they depend so greatly can greatly reassure patients and families. Patients may be reminded that their plight has not totally isolated them from the rest of humanity. Expression of strong emotions can offer confirmation that patients still can evoke important human reactions from those around them. This type of communication may provide evidence that professionals are deeply involved—that they truly care!

Expression of strong emotions to patients and families often should be delayed until its potential effect is examined.

On the other hand, the immediate expression to patients and families of spontaneous strong emotions generally is to be avoided. This is because the existential issues in terminal care settings often evoke reactions primarily relevant only to the person experiencing them. A general rule is to examine the potential effect on patients of communication of feelings. Great care should be taken if professionals are at all in doubt as regards their own motivations for such expressions. It is essential in such cases to talk it out with other members of the health care team before approaching patients or their families to communicate one's feelings. Once again, if resolution fails to emerge from consul-

When to consult.

tation with colleagues directly involved in the case, outside consultation often can prove invaluable.

CASE ILLUSTRATION

A 61-year-old man dying of metastatic lung cancer was visited frequently by his somewhat officious wife. The attending physician found himself consistently irritated at her constant requests for consultation, information, and additional services. In a staff conference with a consulting psychiatrist, two major observations emerged. First, the physician became aware that the woman's requests probably reflected her sense of helplessness and her need to exert some mastery over this alien environment. Second, he recognized that these interactions highlighted his own sense of frustration in trying to help this likeable gentleman. This knowledge enabled him to deal more gracefully with her in the future by arranging scheduled daily five-minute conferences devoted entirely to addressing her concerns.

Differences in style of emotional expression should be taken into account when modulating professional involvement.

Problems often arise in situations in which there is a significant difference in personal styles of emotional expression between those receiving care and those providing it. Such instances may prove highly frustrating for all involved if a workable compromise is not evolved early in the relationship.

At times, clinical judgment may indicate to professionals that the long-term mental health of certain patients and families may be better served by a radical change in their patterns of relating. However, styles of communication of feelings may be very deeply rooted in personality structure. These patterns may be so fundamental as to be approachable only with difficulty by the most skilled of psychotherapists. Thus, when tentative and gentle introduction of such topics fails to elicit any corrective response, it is time to reconsider.

At times, the concluding judgment after careful thought and discussion by the health care team may be that the interests of patients and families are seriously jeopardized by their patterns of relating. In these cases, a more direct and forceful presentation of the profession-

When to refer.

als' viewpoint of the problem and its possible sequelae can be attempted. If patients and families still resist reexamining their current patterns, the next step is to consider referral to an outside psychiatric consultant, provided those receiving care are willing. If they are not, it may be necessary to abide within the limits of interactional styles that are comfortable to the patients and families in question. Unfortunately, the tension generated within and among health care personnel by such a situation can have a profoundly negative influence.

CASE ILLUSTRATION

A 52-year-old woman was dying of recurrent breast cancer. She had lived for the past 34 years in a very dependent relationship with her husband, a forceful and successful engineer. After the third recurrence of her disease, she was exhausted and strongly opposed to any further treatment not directed toward easing her symptoms. Unfortunately, she felt unable to communicate this to her husband, who adamantly pressed to prolong her life at all costs. Attempts by staff members to address this problem with each of the couple separately only confirmed the polarity of their respective positions. An attempt by the attending physician to mediate the issue in a family meeting failed when the wife refused to speak out against her husband's opinion. Psychiatric referral finally was made.

In separate sessions with each of the couple, the consultant confirmed the extreme communication problem. She also uncovered the husband's overwhelming sense of helplessness, dependency, and inability to express directly his love for his wife. In his mind, pressing her to "fight on" and not succumb to any "weak thoughts" was the best demonstration of his love. The wife revealed a relative acceptance of her fate, enormous anger at her spouse's disrespect for her feelings, and absolute frustration at her inability to communicate. In a couple's therapy session, these issues at last came into the open, allowing some very important communication to take place over the next few weeks. In the end, all parties involved felt that some fundamental issues were resolved, significantly enhancing the quality of the last few months of the woman's life.

Physical Contact

Expression of feelings through physical contact is a special concern. (7)

The sensitive issue of physical contact between health care personnel and their patients deserves special consideration. A great deal of touching ordinarily takes place in the process of carrying out the technical aspects of providing care. This is, however, rather sharply differentiated from the use of touch as a means of communication. Of the nonverbal means we employ to convey emotions, touch is the most intimate. Often, it can be the most powerful as well. Within mainstream American culture there exists a pronounced discomfort with physical contact (beyond a handshake) between those not closely related. Thus, the clinician may be presented with a troublesome dilemma. On one hand, professionals may have routine physical contact with some of the most private functions of their charges. At the same time, they may feel excluded from any overt physical expression of their concern and affection.

Although simple resolution of this problem may not be possible, a few guidelines may prove helpful. It is possible to gather cues from the way patients and families interact as to the level of physical contact they find appropriate among those whom they hold most intimate. Many American families are uncomfortable with physical expressions of warmth even within their own bounds. In such cases, the likelihood is small that members will welcome physical expression by an outsider. Equally useful are more immediate cues regarding the reactions of those receiving care to otherwise innocuous physical contacts such as a touch on the hand or arm during conversation with the professional. Someone who demonstrates withdrawal or unresponsiveness to such actions is an unlikely candidate for *hug therapy* for depression.

Cues regarding the propriety of touch as a means of communicating feelings to patients include (1) observing patient–family interactions, (2) asking directly, and (3) recognizing the limits of one's own comfort.

There may be times when clinicians feel the urge to provide physical comfort to terminally ill patients or their families by holding a hand. Many times, giving a consoling hug seems the appropriate thing to do. At such moments, it is usually permissible to ask openly whether such a gesture would be welcome. If there is any doubt in the professional's mind, he or she can say something like, "I feel touched by what you are experiencing and would like to hold your hand (or give you a hug) if you feel comfortable with that." If those being asked have already identified the professional as someone with whom they can deal openly, then an honest verbal response, either negative or positive, should not be too difficult to make.

In the reverse situation, the professional may feel ill-at-ease with physical contact initiated by the patient. Caregivers should not feel obliged to maintain such interactions if they cause discomfort. A graceful means of disengagement should be sought, particularly if the contact initiated seems at all inappropriate. There may indeed be instances where there is a question of whether or not the patient was acting reasonably in touching the caregiver. In these cases, the professional should talk it over with others involved in the case. Such a discussion may yield a consensus that the patient was not taking undue liberties. When this happens, it is incumbent upon professionals to examine closely their inner source for such reactions.

We have examined the elements of a strategy which may lead toward better communication. In the last half of this chapter we shall present a set of specific techniques aimed at further enhancing the effectiveness of communication.

Development of Specific Communication Skills

Need for Communication Skills

It may seem rather strange even to consider *communication* as particular set of skills that may be cultivated. However, the sad fact is that whereas the senses of the average health care professional may function more than adequately, effective assimilation of what has been perceived seems far rarer than it should be. One particularly useful attempt to bridge this gap between observation and understanding has been made by Ivey and Authier (1978). They have formulated a set of individual communication skills that can be learned and practiced separately until they are integrated into one's individual style. Some specific elements of this model include nonverbal communication, minimal encouragements, open and closed questions, paraphrasing, reflection of feeling, and summarization. We will discuss each of these concepts at length, even though much (or even all) of what follows may be second nature in practice to a large portion of our audience.

Nonverbal Communication

A basic process in the interaction between patient and professional involves nonverbal communication. Specifically, it is largely through media other than words that the message "I am interested in what you have to say," or its converse, may be transmitted. We have all encountered the physician whose primary attention seems to be on the chart, or on the next scheduled patient. The clear message to the patient in such an instance often is "You are a problem I have to solve," rather than "You are a person whose problems we can address together."

Attention is communicated nonverbally by eye contact, body position, and body movement.

This brings up the first point in effective body language between professional and patient: namely, how we communicate *attention*. Partly, this is accomplished by gaze. Patients whose caretakers never look directly into their eyes cannot help but question the extent to which they exist as persons in the mind of the professional. Conversely, people who are constantly transfixed by a penetrating stare may begin to feel as though they are specimens. Comfort with eye contact is quite variable between cultures, and between individuals within a given culture. Professionals do best to start with a level of eye contact with which they personally feel at ease. This can be modified when necessary by using the patient's own variation of eye contact as the cue for what feels comfortable to that person.

This rule of thumb applies to other aspects of nonverbal interaction as well. More specifically, although clinicians may look patients squarely in the eyes, their body positioning may tell a different story. For example, turning your body at right angles to the patient and leaning toward the door may clearly communicate a desire to break contact. During some portions of an interaction such a posture may be antithetical to optimal communication. Toward the end of a specific contact, however, it may serve as a gentle reminder that a "goodbye" is imminent. This can allow patients an opportunity to finish communicating any points which are unresolved.

Another important aspect of nonverbal interaction is the general level of movement on the part of the professional. Total stillness or rigidity of body or expression, or constant fidgeting or habitual movement of any sort, can intimidate or communicate discomfort whether or not either is intended. Unfortunately, most of us do not have a high level of awareness of our own movements during conversation. Observing a videotape of an encounter with a patient can be of considerable value with respect to increasing awareness of one's own nonverbal communication.

A frequent complaint about physicians concerns their tendency to read or write in charts during conversation with patients. Such behavior often enhances the sense of dehumanization which is so often evoked in the lay population by medical settings.

Minimal Encouragements

Empathic listening encourages patients to communicate. (20)

The second skill is the use of minimal actions and words on the part of the professional. This encourages the patient to communicate by providing reassurance that the flow of the conversation is being followed. Clinicians can indicate attention largely by the usual simple supportive nods and sounds that most people use quite naturally in everyday conversation.

The first issue here is that of *silence*. It is sometimes difficult to remember that the most basic invitation to speak is the creation of some space for that speech to occupy. Most of us have encountered the phrase "I could not get a word in edgewise." That concept illuminates the need for professionals to leave plenty of *listening spaces* in the flow of questions and explanations. This provides vital opportunities for patients to insert unprompted communications that can supply important information in areas the clinician may not have anticipated.

Silence may seem particularly uncomfortable in settings surrounding terminal disease. This is perhaps because we are more sensitive than usual to the awesome nature of what may underlie the absence of vocalization. Hence, professionals often lay down barrages of information that result less in knowledge for patients than in some sense of control for uncomfortable clinicians. Although this reaction is quite natural, it can end many vital possibilities for understanding on the part of all involved.

In order to use silence effectively, the professional must in fact be reasonably comfortable on a personal level with the existential and emotional implications of terminal illness. The achievement of such comfort is discussed in Chapter 1, and is by no means a trivial accomplishment.

Simple nods and sounds are principle mechanisms of minimal encouragement.

Key to the concept of minimal encouragements is that the expression of simple nods and sounds—be they affirmative or negative—must facilitate patients' communication rather than distract them. Because there are many widely varying personal styles of communication, we suggest that professionals observe the patient's style and reactions to guide the interaction.

In order to be most effective, professionals should be aware of and alert to a few specific points. First, they should avoid stereotyped gestures or phrases. These often tend to distract more than to encourage. Even conventional supportive statements such as "I see," and "I understand," bear close examination. For one, they tend to call attention to the speaker, when in fact the goal is for the professional to be as unobtrusive as possible. Additionally, such phrases may actually retard communication in a more active manner. They can do this by implying that the omniscient professional in fact sees and understands even though a complete thought or feeling has not yet been presented by the patient.

Ordinary supportive phrases can obstruct open communication.

In general, the watchword here is not so much the adoption of any specific behavior by the clinician. Rather, it is the need to be sensitively aware of each patient's response to the professional's own communication style. That style then can be modulated to maximize the therapeutic value of the interchange.

Open and Closed Questions

Another important parameter of communication involves the use of *open* and *closed* questions. The degree of openness of a question does not reflect a value judgment on the nature of the question or the intent of the questioner. Rather, it defines a *spectrum of specificity of answer sought*. An inquiry into someone's birthdate or current address ordinarily would be regarded as an almost entirely closed question; the specific pieces of information sought are usually the only answers that will satisfy the intent of the questioner. An almost open question, on the other hand, would be an inquiry such as "What prompted you to come to see me today?" Such a request for information allows a vast scope for response, and implies little expectation on the part of the interviewer concerning an acceptable form of a reply. A certain limit, however, has been established in that the information sought has been defined as relevant to the act of visiting the questioner. An inquiry such as "What's on your mind?" is nearly completely open. In fact, it can at times be so open as to hamper communication by being overly threatening.

Clinicians should be aware of the degree of openness of their questions, and of the possible effects of this dimension on comunication.

Questions of various degrees of openness are appropriate at different points in the interaction between the patient and the professional. Hence, the operational rule is for the clinician to be aware of the place on the spectrum that a given question occupies. They are thereby enabled to assess more accurately whether a given inquiry is appropriate to achieve the desired purpose. For example, many professionals will begin interviews with a long series of queries for specific information. This often implies to patients that professionals prefer them to take a passive role in offering information. Additionally, such an approach places on the professional the burden of always asking the correct specific questions.

It is usually preferable to begin interviews with more open questions, followed by a focusing process.

Wise clinicians begin interviews with more open questions that invite the patient to acquaint them with a broad area of concern. As the interview progresses, the inquiries can cone down to address the specific issue at hand in an efficient way as directed by the expertise of the professional. In emergency settings this focusing process may be appropriately quite abrupt. However, in the setting of terminal illness it often should not be. This is because the role of the professional is usually more supportive than technical and the issues at hand are frequently ill-defined.

The concept of a continuum of openness of questions can be used to manage interviews in other ways as well. For example, we have all encountered the garrulous individual for whom the polite "How are you?" releases a flood of reveries and descriptions of problems. With such a person, it is possible to streamline the interviewing process by tending more toward closed questions once the area of concern has been established. It is even appropriate to interrupt and say something to the effect of: "I am aware that this topic is important to you and will be glad to discuss it at another time, but I think now we need to focus on . . ." This response leaves the patient feeling heard, and may

Open questions are often more threatening than closed ones.

allow the professional to feel much less frustrated and accordingly be a more effective helper. On the other hand, some patients may have difficulties responding to more open questions such as "How are you feeling about that?" This can be addressed by recalling that closed questions are usually less threatening than open ones. Such a patient can be given an opportunity for an easier response, even a simple "yes," or "no," by beginning with a more closed question such as "Do you have any feelings about that?"

A final point about the open-to-closed question spectrum concerns ending an interview. More often than perhaps we would like to admit, we ourselves conduct entire examinations and interviews during which we totally miss important points or concerns of our patients. One way of ameliorating this problem is to end the session with an open question such as "Is there anything else of concern to you that we have not addressed to your satisfaction today?" If during the preceding interaction the professional has become identified as someone truly present to listen to the patient, this sort of inquiry will often net surprising and important information.

CASE ILLUSTRATION

A young wife was dying of a recurrent brain tumor that had left her partially paralyzed but otherwise intact and pain-free. She and her husband came to a clinic appointment and showed signs throughout their visit that something was on their minds. Finally, at the end of the interview the physician remarked that she sensed some tension, and that she wondered if there was anything else troubling the couple. The wife burst into tears, and it emerged that this previously quite passionate couple had been celibate for six months on the presumption that sexual excitement might be dangerous for the wife. Once this apprehension was cleared up, everyone parted in much better spirits.

Paraphrasing

Paraphrasing is useful for verifying that patients have been understood, and for reassuring them that they have been heard.

The ability to paraphrase is particularly vital in the interaction between professional and patient. It may be defined as *the repetition in the listener's own words of the gist of what is being expressed by the speaker.* Paraphrasing has several important uses in communication. One is to ascertain whether the professional has in fact understood thoughts as the patient meant to convey them. Additionally, paraphrasing can reassure patients that they are being listened to and understood.

Paraphrases should be presented in a tentative manner so that patients will feel comfortable correcting them. A principle reason for this is the status which many people assign to professionals in a medical setting, as described earlier in this Chapter. This can result in thoughts such as, "Well, if that's how the doctor says it is, then that must be right." Hence, it is advisable to pepper one's paraphrases with disclaimers such as "Let me see if I have this correctly . . ."

Although universal generalizations about the frequency and duration of paraphrases are not possible, here are some pointers concerning their use. Patients with otherwise normal mental status may become repetitious about a particular topic. This often indicates that they are uncertain whether or not the professional has understood them. A paraphrase at such a point serves both to provide reassurance and, if it is correct in timing and content, to allow the interview to move on to other topics.

In most instances paraphrases should be kept to a sentence or two in length. This avoids undue interruptions of the flow of interchange, and helps to ensure that important information is confirmed fairly frequently.

Paraphrases should be very brief.

Reflection of Feelings

Reflection of feelings is perhaps the communication skill that is most specific to the care of the terminally ill. A principle reason for this is that the professional in such settings often is occupied with facilitating emotional adjustment for patients and families.

Reflection of feeling is a variation of the paraphrasing technique described above. The specific emphasis, however, is shifted to emotional rather than informational content of the communication. A reflection of feeling might be, "You seem to be angry (or sad, or frightened) about that."

This type of statement serves a number of purposes. It provides implicit reassurance to the patient that the professional finds the specified feeling to be appropriate enough to be recognized and discussed openly. Clinicians making such statements identify themselves as available to discuss the specific feeling involved as well as emotional issues more generally. In our experience, such reflections can serve as a sort of *feedback amplifier* of the emotion to which they refer. This can enable the patient to venture more deeply into that feeling and its ramifications. Hence, the professional can encourage existing emotional strengths and healing mechanisms. This is accomplished by allowing patients to follow their internal processes with lessened fear of external judgments or limitations. Of course, if the professional is more angry or sad or frightened about the issue than is the patient, neither may benefit from such reflection.

Reflection of feeling serves to encourage experience and discussion of emotions, and to strengthen existing emotional healing mechanisms.

Reflection of feeling is easier when one is responding to explicit verbal communications. Indeed, the more implicit a feeling is in its expression, the more room for interpretive error on the part of the listener. Therefore, clinicians should be extra careful when reflecting feelings that are not expressed openly. In such cases, it is wise to be tentative in proportion to the degree of difficulty the patient appears to be having with the expression of the emotion.

Be tentative when reflecting feelings not expressed overtly.

Sometimes it is possible to facilitate the interchange by overtly giving the patient permission to have such a feeling. For example, a permissive reflection might be the statement that: "This may not be the case for you, but in your situation people often experience . . ." The professional should remember the potential value of such an exchange even if the patient is unable to respond on the spot. The questioner will be recognized thereafter as someone who is comfortable hearing such thoughts, and to whom it may be possible to turn at a future time.

Summarization

Summarization ties up an encounter in a package that is efficient and neat enough to leave all parties with a sense of completion and satisfaction.

The final communication skill to be considered here also is related to the paraphrase. It is used to confirm a larger body of communication, and is appropriately termed *summarization*. The technique is useful at breaking points in interactions between patient and professional such as the end of the elicitation of the history of present illness, or after the physical examination. The professional says something like "Now let me see if I have the story correctly. It all started with . . ." This is then followed by a few-sentence synopsis of the substantial portion of the interchange.

Summarization can cover a much larger body of information than paraphrasing. Therefore, it requires more consolidation and interpretation on the part of the professional. It follows that a certain level of tentativeness almost always is appropriate. Summarization provides patients with a final opportunity to correct any misconceptions or to clarify any unclear communication. In addition, it provides reassuring evidence that important information can be transferred effectively.

This technique also is useful in interview management, because an effective summary usually is recognized as drawing a particular interchange to a close. Summarization may be followed with a statement of desire to close the conversation for now, or to move on to the next topic without seeming abrupt.

Part 2 Summary

In Part 2 we began by exploring some psychological aspects of death, grief, and mourning. Then we took a brief look at some existential viewpoints relevant to care of the dying. Next, we examined aspects of interpersonal communication, noted some circumstances under which communication tends to break down, and looked at common effects of such disruption. Then we discussed elements of a strategy to bring about better exchange of thoughts and feelings. Finally, we examined a group of specific skills aimed at enhancing communication in any clinical setting. Now, in Part 3, we are ready to explore a practical model for helping dying patients and their families.

References

Ivey, E. A. and Authier, J. 1978. *Microcounselling.* Springfield, Illinois: Charles C Thomas, Publisher.

Section 2 of this book presents a systematic educational model of specific communication skills that should be part of the therapeutic armamentarium of all clinicians. Skills of attention and influence known as "microcounselling" are described in detail. Although the organization of material leaves much to be desired, this is probably the best book published to date that elucidates the applied helping process. Its value for health care practitioners is enormously increased when it is coupled with *Respectful Treatment* by Lipp.

Lipp, M. R. 1977. *Respectful Treatment: The Human Side of Medical Care.* Hagerstown, Maryland: Harper & Row, Publishers, Inc.

This book complements *Microcounselling* by providing a frame of reference within the medical setting. In large part, it deals with barriers to effective communication between patients and those responsible for their care. It is replete with concise problem solving suggestions aimed at dealing with obstacles to the management of illness, and should be in the libraries of all those involved in health care.

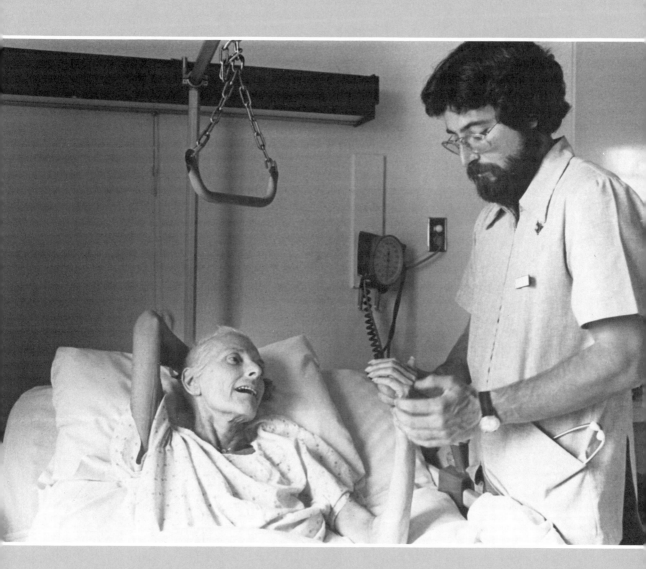

PART 3

A Practical Model for Helping Dying Patients and Their Families

In this section we address specific problems in the care of the dying and their loved ones roughly in the sequence that one might expect to encounter them. First, in Chapter 4 some issues involving initial adjustment to life-threatening illness will be elaborated. In Chapter 5, the problem of balancing medical interventions in order to maximize quality of life is discussed. Chapter 6 approaches a number of clinical concerns that arise in the course of coping with chronic disease. Specific issues arising in the support of the patient who is very near death are presented in Chapter 7, followed by an examination of the moments at life's end in Chapter 8. Finally, in Chapter 9 we address the appropriate management of grief and mourning. Overall, in this section we will follow the course in time of a generalized terminal illness, with practical suggestions at key points along the way.

Sharing the Diagnosis: Initial Adjustment to Life-Threatening Illness

4

Overview

Difficult and important problems are met at many junctures during the progression of a life-threatening illness. These often begin with patients' decisions about whether and when to seek medical diagnosis for disturbing symptoms. We pick up our discussion of practical clinical issues faced by health care professionals after a diagnosis is made of a condition that is likely to end in death. This is the time when patients face what Pattison (1977) terms "the crisis of the knowledge of death." In this chapter, we discuss guidelines for initial sharing of the information that a life-threatening condition exists. Then we examine common immediate reactions of patients and families to this news, including shock, denial, and anger. Finally, we look at some special problems of prognosis as related to the maintenance of hope during this early period in the course of a terminal illness.

Improving the Clarity of Initial Communications

Breaking the News

The manner in which the news of a life-threatening illness is broken is of extreme importance to subsequent treatment. (18)

The interaction in which the diagnosis of life-threatening disease is communicated can be of vital importance to the evolution of an effective caring relationship between patients and professionals. Patterns that may persist throughout the course of a terminal illness often are established in this critical initial encounter. Even when a relationship with the patient and family in question already exists, potentially fatal illness constitutes a new context in which nothing can be taken for granted.

Such earthshaking news should rarely, if ever, be broken over the telephone. If possible, it should be done in private, with all parties present being seated. Assessment of who should be present in the room is possible only on a case-by-case basis, but the presence of at least one family member or close friend is often useful.

Initial shock may interfere with the patient's understanding of what is said.

Breaking the news of a life-threatening illness is particularly critical in that initial shock may cause extreme distortions or even amnesia for much of what is said following the opening remarks. One sensible approach is to try to prepare patients and families with initial statements such as, "We are going to be discussing some very important information, so I would like you to pay close attention and interrupt me if there is anything you don't understand. You may wish to take notes if you feel it would be helpful." This latter suggestion is made because the demonstration that a professional feels that patient and family should understand clearly implies that their own actions and participation are important. This sets the groundwork to address some of the issues of powerlessness that so often arise as an illness progresses. It should be born in mind, however, that the notes taken by patients or family members in such highly charged sessions often chiefly reflect their own anxieties, and may correspond poorly to what was actually said.

Bad medical news usually should be presented straightforwardly with carefully chosen, simple words. (15)

The actual communication of the news can be made in a number of ways, depending on the styles of the persons involved. One way is to begin with something such as, "I have some bad news for you. There is good reason to believe that you have a disease that may shorten your life. It is called ———." It is not necessary to give precise medical names in this initial communication. Indeed, words should be chosen that are judged most likely to give patients and families a clear picture in simple language of what is going on. If malignancy is involved, it is important to use the word *"cancer"*. This is because the euphemisms for this disease (such as "growth" or "tumor", or the more technical "neoplasm" and "malignancy") will confuse many patients. If it is known, the organ system involved should be named by saying, for example, "It is called *cancer of the breast*." At this point, clinicians should be silent and allow some time for reactions.

Breaking the news usually should be delayed until there is reasonable time for assimilation.

A most important variable in this initial encounter is *time*. Regardless of how empathic or emotionally adept health care professionals may be, these assets are likely to come to naught if there is not sufficient time in which to exercise them. Except in emergencies, there is seldom such a rush to begin treatment that an interview cannot be postponed until a reasonable amount of time is available. At times, it may even be appropriate to delay this communication as much as a day or two. In most instances, the beneficial effect on the course of treatment resulting from increased patient–professional cooperation will outweigh any advantages of starting treatment earlier after a hurried communication of the diagnosis. It is difficult to generalize as to the specific time required to negotiate this interaction successfully. It is wise, however, to allow at least one hour for the communication of a grave diagnosis. Further, it is preferable that clinicians conduct such conversations at times when they have no subsequent pressing commitments.

Once basic information has been communicated, silence is an important tool.

In an attempt to cover their own discomfort with breaking bad news, clinicians sometimes bombard their patients with a barrage of information. This approach is likely to fail in the purpose of communicating useful knowledge to patients and families. In addition, it frequently precludes more complete exploration of the feelings and reactions of patients and families by limiting the time in which such a process can take place. *Silence* becomes a useful tool in the armamentarium of the astute clinician in such anxiety provoking settings. Once the basic vital information has been communicated, it is appropriate for professionals to be silent for a few minutes and allow patients to express their concerns. A caretaker's willingness to sit quietly for periods of a minute or even two and wait for patients or families to respond is important. It communicates that busy schedules are less important than human feelings. Further, it provides tacit reassurance to those facing terminal disease that their emotions and reactions are significant. Perhaps more so in this encounter than in any other clinical context, there is little to be gained by rushing, and potentially much to be lost.

Answering Questions

Questions from patients and families should be solicited early and directly.

Whereas some patients and families are prone to ask numerous questions spontaneously, others are not. With the latter, professionals can expedite the process of initial communication of and adjustment to a life-threatening condition by encouraging questions. This often is done best quite directly and relatively early in the encounter. The format might be something like, "Many people find this kind of information overwhelming, and it is quite easy to become confused. Because it is vital to us that you have a clear understanding of what is going on, I would like you to ask any questions that may come to mind." This kind of communication gives patients and families permission both to acknowledge their confusion and to seek to alleviate it. It transfers some sense of control back to them by making it clear that their understanding is important to their caretakers.

Even patients or families who ask relevant questions should be queried as to what they have heard. (8)

Often, patients and families will ask many questions that may make the task of clinicians somewhat easier by allowing them to interact in a strictly responsive mode. It is important, however, that professionals not assume from such questioning that their patients are understanding all that is being said. One question should be asked a few minutes after the initial communication has been made, regardless of whether patients and family members have been silent, tearful, frantic, or questioning. Clinicians should inquire, "What have you heard me say?" The response to this question can prove to be invaluable in clarifying misinterpretations and in circumventing communication problems before they become insuperable. Naturally, any misconceptions should be corrected gently and patiently before proceeding.

It is also valuable to solicit questions directly about important points that are communicated as the interview progresses. Care must be taken not to be at all brusque about asking for questions, or patients may feel compelled to deny confusion in order to be pleasing. If there is any doubt about whether or not a key point has been understood, the patient or family member should be asked to repeat the information back in their own words. This should serve as a basis for clearing up any misconceptions.

Closing the session in which the news is broken can be made a supportive, forward-looking experience.

Toward the end of this critical encounter it may be useful to ask some more general questions aimed at reviewing the key points that professionals wish to be remembered. This is a practical check of how effectively they have communicated the points that they intended to emphasize. It also ensures that major *take home lessons* have been received.

We also encourage clinicians to jot down important points themselves, and share the content of them with or even give these notes to their patients. A few numbered, simple sentences illuminating the most important points may serve to avoid a good deal of miscommunication. Such information usually should include specific diagnosis, treatment options, diagnostic procedures, and relevant appointment times and telephone numbers. A good time to write this is near the end of the encounter, during the review session. Earlier, it may prove distracting or distancing.

Finally, clinicians should try to map out roughly a course of possible treatments. Special attention should be paid to areas in which the patient and family can contribute to the medical regimen. This can address directly their sense of helplessness, as well as providing important initial information as to the shape the future may take.

Facilitating Emotional Responses

Effective management of their own discomfort is a first step for professionals in supporting their patients' emotional responses.

Facilitation of emotional response is equally important to the accurate transfer of information. The ability of patients and families to express their thoughts and feelings is in part determined by how they perceive the receptivity of professionals toward them. It is understandable that clinicians will feel uncomfortable communicating such devastating information as the existence of life-threatening illness. Even deeper feelings may be evoked if long-standing relationships exist between the parties involved, or if the circumstances touch off distressing memories or feelings from the professional's past. Patients and families are likely to be aware that those who must communicate this fearful reality are disturbed by having to do so. Unfortunately, many clinicians cope with such discomfort by distancing themselves emotionally from the situation.

We do not imply that an emotional breakdown on the part of a professional is likely to make a positive contribution. Such occurrences probably would cause even more confusion for patients and families. Further, it often focuses attention on the emotions of the professional, and thereby may reverse the caretaking roles at a particularly inopportune moment.

The guiding principle governing communication of the uncomfortable feelings of clinicians who are delivering bad news must be that *the interests of patients and families come first*. If professionals experience genuine feelings, they are likely to be sensed at some level by all of those present. Brief and nonhistrionic communication of these emotions is often useful in breaking down some of the barriers to clear exchange of information and emotions. Direct acknowledgements of humanness by professionals frequently serve to reduce the level of patient anxiety inherent in the crisis of the knowledge of death.

Under such circumstances, some patients and families are likely to feel that it is unsafe for them to express their emotions openly. Others perceive the clinician's ineffectively managed discomfort as a signal to protect a seemingly fragile professional from their emotions, which they must then keep to themselves. Feelings of abhorrence and withdrawal by patients and families may be projected outward more readily, and then perceived as coming from clinicians. In this situation, any lack of clarity or ambiguity can have profound negative sequelae for relationships throughout the course of a terminal illness.

Professionals also can assist the patients' initial adjustment by overtly granting permission for them to express strong feelings. This

Explicit permission should be given for the expression of feelings. (8)

can be done very simply with a statement such as, "Many people in situations like yours have feelings which may be hard to express." This implies very directly that the speaker is open to hearing about these feelings. It also leaves room for patients not to respond by simply acknowledging the difficulty of making such communications. By avoiding specification of a particular emotion, words are not put in the mouths of patients or families.

When professionals clearly sense patients have a specific feeling that they find difficult to express, a tentative reflection of that emotion may be in order. Clinicians can say, "I wonder if you might be feeling ————[sad, angry, confused, overwhelmed, et cetera]?" This question does not require patients to respond if they are unable to at the moment, but it acknowledges the emotion and tacitly conveys the message that it is acceptable.

Often, professionals are frankly unsure of what emotions are experienced by patients and families in this setting. A direct admission of this fact can prove useful: "It is important for me to understand what is going on with you, and I am not certain that I do right now." This communicates that clinicians care about the emotional reactions of patients and families, and identifies their expression as important. Further, it gives some power back to those inclined to feel most powerless by enabling them to help overtly in their own care.

Communication Beyond the Basic News

It is not necessary to communicate "everything" during the initial session.

The issue of timing of communications beyond the basics of a life-threatening diagnosis is probably as vital as the content of that message. Regardless of the eloquence, accuracy, ease, and force with which information is presented, it is likely to fall on deaf ears if conveyed at an incorrect time. This is particularly so given the emotional turmoil that generally prevails during the crisis of initial adjustment to life-threatening disease. Until it is apparent that patients and families are beginning to accept the reality of their situations, it is wise to keep communications as *simple* as possible. It is vital that all important points be communicated during the visit when the news is broken. It is preferable, however, that these points be made with the minimum necessary detail. In this way, those confronting a terrifying reality are not forced to decide what is important to assimilate and what can be left for a later time.

Patients often provide cues as to the proper timing for key communications.

Further specificity and detail can be developed as the relationship progresses and as patients or families request. Often, the terminally ill or their families will make the correct timing obvious through their lines of questioning or through their emotional tone. When there is any doubt at all, professionals seldom will go wrong with a statement such as: "I wonder if this is the right time to talk about these issues?" If reasonable assurances can be given that adequate opportunities will exist later, then no one will feel pressured into exchanges for which they are not prepared.

Once professionals are satisfied that there is consensus regarding key points, the initiative regarding further elaboration can pass more to the patient. Some people are reassured by knowing as much as they possibly can regarding their conditions. Conversations at a level of detail that could not possibly be of practical use may prove emotionally valuable by developing in them a sense of participation in treatment. Others may find medical details daunting and alienating, and may prefer to know only the very basic facts regarding their condition. Neither of these stances should present problems as long as they are anticipated and worked out directly. However, professionals often may make assumptions regarding such highly charged issues that reflect more their own uneasiness than the desires of patients or families. If there is any doubt, the clinician can ask patients how much they wish to know. Professionals should add the assurance that changes in level of disclosure can be made, after appropriate discussion, whenever the patient or family member wishes.

Follow patients' lead in elaboration of details. (20)

Immediate Reactions of Patients and Families

Range of Variability in Form and Intensity of Response

Health care professionals are likely to meet with a broad spectrum of reactions when first discussing a life-threatening condition with patients and families. It may be that these emotional responses foster some sense of power, however illusory, in situations that remind clinicians of the limitations on their control over their own lives. As is the case in many of the issues we have addressed, the variation in styles of reacting among individuals, families, and cultures is often too broad to permit the useful institution of simple rules. Our suggestions should be taken as loose guidelines that require adaptation to each particular situation.

The first point we wish to emphasize is that a powerful expression of negative emotions is generally appropriate on hearing that one's demise is imminent. In fact, the lack of a reaction should in most cases cause more concern than its presence. To be sure, these statements are too general to be applicable to all patients and families. The backgrounds, personalities, and ages of the individuals in question must be taken into account. We feel no more comfortable with placing even a tacit requirement on anyone to express strong feelings than we do with efforts to suppress them.

Absence of emotional response to the news of terminal illness should cause more concern than its presence.

Another important issue is that the patient's expression of strong feelings on hearing this news often results in uncomfortable moments for clinicians. Few persons are likely to be entirely at ease when others are experiencing great pain and shock. Perhaps because of this discomfort, many people tend to attribute strong expressions of feeling to a lack of self-control, even in such extreme settings. Patients and families may even find themselves apologizing to obviously nonplussed professionals, or attempting to shush their more expressive relatives. Once again, the guiding principle must be that the interest of patients and families, rather than the uneasiness of professionals, takes precedence.

Common Specific Reactions

A sensation of numbness is the most common immediate reaction to news of a life-threatening illness.

Probably the most common response on hearing news of a potentially fatal illness is a deep state of shock that patients often characterize as a *sensation of numbness.* This may be a means whereby individuals protect themselves from the immediately overwhelming feelings that are likely to be evoked by this information. Patients and families may seem almost stuporous, and this state may be so intense as to render communication quite difficult. It is important to be patient with those who react in this manner. A gentle reflection of feeling, such as, "This must be awfully overwhelming for you," can help patients and families to break loose from an acute state of shock. Once this has happened, more useful communication can begin; until it does, much of what is said is likely to be forgotten. We have observed many instances wherein professionals continued with their interview in an apparently oblivious manner in spite of the fact that patients and families were clearly overwhelmed. An unfortunate result of this is often a serious disparity between what clinicians think has been communicated and what actually has been received.

Denial *is another common means of protecting oneself in such crises.*

A second common reaction is *frank denial* of the overwhelming information being presented. This can range from momentary expressions of disbelief ("This can't be true!") to hostile rejection of the diagnosis and even of the bearer of such ill tidings. It is often difficult for professionals to contend with such responses, particularly because they are already acutely aware of the limits of what they have to offer to patients with terminal illnesses. Thus, the implication by patients or families that the diagnosis is inaccurate may touch on any sense of inadequacy already present in attendant clinicians. This sometimes results in the professional's subtly expressed anger or withdrawal, which could not come at a more inopportune moment.

Once again, clinicians can address these situations by verbalizing the patients' sense of being overwhelmed that probably underlies the reaction. In most instances, by attending to the emotions that precipitate the response, it is possible to get on with the interaction without jeopardizing the patient–professional relationship. Our experience is that rejection of health care personnel in such settings reflects the tendency of many to deny an overwhelming and ultimately threatening reality. If clinicians can remain supportive through such an encounter, a solid foundation for a trusting relationship is likely to be developed.

In most cases, the reaction of *anger* also is a manifestation of the sense of being overwhelmed, and may most usefully be addressed as such. This frequently can be done by reflecting the underlying feeling of being totally overwhelmed before addressing the anger itself. If anger persists in the face of this tactic, directly acknowledging it often helps to defuse the situation. Rage, like guilt and blame, can be a reaction to the helplessness experienced by those confronted with the reality of life-threatening disease. Anger specifically expressed toward the clinician at this stage is frequently nothing more than a primitive reaction analogous to executing the bearer of bad tidings.

Anger also is often encountered in this situation. (11)

Strong expressions of *fear* on an overt level are somewhat less common than the above reactions at the time when patients and families are first informed of a life-threatening disease. It often seems that the more primitive denial-oriented defenses against potentially overwhelming anxiety need to subside somewhat before the reality of the situation is discoverable. Then fear may be experienced and possibly even openly expressed. Indeed, the ability to connect directly with the appropriate primordial reaction to such news may reflect psychological strength.

Initial reactions of fear and sadness to such news often reflect psychological strength.

The frequency of direct expression of *sadness* during the initial sharing of the diagnosis is similar to that of fear as compared with other common reactions. This is probably because sadness is a relatively mediated reaction to such news. Certainly, sadness requires some level of acceptance that often is absent at the outset. The expression of fear or sadness in such contexts should be supported by health care professionals unless it becomes disabling. In the latter instances, it should be addressed by empathic reflection of feelings and reassurances that such emotions are natural and appropriate.

Maintaining Hope in a Realistic Context

Defining the Realistic Context

Most health professionals are acutely aware of the importance of hope in motivating patients and families to cooperate actively in their own care. This is no less the case in the setting of life-threatening

The key to maintaining hope in a realistic context is to shift the object of hope to a shorter range of time. (17)

disease. The difference is that here the probable outcome is more clearly defined. Even when there is not a shadow of a doubt in the mind of the professional that the present illness will end in the death of the patient, it still proves possible to maintain hope in a realistic context. The key is that the object of hope is shifted to a shorter range. Patients will begin to hope for a longer remission between therapeutic courses, or for survival until a particular goal has been achieved. As things advance, the focus of hope can shift even further toward the immediate. Patients and families hope for relatively symptom-free days, or for one last period of being at home. They may hope for a relatively peaceful and dignified death. The point is that hope springs eternal barring the presence of psychopathology. If given the opportunity and the encouragement, terminal patients will find a way to remain hopeful, often right until the moment of death.

CASE ILLUSTRATION

A 66-year-old woman was informed that she had an inoperable uterine tumor that was quite likely to take her life. She was initially depressed, but rallied to focus her hopes on a course of chemotherapy. Although her doctors cautioned her to temper her optimistic expectations, she steadfastly maintained that she would "beat the odds." When her disease continued to advance, her family and physicians feared she would collapse emotionally. Instead, after a depression that was briefer than her initial one, she turned her hopes toward surviving to see the birth of her fifth grandchild. Against medical odds, she lived the intervening five months and died peacefully less than a week after welcoming her granddaughter into the world. In retrospect, all involved realized that this woman knew that she needed to have hope in order to cope.

Communicating Prognostic Information

Statistics should be used with great caution and appropriate disclaimers when discussing prognoses.

The issue of determining and communicating prognoses usually arises during the course of a terminal illness. Many times, this initially takes place when the diagnosis is shared. To be sure, prognostic information is important to patients and families because it allows them to make more realistic adjustments and plans. Communication of statistical prognoses, however, can be particularly inappropriate when the news is first broken. It is advisable to keep prognostic statements more general at the outset when patients or families inquire as to what course their disease will follow. For example, let us assume that a matched group of patients has a five-year survival rate greater than, say, 30%. It would be reasonable to tell patients that their situation is grave, but that they stand a good chance of survival. For those whose matched cohorts survive less than 10% of the time, it is appropriate to say that the disease is likely to shorten their lives, but that they stand some chance of survival. If clinicians are pressed to report numbers, then these can be communicated if they are known. It is crucial, however, to preface such accounts with clear disclaimers. We must constantly remind ourselves that although statistics provide information about others with similar illnesses at similar stages, they neither describe the patient at hand nor predict the future.

Specific time predictions are unwise, especially soon after the diagnosis has been made.

When the information that an illness is serious and life-threatening is shared, there usually is no compelling reason to make specific time predictions regarding the course of the disease. If patients seek such information, clinicians can fairly state that it is impossible to predict in the absence of a period in which to observe the course of the disease. This is not done to evade giving a response, but in absolute honesty. In fact, there are relatively few cases in which even the most astute clinicians can make predictions with a high degree of accuracy at the initial diagnosis. It may be possible to talk more generally, with hesitancy, about survival in terms of years, or months, or perhaps days, without assigning specific numbers. One good approach is to use statements such as, "I cannot read the future, but it seems more likely that you will live for months rather than years," or any appropriate time units such as weeks versus months, or days versus weeks.

There are few occasions when it is necessary to offer opinions about the amount of time patients have left, especially when they are not specifically requested. These predictions seldom are applicable during the early period of a disease. However, if professionals sense that patients or families are making plans not consistent with the most probable course of the illness, it is often appropriate to broach the topic gently. In summary, the *style* in which these difficult communications are handled is what differentiates between the truth that wounds and the truth that heals.

Addressing the Issue of Abandonment

Realistic reassurance should be provided that caretakers will be there to help, whatever happens. (6, 7)

Feelings of abandonment are among the most difficult emotions for those confronting terminal illness. Not only are patients faced with the loss of the entire world, but they often feel a profound sense of isolation from the rest of humanity. This makes any unnecessary losses particularly painful to such individuals. It is vital that professionals involved in terminal care settings are aware of and prepared to address issues concerning abandonment.

We should reemphasize the sense of powerlessness that patients often feel in the face of terminal illnesses and the confusing medical interventions that are often associated with them. Given this, the assurance that those whom they trust to guide them through this intimidating maze will remain with them is imperative.

If it is possible for each patient's usual primary care physician to remain at the helm, this is desirable. However, technical realities may dictate a shift in primary responsibility to a specialist (see Chapter 14). When this is the case, some continuing involvement and contact with the more familiar physician is often quite reassuring. Clearly, continuity of care is of particular significance in terminal care settings.

References

Alsop, S. 1973. *Stay of Execution: A Sort of Memoir.* Philadelphia: J. B. Lippincott Co.

The author, a capable journalist, describes his experiences after the discovery of his leukemia. His autobiographical sketch of a final period of life that lasted longer than his doctors predicted is a well written account of the thoughts and feelings of someone facing a terminal illness.

Caplan, G. 1964. *Principles of Preventive Psychiatry.* New York: Basic Books, Inc., Publishers.

Chapter II and Appendix B of this book are highly recommended to those working in terminal care. Chapter II deals with a conceptual model for primary prevention of psychopathology, with most cogent material on life crises. Appendix B, by Vivian Cadden, is on crises in the family, and contains practical information on how to help friends or relatives in crisis situations.

Pattison, E. M. 1977. *The Experience of Dying.* Englewood Cliffs, New Jersey: Prentice-Hall, Inc.

Initiation of Treatment: Making the Difficult Choices

5

Overview

The next milestone along the course of our generalized terminal illness involves decisions relating to the initiation of treatment. Shortly after the initial adjustments to a serious disease have begun, professionals, patients, and families are faced with the choices that largely will define the quality of remaining life. We now present some practical guidelines for facilitating such decisions.

Prerequisite for Realistic Choices: Open and Accurate Communication

Ethical Considerations

We have discussed a number of issues concerning the importance of open and accurate communication in guiding patients and families toward appropriate decisions. In the context of the choices made early in a terminal illness, this concern becomes particularly relevant. The courses embarked upon at this time will strongly influence the way in which patients and families experience the entire process of dying. It is vital for clinicians to be as certain as possible that the decisions undertaken at this juncture reflect accurately the personalities and desires of those most affected by them.

In most cases, withholding vital information concerning the shape of the remaining days of someone's life is difficult to defend.

Serious moral and ethical dilemmas are created when patients and families are inadequately informed. The possible negative sequelae of failing to inform patients about the likely consequences of each of the choices offered to them generally far outweigh any possible benefits. If such a path is chosen, the responsibility for ordering the last period of life of another human is taken away from its rightful holder: the patient. Given the emotional charge that usually is present, the likelihood of the clinician making incorrect decisions for the patient during treatment of life-threatening illness is greater perhaps than in most other situations.

One can estimate the extent of discomfort professionals are likely to experience if they withhold vital information by examining the situation of the comatose patient. Major ethical dilemmas arise when anyone is forced to make life-or-death decisions for another person. The distinction between problems involving comatose patients and those arising from implementing decisions made by inaccurately informed patients is more one of degree than of substance.

Avoiding Hidden Agendas

Hidden agendas often interfere with appropriate decision-making.

Clinicians frequently have clear opinions as to how patients should decide about particular issues. This is often quite appropriate, given the nature of the caretaking relationship. Problems arise, however, when such opinions are not openly acknowledged, as patients may feel subtly pressured into making specific choices. Professionals do better to state openly their own opinions when presenting alternatives. In that way they are more likely to avoid hidden agendas and to present all options accurately.

Hidden agendas are often signaled by emotional reactions disproportionate to the immediate stimulus.

Problems may arise in the terminal care (or any other) setting when a particular action is motivated by concerns rooted outside of the therapeutic relationship. For example, the patient who has a long-standing hatred of the medical establishment will be difficult to work with even for the most responsive and sensitive clinicians. This is because such individuals are not dealing with the professionals as they are, but with what they represent. Hidden agendas of staff members often are evidenced by reactions to situations or personalities which are markedly out of proportion to the stimuli that elicited them.

Such phenomena are bound to arise in the emotionally charged atmosphere surrounding life-threatening disease. Professionals may be able to deal with hidden agendas by modeling open communication about emotional issues for their patients (and each other). This gives the message that such behavior is understood, and that communications of this type are safe to make.

When professionals are overwhelmed with their own frustrations regarding a specific patient, however, it is important to consult with other staff members before communicating these feelings directly to patients. This helps avert possible exploitation of patients or families by clinicians who ventilate emotions that may have nothing to do with the present situation. Times will arise, however, when such conferences reveal a consensus that the problem does arise from the relationship between the specific individuals concerned. Open exploration of the area of conflict, with mediation by a consultant if the issue is too highly charged, usually will resolve such issues.

CASE ILLUSTRATION

A nasty exchange took place on rounds at a prominent teaching hospital between an oncology fellow and a nurse who inadvertently broke some equipment. The fellow realized immediately that his fit of pique was inappropriate, and that he was in a lousy mood because of an argument he had had the previous evening with his wife. In front of the patient, the fellow sincerely apologized to the nurse, saying that his behavior had been out of line and that he was just feeling down for personal reasons. She accepted his apology with grace and humor, and rounds continued in a much less tense atmosphere.

When professionals suspect that patients have hidden agendas, they should encourage patients to express underlying feelings.

Health care professionals can help overcome hidden agendas by encouraging patients and families to communicate their underlying feelings and motives more openly. For example, if staff members feel as though they are being related to in terms of their roles rather than as people, the following statement may be helpful: "I feel uncomfortable with the way we are interacting. This could be off base, but it seems to me that you respond more to my uniform than to me. Is there something going on?" This kind of inquiry may be initially difficult for the individual who is unused to giving or receiving such direct communication. If it is done in a supportive and gentle manner, however, the long-term results are likely to be positive even if the immediate attempt fails.

Balancing Responsibilities

With appropriate help, most patients can assume executive responsibility over their own lives.

Patients and families can arrive at realistic decisions only if they are armed with accurate and understandable information as to the implications of each possibility. There are people, however, who may wish to delegate their authority entirely to the professionals involved. When a patient makes this request, clinicians can resort to the technique of exploring the patient's underlying feelings before addressing the content of the request. The emotions spawning such a choice are likely to include a feeling of helplessness and a desire to be taken care of.

Usually, through full exploration of the possible underlying motives, most individuals eventually resume executive authority over their own lives. If not, clinicians may need to assert directly that they will be better able to carry out their caretaking functions with an actively involved partner. If this sort of exchange fails to elicit a positive response, it may be necessary to accede, at least temporarily, to patients' desires to yield their authority. Even in such cases, however, it will be important to review frequently the appropriateness of treatment decisions, and to ascertain whether patients are willing to resume responsibility for their own lives.

CASE ILLUSTRATION

A 50-year-old plumber discovered a lump on his neck, and within the next week was diagnosed as having a metastatic carcinoma of the pharynx. His doctors noted a very passive attitude on his part, characterized by the statement, "Whatever you think is best, Doc." A conversation with his wife revealed that this was typical of his behavior toward physicians throughout his life, regardless of the situation. Further, she said that he was very uncomfortable with emotional expressiveness in any context. Attempts to reflect feelings of helplessness were greeted amiably and with his usual blanket acquiescence, but produced no change in his passivity. Finally, after a gentle direct invitation to participate more actively in his care was greeted only with discomfort, those involved gave up efforts to change this pattern. He evidenced clear relief at not being called on to behave in ways that were beyond his scope, and the remainder of his medical care proceeded smoothly.

The Clinician's Role as Advisor

The industrial consultant model serves well in returning final decision-making power to the patient. (15)

We have found it useful to conceive of one important aspect of the role of primary health care professionals as paralleling that of the industrial management consultant in the business setting. When companies encounter problems that are beyond the scope of their own expertise, they hire consultants to provide expert advice. The final decision on the implementation of these suggestions resides with the parent company—or, in any medical setting, with the patient. To be sure, the consultant whose recommendations are ignored with regularity may feel reluctant to sign on again with the same corporation. Although this model is too simple to characterize accurately the complexities of the caretaking relationship, it offers a path toward understanding some of its important aspects in the context of terminal disease.

Patients hold the ultimate right to decide what is done to their own bodies.

Under most circumstances, the ultimate power over what happens to the patient's body rightfully resides with that individual. When a professional's services are hired, the right to refuse any particular aspect of those offerings belongs equally to the individual in question. The ability to make appropriate decisions as to whether or not to follow the advice of a medical consultant, however, is contingent in part on understanding the various implications of those recommendations. If patients are to have the basis to make such decisions rationally, professionals must assume the responsibility of informing them accurately as to the implications of each option.

The patient's ultimate responsibility and right to decide do not preclude clinicians from venturing professional opinions, or even presenting their views strongly. In fact, a more balanced presentation often is made when any agenda the clinician may have is made overt. Further, we do not imply that staff members should dwell on the possible secondary effects of treatments. One objection to obtaining informed consent by stressing side-effects is the resultant negation of the significant placebo effect that positive statements about the actions of specific therapies may have. It is usually possible to make an honest statement of both positive and negative potentials of therapy, followed by the assertion that the recommended therapy, all told, is likely to have beneficial results. The power of the words of respected professionals generally is sufficient to enlist both conscious and unconscious cooperation from patients and families in the absence of intervening emotional conflicts. In addition, a study by Corby et al. (1983) has demonstrated no significant detrimental reactions in a population given a detailed discussion of potential side effects when compared with a control group receiving no special instruction or information.

Management decisions in terminal care settings are seldom clear-cut, particularly at the earlier stages of an illness. Thus, if clinicians frequently find themselves unable to support patient choices that run contrary to their own opinions, some self-examination may be in order. Such conflicts often reflect the professional's need to maintain at least the illusion of control in certain situations. If difficulties persist, psychiatric consultation for the professional may be in order. Finally, if an honest look at their own motives and at the patient's situation still leaves clinicians too uneasy to continue in attendance, referral for further care should be expedited in as supportive a fashion as possible.

When to refer.

Effects of a Climate of Openness

Open communication leads to mutual trust, teamwork, and better problem solving. (13)

One particularly valuable result of a climate of open communication of essential information in any medical setting is the creation of an atmosphere of teamwork and trust among all involved. Ideally, a feeling evolves that patients, families, and professionals are all colleagues working together to provide optimal care. Each member of this team has vital contributions of information and skills to make, and each can benefit from the actions of every other. Such a spirit often is impossible to achieve if only some individuals are in the know regarding essential information.

This sense of mutual collaboration between professionals, patients, and families has another important positive effect in terminal care settings. It is almost inevitable that conflicts will arise as the difficult issues evoked by decline and death are confronted. If the lines of communication are open between people who share a fundamental mutual trust, these problems are likely to be resolved more smoothly.

Issues in Making and Implementing Decisions

The Patient's Right: To Chart One's Own Course

Professionals should defer to the patient's definition of quality of life when making and implementing treatment decisions. (20)

Facing a terminal illness is likely to be the most direct confrontation with powerlessness that most individuals will experience. Given this, clinicians should do as much as possible within the limits of professional judgment to support patients' control over the course of daily living. A fundamental aspect of this enfranchisement is an understanding of the factors contributing to each patient's definition of the quality of life. Solicitation of and deference to these views is particularly important in the context of terminal illness. This is because therapeutic modalities employed in this setting often have profound effects on a patient's sense of well-being.

Generalizations about what constitutes an acceptable *quality of life* during the period of treatment for a terminal illness can serve only to cloud the picture. This definition, and its therapeutic consequences, must properly reside with the individual in question whenever possible. The task for clinicians becomes one of determining where this balance between positive and negative effects of a given therapy lies for each patient at any particular moment. Satisfactory accomplishment of this goal requires open communication between all centrally involved parties regarding all key decisions. Once this is achieved, professionals may feel more confident that the courses they recommend are appropriate to the situation at hand.

There are as many styles of dying as there are of living. (20)

For some people, the sense of purpose inherent in fighting their illness to the bitter end may be of tremendous psychological value. These individuals may endure severe symptoms related to their treatments with equanimity as long as they feel that the fight is being carried to its finish. For others, the diagnosis of a probably terminal condition serves as an impetus to redirect their priorities toward optimization of the quality of their daily lives on physical and emotional levels. Such patients may seek primarily palliative and pain-relieving interventions from health care personnel. They may choose to focus their efforts during this twilight of their lives toward loved ones, favorite activities, enjoying the world around them, or even just sitting and dreaming. There are as many styles of dying as there are of living.

Influence of Emotions on Decision-Making

Emotional states of patients and families must be assessed before significant treatment choices are discussed. (5)

The emotional state of patients and families facing terminal illness is likely to fluctuate widely throughout the course of a disease. It is important to be as certain as possible that decisions with far-reaching consequences are not based on momentary extremes of feeling. For example, in moments of despair patients for whom therapeutic intervention offers reasonable chances of significant remission or actual cure may choose to forego treatment. On the other hand, clearly mor-ibund individuals in the grip of a transient denial of their conditions may opt for highly toxic regimens that they might otherwise have rejected. In either case, patients and families may become saddled with the consequences of choices that they would not have made if their judgment had not been obscured by their emotional state.

Many such situations can be averted if clinicians regularly address the underlying feelings of patients and families before important choices are made. More often than not, the simple chance to ventilate fears and hopes to an empathic listener will allow patients to make more appropriate decisions. Clinicians may sense that treatment decisions in this highly stressful setting reflect desperation more than clear thinking. In such cases, a simple reflection of that emotion should be attempted. The same applies when evident apathy or denial underlie apparently inappropriate requests or choices. Once these feelings have been empathically and nonjudgmentally explored, it is likely that the process of arriving at mutually acceptable treatment courses will pro-ceed uneventfully.

CASE ILLUSTRATION

An 82-year-old woman was brought to the hospital from her nursing home by her distraught family. They had noted a steady decline in her alertness and weight over a few months, and medical evaluation revealed an enormous abdominal mass that probably represented dissem-inated tumor. The woman was totally demented and had been so for a decade. In spite of this, the family pressed strongly for aggressive intervention. Gentle probing by the attending physician revealed much guilt on the family's part regarding their decision to institutionalize their mother when she became incoherent and incontinent. Once they were given the oppor-tunity to clearly express these feelings, as well as some reassurance that they had acted appro-priately, their attitude changed. After some vacillation, they arrived at a reasonable decision to initiate only supportive care measures. The elderly woman died peacefully within a few days, and the family went through an uncomplicated mourning process.

Settling Accounts

Putting one's affairs in order can be of great psychological and spiritual value.

It is old wisdom that putting one's affairs in order can be of great comfort to those facing the probability of an imminent death. The activity of settling one's accounts promotes a sense of mastery and control on many levels in a very helpless situation. In addition, this action may in itself promote resolution of emotional issues. This is because it constitutes a powerful and universally recognized metaphor for preparing to die. As a result, patients or family members who are having difficulty accepting the situation may be enabled, as they resolve their material issues, to address unresolved emotional ones more effectively.

The health care professionals who are of greatest value in facilitating this process are specially trained social workers or nurses armed with information from the other members of the health care team. They have knowledge of and access to resources that often prove invaluable to emotionally shocked patients and families in sorting out what needs to be done. Further, as social workers and nurses receive increasingly advanced training in emotional counseling, they provide additional support in resolving psychological issues stimulated by this process.

Putting affairs in order can be a gift from patients to loved ones.

There are significant advantages after the death of the patient for the bereaved if the deceased has carefully settled worldly affairs before dying. It frees loved ones to attend to the important business of grief and mourning during a critical period. The chore of sorting through often unfamiliar financial affairs is not simple even for someone who is emotionally uninvolved. Completion of funeral arrangements can be equally disturbing and taxing. When the state of shock and the strong emotions of grief are added to the picture, these tasks can become a true ordeal. Patients can be assured that they are performing a great service to their loved ones by taking care of these matters early in the course of a terminal disease. In this way, unexpected medical turns are unlikely to prevent the process from being completed. Further, the dying can derive much satisfaction from giving their loved ones this final gift. As one colleague put it, "Many families have told me that my urging them to make these arrangements was the single most important service I performed. However, it is not easily done, especially when the family sees it as giving up. It requires great sensitivity and timing."

The negative feelings toward the deceased that arise on sudden discovery that one major legacy is a tangle of unresolved affairs frequently complicate mourning. Too many times we have seen situations in which survivors thought themselves to be financially better off than in reality they were. Most tragic probably are the instances in which the bereaved thought themselves secure only to discover that few arrangements existed for their support. If financial affairs are addressed early on, it allows at least some time to prepare more realistically for the future. This can avert unpleasant surprises at a most inopportune time.

Conflicting Motives Between Patients and Professionals

Professionals' need to do something positive may conflict with the patients' interests. (4)

There are a number of circumstances in which the needs or interests of professionals may come into conflict with those of patients and families. Underlying such circumstances often is the sense of helplessness that is so common in terminal care situations. Ours is a culture where the watchword is *Don't just sit there, do something!* Health care team members often become frustrated and sick at heart when their interventions "fail" to produce better results. They may feel compelled to promote more or different treatments (*minor medical heroics*) even against the interests of the patient's quality of life. Right to die legislation has been enacted in several states in an attempt to resolve this sort of conflict (see Chapter 7).

It is vital to agree when to shift from curing to caring as the primary focus of medical interventions.

In any event, it is important to explore the motives behind urges among health care team members to institute further treatments that may decrease the quality of life of patients. Examination may allow the expression of underlying feelings that are blocking a more realistic solution. Patients and families are too often taxed by inappropriate therapeutic interventions that are primarily expressions of staff helplessness. Thus, if any serious doubt exists as to the realistic basis of the push for further treatment in a given situation, consultation with an uninvolved expert may be useful as well.

When to consult.

Another way of addressing this need to do something positive in terminal care settings is to refocus health care team goals away from defeating disease and toward providing an optimal experience for patients and families. This can be done by emphasizing symptom control and supportive care interventions. Professionals' willingness to provide safe passage through this difficult time by abiding peacefully and responsively with their patients may be the greatest service they can offer. Very often, the golden rule in terminal care may be *Don't just do something, sit there!*

Research Studies

Medical research can cause conflict between patients and professionals.

We ordinarily think of research as an activity that goes on only in the rarefied atmospheres of a relatively few prestigious medical centers. This is not entirely the case. In cancer research particularly, where national protocols exist for a large number of studies, local physicians from virtually any community may take part. It is only by studying large numbers of patients that statistically significant answers can be obtained for certain subtle questions. Therefore, primary care clinicians may have the opportunity to participate in such studies, and even may become emotionally invested in them.

For the most part, involvement in research protocols is not problematic. Committees for the use of human subjects in research rigorously review ethical and practical aspects of study proposals before experiments begin. Further, the research protocols requiring larger numbers of patients than are available at single institutions are often those that investigate the less controversial distinctions among currently acceptable alternative treatments whose differences in outcome might be too small to assess in studies of fewer patients.

Patients may be subtly and unintentionally persuaded to assent to measures that are not in their interests. (6)

The potential for conflicts of interest between professionals and patients, however, always exists when either has an agenda that derives mainly from outside of the therapeutic relationship. In addition, those faced with the abyss of lifethreatening illness may be particularly vulnerable to implications that an experimental therapy may offer a miraculous cure.

Therefore, it is incumbent on professionals to be very clear about their own motivation for offering treatment under a research protocol. This is not to say that patients cannot derive satisfaction from participation in research. One of the ways in which many persons cope with difficult realities is to look for a way in which their suffering has benefited others. Participation as a subject in research or teaching offers such an outlet. We believe strongly, however, that measures should be taken to safeguard against exploiting the desperate patient. Professionals involved in studies should be open about their own desires for patients to participate. It must be stated that no negative consequences, either overt or subtle, will result for those who wish to refuse.

Patients can derive satisfaction from helping others. (6)

Finally, there are significant ethical questions to be faced when teaching or research are combined with medical care. It is not trivial to assess in any given case whether or to what degree the potential of benefit for the many outweighs the benefit to the patient. Clearly, it is only possible in individual cases to assess this balance, and then only in open collaboration with patients and families. When there is any doubt or conflict, the interests of the patient must take precedence.

Nontraditional Therapies

There are many nontraditional modalities now available for treatment of life-threatening illness.

We will not attempt to provide a complete survey of the various alternate therapies currently available, because they are numerous and sometimes difficult to characterize. However, we will catalog a few of the most popular nontraditional modalities now used in the area of cancer.

The *Simonton* method involves an effort to enlist the body's immune defenses against cancer through meditation and guided fantasies. Although no definitive studies have been done to assess its effectiveness, this approach generally cannot do a great deal of harm. One exception to this arises from Simonton practitioners who do not guard against (or even may actively promote) feelings that those whose diseases worsen have somehow *failed*. We have seen very negative effects on quality of life from the resulting sense of guilt and confusion.

There are other meditative therapies available, some involving colored lights or massage or the laying on of hands. All of these are

Most alternative therapies cause problems only if they lead patients to forego or delay vital mainstream treatments.

probably equally benign from a medical standpoint, although they may prove financially exploitive. Problems can arise, however, if these options lead patients to circumvent potentially helpful conventional treatment modalities.

There are a number of medicinal approaches available. The most prominent of these are vitamin C and laetrile. In the case of the former, the chance of any direct harm being done or of it resulting in any interference with standard therapies is relatively small (this is true only with doses below a few grams per day, as higher amounts can cause renal problems). Laetrile, however, has potential for toxicity if the compound is inadequately purified. Further, increasing evidence points toward the uselessness of laetrile as an agent for fighting malignancy (Moertel et al., 1982). The various other herbal and medicinal remedies are too numerous to review, and there is no convincing demonstration of their effectiveness.

Finally, there is the issue of foreign clinics that offer alternative therapies. Historically, they have represented one of the more noticeable attempts to exploit the desperate. We have not the information to pass judgment on specific clinics currently in operation, but the findings concerning their predecessors do not augur well. From our viewpoint, patients and families should be discouraged from squandering precious time and resources on fruitless expeditions. When the issue is brought up, the approaches described below may be employed to attempt to resolve any arising contentions. If agreement is not forthcoming, clinicians may have to deal with the frustration of seeing their patients taken advantage of in this particularly heinous manner.

There are logical reasons for patients and families to seek nontraditional therapies.

Many times, health care professionals find themselves feeling hurt or angry when a patient chooses to attempt a therapy not recommended by the attending clinician. This is quite understandable in the face of the implication that their patients view the offerings of the clinician as inadequate. In truth, this choice may reflect a rejection on the part of some patients or families. Equally, however, it demonstrates the natural tendency to look elsewhere as mainstream alternatives begin to fail. Many alternative therapies are characterized by their lack of toxicity, and by the fact that control is more likely to reside with the patient than with the person administering the treatment. It is not surprising that such factors would look particularly attractive to patients and families suffering from the side effects and dealing with the technological complexities of current diagnosis and treatment. The desire to look into the various alternative or unorthodox therapies does not necessarily reflect on the skills of involved professionals.

Exploration of feelings about conventional therapies is the first step in dealing with patients who seek nonconventional treatment.

The initial course that clinicians should follow when the issue of using a nonconventional alternative remedy arises is to address possible feelings of helplessness and resentment about medical treatments. Many times, the resulting ventilation lays the issue to rest indefinitely. When this does not happen, some clinicians may feel compelled to take a stand, giving patients the choice of abiding by their recommendations or going elsewhere.

This sort of response usually is not necessary! Many of the most prominent alternate approaches, such as Simonton's techniques, physical therapy of various kinds, psychic healing, or vitamin C therapy, can be utilized by patients who still continue their medical regimens. Clinicians should be able to understand the use of these modalities as long as patients are not prompted to forego standard treatments. If the nontraditional methods begin to interfere with standard treatments, once again the issue should be approached by addressing feelings before content. The opportunity to explore these underlying emotions often permits a more reasoned exchange between clinician and patient. If the conflicts still are not amenable to resolution, it may be necessary to treat the patient within the limits acceptable to that individual. If such a course is not ethically reconcilable for the clinician, referral may be necessary. This should be done in a gentle and supportive manner.

When to refer.

Addressing Concerns Related to Families

The Family's Sense of Helplessness

Active cooperation and support from loved ones is often more important during this period than at any other time of life. Clinicians perform a great disservice if they fail to take family issues into account beginning with the initial diagnosis of a life-threatening condition.

Early involvement of family members in information and decision-making addresses their sense of helplessness and assists in the treatment of patients. (4)

Involvement of family members in information and decision-making from an early point in the course of a final illness helps to address the issue of helplessness close to its onset. A terminal disease is as likely to evoke this feeling in family members witnessing the deterioration of a loved one as it is to produce this state of mind in the patient. Because the patient is legitimately the focus of a great deal of attention, some family members may have additional reason to feel neglected and helpless.

As we have stated, the possession of information about what is going on seems to allow most of us to feel more at ease even if we are unable to alter significantly the course of events. This applies equally well to loved ones as it does to the terminally ill. If clinicians solicit input from families, they stand to benefit on two further counts. First, information from the family can provide a valuable perspective that may not be available from any other source. Second, if loved ones feel that their thoughts have been taken into account in setting a course, they are more likely to contribute actively toward following it. The emotions and thoughts of family members should be addressed with empathic listening and nonjudgmental exploration of unresolved feelings.

Conflicts Between Patients and Family Members

There are likely to be instances during the course of a terminal illness when conflicts arise between patients and family members. Such occurrences are to be expected in highly charged situations when emotionally close individuals are placed under extreme stress. Therefore, it is incumbent on health care professionals in terminal care settings to develop methods of dealing with such difficulties. The following are some guidelines that we have found useful in such instances.

When conflicts arise between patients and family members, each person usually should be seen individually first.

When a conflict arises, it is often helpful to give private forum to each person's feelings. This tactic alone may suffice to cool things off enough to enable those involved to realize that their emotions are motivated more by situational stresses than by their loved ones' behavior. Professionals do well once again to address feelings before content in the process of exploring such conflicts. A nonjudgmental effort simply to sort things out is recommended, and usually will lead to a reduction of tension even if the underlying issue remains unresolved.

CASE ILLUSTRATION

A 25-year-old man was rapidly dying of a rare neural tumor. On admission to the hospital, it became apparent that there were some severe conflicts between the patient and his parents. The patient felt that his father had always compared him unfavorably to his older brother, and had taken an authoritarian attitude toward him (particularly regarding his illness). The parents were heartbroken at the impending loss of their son, and had focused on a regimented adherence to "doctor's orders" as a means of gaining some sense of control. After each of the parties were allowed the opportunity to express their feelings in private (at times quite loudly), a breakthrough took place. The son and parents ended this encounter in a useful and poignant session culminating with all in tears and mutually expressing appropriate love and sadness.

Once this cooling off process is complete, those in conflict should be encouraged to communicate directly about their difficulties. This will often proceed much more smoothly once the immediate heat of the situation has been dissipated by the chance to talk it out with an impartial but supportive listener. If the adversaries feel uncomfortable about addressing each other face-to-face, they may be more willing to do so in the company of the professional who has talked it out with both of them.

Direct conflict mediation is within the scope of most nonjudgmental clinicians.

The actual process of mediating such a conflict directly is a delicate one. It is, however, by no means beyond the abilities of most sensitive health care professionals. The key rule to follow when involved in such situations is that the clinician is present to provide, as much as possible, safe passage for everyone present. Those in conflict should be encouraged to speak directly to each other, rather than to address the clinician. Further, they should be guided to express what they feel rather than to make judgments or draw conclusions about the other person. This rule must be equitably enforced if the professional is to remain useful as a mediator.

One particularly important function that an impartial observer can serve in such settings is to ensure that each of the quarreling parties actually has been heard. Often, in the heat of argument, and especially in emotionally charged situations, individuals will tend to concentrate on their next retort rather than on what is being said. A real service can be performed merely by asking such a question as, "What did you hear her say?" Even the simple knowledge that one is being heard sufficiently so that words and ideas can be repeated back often suffices to reduce the tension level.

If one person begins to be abusive to another, it is usually appropriate to intervene. This can be done effectively with a statement like, "I feel uncomfortable with what is going on right now. What are you feeling at this moment?" This question usually should be directed toward the aggressor. Such an inquiry does not escalate the encounter by accusing anyone, and models the open expression of discomfort.

When to refer.

There may be instances in which this sort of mediation fails to achieve a reduction in the level of hostility. When this occurs, the problem may be addressed by meeting separately with each adversary and encouraging further ventilation. If this does not allow for an open reconciliation, the situation may have to be managed by periodic private meetings with each of the involved parties. During these sessions expression of feelings can be encouraged, and support should be given openly to the person with whom one is talking. If major conflict remains, referral to an outside expert counselor may be necessary. Finally, if all measures fail, the interests of the patient usually should take priority over those of the family. Fortunately, clashes usually can be headed off well before this choice must be made.

The shift in roles within the family commonly results in family conflicts during terminal illness. As an illness progresses, the patient often becomes incapable of performing accustomed family tasks. These then must be taken on by other members, who may feel unprepared for them. We have often seen husbands floundering in an overwhelming sea of day-to-day care of the home. Perhaps as common is the wife who quails before the daunting world of business and finance. The situation is further complicated by the guilt and resentment of the patient whose role has been usurped.

Professionals can address these problems in a number of ways. They should anticipate problems with role changes, and should make special efforts to elicit feelings surrounding them from all parties. This ventilation can reduce tensions and create a more receptive atmosphere for concrete problem-solving interventions. Periodic followup of role change problems often can head off new conflicts before they become serious.

Enlisting Families in Support of Treatment

Family support should be enlisted early. (7)

As we have noted, family members should be enlisted early and recognized overtly as vital members of the treatment team. The earlier they become actively involved, the more easily they are likely to negotiate the many transitions that are inevitable. As a terminal disease progresses, family members become increasingly crucial contributors to the quality of life of the dying. This is because emotional support and the less technical expressions of caring assume a more important role in providing comfort and consolation.

The other side of this coin may be observed when family members are excluded from participation in information and decision-making. When this occurs, they may witness the side-effects of therapies without ever having been told the positive results that are expected. Loved ones may come to associate medical interventions with negative consequences for themselves and the patient. Too often this results in their active opposition to the efforts of health care professionals.

Family Pressures to Persist in Curative Attempts

The shift from cure to care may be difficult. (13)

Family members frequently apply pressure to persist in curative attempts past the time when these are in the patient's interest. This behavior often is a reaction to the sense of guilt and helplessness that family members usually experience. Additionally, it may be a desperate attempt to ward off the inevitable loss that looms so frighteningly in the near future. When pressure of this sort is applied, professionals should again first respond by addressing the underlying feelings with nonjudgmental exploration. This will often suffice to reduce the emotional intensity enough so that a simple explanation of the indications to alter further treatment from the *cure* to *care* modality will be heard and understood.

If this type of intervention is ineffective in clearing up the issue, it will become important to separate clearly the wishes of patients from those of family members. This determination should be attempted with each of the parties separately, in order to minimize the pressure

Family pressures to persist in curative attempts must be explored, but the wishes and interests of the patient generally come first.

that may be applied. When it is clear that a conflict will not be resolved by exploration and explanation to the involved parties separately, direct mediation may be in order. If such efforts—either by involved clinicians or by outside consultants—fail, the interests of the patient must assume priority.

References

Baer, L. S. 1978. *Let the Patient Decide*. Philadelphia: The Westminster Press.

This rather short, thoughtful book by a family doctor with 40 years of experience deals primarily with patients over age 65 years. The first part describes dilemmas surrounding treatment decisions, and has many case illustrations. The second part analyzes the possibilities open to patients who do not want their dying needlessly prolonged. This book is very worthwhile for health care professionals, as well as for most older persons.

Balint, M. 1964. *The Doctor, His Patient, and the Illness*. London: Pittman.

A worthwhile book aimed at teaching psychotherapy to the family doctor. Principles are well illustrated by clinical examples. Much of the content is applicable to the interpersonal aspects of therapeutic relationships during the care of dying patients.

California Natural Death Act. State of California Health and Safety Code. Division 7, Part 1, Chapter 3.9, Section 7185.

Corby, J., Leiderman, P. and Bernal, P. 1983. Informed consent for psychoactive medications. *Proc. Amer. Psychiatric Assn*. Page 241.

Glaser, B. G. and Strauss, A. L. 1965. *Awareness of Dying*. Chicago: Aldine Publishing Co.

One of the pioneering systematic sociologic studies of hospital settings. The emphasis is on interactions between patients and staff after the transition from curing to caring has taken place. The valuable concept of "mutual pretense" was first elucidated here. Many practical examples illuminate their theoretical model.

Moertel, C. G., Fleming, T. R., Rubin, J. et al. 1982. A clinical trial of amygdalin (Laetrile) in the treatment of human cancer. *New Eng. J. Med*. 306:201–206.

The Downhill Course: Coping with Chronic Disease

6

Overview

Once the period of diagnosis and initiation of treatment has passed, persons with life-threatening illnesses enter a difficult new phase. This may be thought of as the period of chronic disease. During this time, which is extremely variable in length, there often arise great uncertainties as to the effectiveness of initial therapies. Therefore, there may be no clear means of anticipating the amount or the quality of life remaining. During this downhill course, however, patients' experience of their illnesses depend heavily on their emotional state.

Realizing That the Illness Will Prove Fatal

Interdependence of Emotional State and Experience of Illness

Glaser and Strauss (1968) likened the course of a final illness to the path of a projectile—a "trajectory of dying." Unlike simpler trajectories followed by ballistic projectiles, this course is complex and often difficult to anticipate even from day-to-day. Nonetheless, we often may be lulled by our expectations into assuming that the timing of a terminal illness has been established with certainty. We may even become angry when a reprieve occurs and our "projectile" fails to follow the course we anticipated.

It is vital for clinicians to assess when extension of living becomes prolongation of dying. (4, 15 and Figure 6-1)

The Chaplain to the Stanford University Medical Center, Ernle Young (1976), has elaborated a particularly useful version of this trajectory. His model, diagrammed in Figure 6-1, emphasizes a clinically important crossover point. This is the juncture at which additional medical therapy ceases to extend living, but only prolongs a difficult process of dying. Past this point, the value of persisting in treatments that are not directed toward maintenance of quality of life becomes questionable at best.

The issue then becomes one of defining as precisely as possible when this transition takes place during the course of each illness. This is an intensely individual matter that is highly contingent on the per-

Figure 6-1: The trajectory of dying: Point *A* represents birth, *X* denotes the diagnosis of a life-threatening condition, *Y* is the point past which medical interventions act to prolong dying rather than living, and *Z* indicates death.

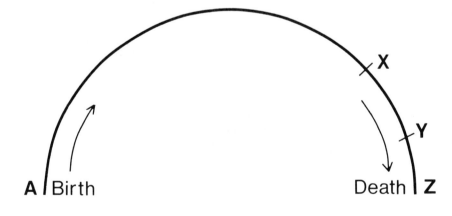

Patients should have the main voice in changing the primary objective of therapy from curing *to* caring. *(15)*

sonalities of the patient and the involved clinicians. We would like to think that the viewpoints of patients carry the predominant weight in striking this balance. Experience belies this hope to some extent. In reality, the person with the stronger will tends to prevail in such ill-defined compromises. Clinicians should try to be aware of their own tendencies as to aggressiveness of treatment. Particular care should be taken to account for these inclinations when arriving at treatment decisions, especially as regards the determination that this crossover point has been reached. Many professionals regard this decision as throwing in the towel. Those who tend to persist with curative attempts and who have invested a great deal of energy in them may have difficulty switching from *quantity* to *quality* of life as a primary focus.

The way to resolve problems in this area resides once again in honest self-examination, with consultation if any doubt exists, and in clear and open communication between professionals and patients. Paying attention to personality issues early in the course of treatment, before emotional involvement additionally clouds judgment, can bear important fruit. For example, a simple note to oneself that "I can browbeat this patient without intending to, so I have to be careful as things go on," can be of great value in choosing the most appropriate time for the shift from curing to caring.

It is sometimes easy to become so committed to a particular battle plan that the reason for engaging in the war may be forgotten. Regular review with patients and families of where things stand should be coupled with periodic mutual reevaluation of treatment courses. This can help to avert mistakes, and can further cement a positive relationship between all parties involved.

Even the most overwhelming problems can seem manageable in the face of a positive outlook. However, trivial difficulties can plunge a person into despair if encountered during the throes of depression.

Marked variations in emotional state should be anticipated during a terminal disease. (5)

The emotional states of patients and families have a profound impact on the quality of life they experience during a final illness. Therefore, these must be taken into account. As an illness progresses and technical interventions become less relevant, careful management of the emotional arena may be the greatest gift professionals have to offer.

Emotional reactions among patients and families during this phase of a terminal illness tend to follow cycles based upon the status of remission or exacerbation. It is as though the failure of each trial of therapy to contain advancing illness is a recapitulation of the original confrontation with imminent death. Patients and families often may repeat the various emotions they encountered initially, sometimes with even greater intensity. Fears of the unknown, of isolation and abandonment, of loss of a functioning self, of loss of others, and of further suffering frequently recur. So do denial, anger, and sadness. Clinicians should broach the news of each exacerbation of a disease with

Denial, anger, fear, sadness, and other emotions recur in irregular cycles.

much the same attitudes as they had at the original disclosure. Time should be allowed for ventilation and support, and health care team members should not assume that these setbacks are any easier for patients and families than was the initial encounter.

Effects of Denial

Denial is a pervasive emotional reaction in patients and families during the period between initiation of therapy for a life-threatening condition and the realization that the illness will prove fatal. This common response is by no means always maladaptive. There are many instances in which patients and families intentionally suppress or unconsciously repress thoughts and feelings related to their plight. This may persist even when appropriate therapy has been instituted and patients are conscientiously following medical regimens. In such cases, damage is seldom done by allowing those faced with the ultimate terror of death to enjoy a period, which may well be their last, during which signs and symptoms of advancing disease allow even the illusion of normality. As long as appropriate medical measures are being taken, clinicians often have little to lose by not challenging statements or actions that do not conform to those they expect from terminally ill patients.

Denial *need not be challenged unless it seriously interferes with treatment or causes major problems for the patient or the family. (12)*

There are, of course, significant exceptions to this approach. For example, there are cases in which denial is so great that patients and family members cannot discuss what is going on. Denial of this magnitude prevents practical affairs from being put in order. Even more important, it may result in the evolution of unrealistic and potentially harmful plans and behaviors that are unconsciously intended to belie the terrifying reality. This situation can leave loved ones and clinicians with an uncomfortable choice. Either they collude with these manifestations of denial, or they risk incurring the wrath, or even precipitating the emotional breakdown, of the denier.

When it becomes apparent to clinicians that a clearly pathological level of denial is present, careful intervention is necessary. If the harmful effects of denial are marginal, as, for example, when patients make plans of questionable wisdom, involved professionals should consult each other to be certain that the benefits of intervention outweigh any potential harm. Given a consensus that denial is causing serious enough problems to warrant intervention, the following guidelines may prove helpful.

Underlying feelings should be examined before exploring content when pathological denial is addressed.

First of all, as usually is the case when addressing inappropriate behavior, the *underlying feelings* of patients and families should be explored prior to examining content. Clinicians might begin simply by inquiring how the person in question thinks things are going. If the patient's response offers no opening for broaching the issue, it may be necessary for the professional to inquire directly regarding feelings of helplessness or worry. If this avenue also proves fruitless, the next step should be a gentle and nonjudgmental explanation of why the patient's behaviors or statements have caused concern. If the patient becomes defensive, it is usually appropriate to say something such as, "You seem to be reacting as though I am accusing you of something. I want to make it clear that there is no one at fault here, and that this conversation is only the result of my concern for your well-being." Then, professionals should once again explain why the behaviors in question are troublesome. It is often helpful to use different words in this reiteration from those employed in the initial presentation of the problem. These can be modified on the basis of the denier's own language and level of defensiveness.

When to refer.

Generally, this process will suffice to open the door for resolution of the issue. If not, consultation with an experienced counselor may be necessary. If that measure fails as well, it may be necessary either to work within the limits imposed by the denial, or to refer the patient elsewhere if the situation becomes unconscionable. In either case, professionals should take steps to deal with their own reactions to this frustrating situation.

Denial manifested by noncompliance with treatment can cause anger in clinicians that further complicates therapy.

Denial manifested through medically related behaviors, such as ignoring symptoms or not cooperating with treatment, presents special problems. This is because clinicians may feel blocked in their efforts and may experience hostility toward those whom they feel are thwarting proper therapy. It is recommended in such cases that the issues be talked out with colleagues to allow for sufficient ventilation of angry feelings. This will make it more likely that deniers can be confronted in a nonaccusatory manner.

Patients or families also may bring up problems surrounding denial in conversation with professionals. Once again, a useful approach is to explore the circumstances and underlying feelings before embarking on a course of action. Once the emotional edge has been removed by discussing the issue, a more balanced picture of what is going on may emerge. Then the clinician and the person presenting the problem can examine possible courses of action together.

Effects of Loss of Functional Capacity

Conflicts related to loss of premorbid function usually arise during this phase of a terminal illness. (4, 12)

Another difficult issue arises during this latency period of a chronic, life-threatening disease. It is the effect of disease- and treatment-related loss of premorbid functional capacities. The growing sense of invalidism and dependency that frequently emerges during this period of gradual decline often is highly disturbing to patients and families. Particular difficulty arises when family members convey the expectation that the ill person should continue to perform and fill their needs just as before. There is a delicate balance to be struck in these situations between encouraging graceful withdrawal from full participation in premorbid activities and undermining an already besieged sense of worth. This is no less the case for patients than it is for their loved ones. As a result, conflicts are almost bound to arise in this area at some point during a terminal illness.

A prominent contributing factor to losses of functional capacity relates to the side-effects of treatment. These can be particularly troublesome during this time, because initial therapeutic interventions will often reduce or eliminate the presenting symptoms. As a result, patients and families may be breathing a sigh of relief at the disappearance of overt evidence of the spectre of disease. Particularly in the case of many malignancies, however, proven treatment regimens require the continuation of uncomfortable and at times highly toxic treatments. These often leave patients feeling sapped of energy and forced into invalidism for periods of time following each visit to the clinic or hospital. Similarly, surgical interventions often result in a degree of invalidism or mutilation.

Toxic side effects of treatments can result in patients regarding professionals as tormenters rather than as advocates.

The resulting reduced quality of life can contribute to a strong antipathy toward the entire medical establishment. This, in turn, can assume magnitudes that may interfere with optimal therapy. Clinicians should be aware of this dynamic, and should attempt to address it by promoting ventilation of angry and frightened feelings. The early resolution of these conflicts can prove invaluable in allowing patients and families to continue to regard health care personnel as advocates rather than as tormenters.

Professionals also can address this issue by promoting as much sense of control and active life in their patients as is practical. This can be done by emphasizing the teamwork aspects of treating the illness, and by allowing flexibility in therapy schedules to facilitate as satisfying a life as possible. As far as family members are concerned, this is one instance in which private opportunities to ventilate their frustration and sense of abandonment may be most vital.

Family members are under stresses similar to those of patients.

It may be exceedingly difficult for loved ones to admit negative feelings toward the terminally ill patient. Patience and gentle encouragement are required on the part of clinicians to reassure family members that such reactions are common and appropriate. A chance to talk in private may head off unpleasant and guilt-provoking confrontations with the patient. Group therapy with family members of other terminally ill patients also has proven to be of value in alleviating stress stemming from the loss of functional capacity.

Issues of Symptom Control

Symptoms of Pain

It is important to differentiate between pain behavior and pain experience. (12)

Symptoms of severe chronic pain are present in a significant minority of patients during the course of terminal illness, and constitute an important determinant of the quality of life. Gonda (1962) emphasized that the distinction between patients' experience of this distress and their manner of communicating it to clinicians is central to understanding pain in medical contexts. Whereas the *subjective sensations* of those who suffer constitute pain from their perspective, the professional is made aware of this only through *pain behavior.* The significance of this difference becomes apparent when we realize that pain behavior may constitute a convenient metaphor for eliciting clinicians' attention for many sorts of distress. Further, the manner in which dying patients perceive those who care for them is an important determinant of the quality and quantity of pain complaints.

Another factor that colors pain behavior in this setting is each individual's feelings concerning impending death. Feelings of anxiety, for example, are well known to greatly intensify both pain sensations and complaints. Yet, it is tempting to respond only to the overt content of pain behavior. This is particularly true given our cultural uneasiness regarding sharing of disturbing emotions that may be masked by pain complaints in terminal settings. If medication is forthcoming, patients may indeed feel somewhat relieved and cared for. At the same time, professionals may appreciate the chance to perform a well-defined service in a setting where the visible result of their efforts often is quite limited.

Pain behavior warrants thorough investigation before treatment decisions are made.

Clinicians who are upset by talk about dying may rather hear about pain. Thus, they unwittingly elicit more communication about these concrete symptoms and less about any other aspects of the terrifying reality of death. Unfortunately, if clinicians choose not to look beneath the surface, they may neglect the underlying cause for the symptom of pain behavior. This is poor practice, and is likely to bear bitter fruit in the course of a terminal illness.

When professionals witness pain behavior from terminally ill patients, it is incumbent on them to investigate it as thoroughly as they would any other symptom before treatment decisions are made. Clinicians must bear in mind, particularly when dealing with the dying, that pain behavior may not always be the direct expression of physical discomfort. It is appropriate to begin the inquiry with a statement along these lines: "In order to treat your pain in the best possible manner, I need to understand it fully. Can you tell me about it in detail?"

Once the patient has described the complaint, usual assessment inquiries should follow. One mnemonic for doing this is *PQRST:* **Pre**cipitants, **Q**uality, **R**elieving behaviors, associated **S**ymptoms, and **T**iming. Many times, such an inquiry paints a picture that is consistent with the diagnosis. If other encounters with the patient and family members (as well as the clinical *sixth sense*) do not point toward an underlying emotional complaint, then it may be appropriate to proceed immediately to treatment.

Often, however, there is some inconsistency in the clinical picture, or some hint of another problem presenting as a complaint of pain. If this is the case, a gentle exploration of the possibility is in order. It is usually wise to begin with a disarming statement: "I am confused about this issue, and wonder if you could help me sort it out. Many times in situations similar to yours, my patients have experienced real and excruciating pain as a symptom of an emotional difficulty. Although I am not at all certain that this is the case with you, it would seem wise for us to look into it." If the professional has been identified as one with whom emotions are comfortably shared, this approach will often yield considerable insights.

Great gentleness is necessary to avoid putting patients on the defensive when evaluating for emotional distress presenting as a pain complaint.

Another tack is to say: "It is clear to me that you are suffering. When someone is under emotional stress, it often makes the physical problems worse. Is there anything going on emotionally for you that is making it harder for you to bear the discomfort you now have?"

Once any underlying or related emotional issues are uncovered and thoroughly assessed, they should be dealt with in the manners we have described throughout Parts 2 and 3. Even if such exploration bears no fruit, patients are unlikely to be alienated by an open, non-accusatory, and supportive approach.

To be sure, the foundation of a solid, caring relationship between patient and professional will facilitate a more fruitful exploration of these possibilities. Thus, this extremely delicate issue most often should not be approached on first meeting a patient.

Medical Treatment of Pain

Pain can be addressed medically both peripherally and in the central nervous system.

We begin our consideration of medical modalities of pain control with a discussion of analgesics. The *narcotic analgesics* act on the central nervous system by mimicking the binding properties of the potent intrinsic analgesics produced under certain circumstances by our own bodies. There are, however, other levels of the nervous system at which significant analgesia may be obtained. If pain complaints are related to irritation of peripheral nerves, for example, then *peripherally acting* agents may be employed. The most common of these are the prostaglandin inhibiting compounds such as aspirin. These agents are frequently as effective as some centrally acting compounds for mild to moderate pain. If the medical situation permits, and if patients can tolerate the gastrointestinal side-effects, these simple drugs should be among the first considered. For patients who are intolerant of aspirin or in whom the antiplatelet activity is contraindicated, acetaminophen is an appropriate alternative (although it lacks significant anti-inflammatory activity). The new agent zomepirac (Zomax) is a nonsteroidal anti-inflammatory agent that also may act via prostaglandin inhibition. It has been shown by Forrest (1980) to be more effective than aspirin in treatment of moderate to severe pain. At this writing, however, it is unavailable in the United States.

In current pain control literature, the consensus is that pain that cannot be addressed satisfactorily by peripherally acting compounds should be treated with a narcotic analgesic.

We will not discuss the relative merits of each particular narcotic, leaving that to the experience and judgment of each clinician. Rather, we will underline a few elements of the administration of these drugs that are critical from our perspective.

The negative emotional and social connotations attached to the use of narcotics have detrimental effects in terminal care environments. (12)

All too often, we have seen caregivers, with a syringe already prepared, asking patients if they could "hold out any longer." Through such interactions, patients are placed in a position where they must experience pain, complain of it, and essentially bargain or beg for relief in a situational role of helplessness. The implication is that there is some arbitrary benefit in bearing pain. Particularly for the terminally ill, this attitude is not justifiable. Concern regarding psychological or physical dependency is appropriate in an acute care setting, but it seldom is relevant in terminal care.

One way of reducing problems associated with narcotic analgesics is to avoid intravenous or intramuscular medications whenever possible. This can free sufferers from the need to rely on others for pain relief. In addition, it removes the negative connotation associated with receiving a drug via a needle.

Both PRN and rigidly scheduled pain medications should be avoided in terminal care, unless medication is to be self-administered.

Another important principle is to avoid staff-dispensed *as needed* (PRN) pain medication whenever possible. In some settings, there may be benefit derived from allowing patients to debate with staff members about whether or not they *need* pain relief medication. Terminal care, however, is not one of them. Therefore, clinicians should prescribe medication on a flexible and tailor-made schedule if it is not to be self-administered. The *least powerful* medications commensurate with patients' needs should be prescribed initially. The regimen should be constructed so as to avoid pain as much as possible within the limits of impairment of consciousness acceptable to the patient. Titration of dosage and adjustment of intervals between doses should continue on a regular basis as the needs for analgesia increase or decrease. Such a regimen can be effective in nearly all instances, with methadone and oral morphine being the principal specific medications of choice for severe pain. Oral morphine has the advantage of a shorter serum half-life and easier titration of dosage. This allows patients more readily to balance their level of consciousness and pain control on an hourly basis.

Many of the problems that can arise either with inflexibly scheduled or as needed medications in terminal care settings can be avoided if narcotics are *self-administered* and *self-regulated* by patients. Family members can be of great assistance in such situations, but they must be counseled carefully beforehand. In the end, however, the patient is the final arbiter. That individual usually can assess with the greatest accuracy the appropriate balance between level of consciousness and of pain control that is best for each particular situation. Self-administered oral solutions of narcotic agents often constitute a viable alternative in coping with the pain of terminal disease.

Self-regulation and self-administration of analgesics are ideal for many patients.

We are not entirely comfortable with any of the fixed dose combinations of various drugs (such as the Brompton mixture) now popular in many terminal care facilities as "pain cocktails." The pain of terminal illness is more ideally treated by use of measures that enable specific ingredients to be varied independently.

The *abuse* of self-administered narcotics in terminal care settings is *not* a problem. When addiction occurs, it usually constitutes but a trivial complication in the course of a pain control program that allows patients to carry on reasonably well and to die in relative comfort. Similarly, suicide with such agents is rare when appropriate psychological management is in force.

Addiction usually is a trivial, at times necessary, complication in terminal care. (12)

Problems more frequently arise in persuading patients to take pain medications regularly because of their (1) fear of addiction, (2) desire for therapies to eliminate rather than mask problems, (3) denial, and (4) fear that when they "really need" pain relief they will have used up all of their options. Again, safe conduct within the context of the caretaking relationship is the prime consideration for clinicians. Professionals should address directly each of the above fears, and should let patients know that if any given method of pain control is not acceptable, there are many other options available.

Nausea is a common side effect of oral narcotics, and may be dealt with by concomitant administration of antiemetics from the phenothiazine group. Promethazine, for example, is available in suppository as well as tablet form, for patients who have difficulty holding down any medication long enough for it to be absorbed. Constipation also commonly results from the use of narcotic analgesics. It can be avoided by the prophylactic use of bulk or mild stimulating laxatives if medically feasible.

There are a number of medications that are not a traditional part of the analgesic armamentarium that are useful in dealing with pain

Nonanalgesic medications such as amphetamines and antidepressants may prove of value in pain control.

in the setting of terminal disease. The first of these is the *amphetamines*. In a double-blind study by Forrest et al. (1977), the administration of moderate doses of amphetamine was shown to reduce the amount of narcotic necessary to manage pain. Although the central mechanism for this action is uncertain, its implications for terminal care settings are considerable. Because sedation is a side effect of the most potent narcotic analgesics, the stimulant action of amphetamines also can be of value. We recommend against combining these agents with narcotics in fixed doses, as this could prevent careful assessment of each drug's benefits and drawbacks for specific patients.

Tricyclic antidepressants constitute another group of pharmacologic agents that is useful in reducing pain complaints of terminal patients. The mechanism for their action in this instance is not certain, as the doses required are lower than those necessary to achieve antidepressant effects. A study by Ward and associates (1979) demonstrated that these drugs significantly relieve pain associated with depression. Caution should be used when employing these agents in patients with urinary or cardiac problems because of their anticholinergic and cardiotoxic side-effects. Further, care should be taken not to dispense quantities larger than a gram at a time if any risk of suicide exists.

Tricyclic antidepressants can also cause urinary retention, and their administration should be monitored carefully. Treatment with an antispasmodic agent such as urecholine (Urised) is often effective in dealing with this anticholinergic side effect.

A promising new compound that may be of use in dealing with pain and depression is trazodone (Desyrel), a chemical relative of the phenothiazines. It has been shown by Gershon (1981) to be comparable to the tricyclic antidepressants in relief of depression. Further, it has not been reported to be the agent for any successful suicides, and lacks significant anticholinergic or cardiotoxic side-effects.

Nonpharmacologic Control of Pain

There is a vast array of nonpharmacologic therapies aimed at pain control.

Of course, nonpharmacologic therapies also are key tools in palliation of the symptoms of advancing malignancy. The main thrust of these techniques generally is the control of pain. Hypnosis has been shown by Finer (1979) to be quite effective for the 40 per cent of patients who are susceptible to this technique. There also is an increasing literature on the use of cognitive-behavioral interventions for pain control. These include relaxation techniques, guided imagery, and various other devices which are well described by Turk and Rennert (1981). These methods share the distinct advantage of promoting a sense of power and control in patients by concretely demonstrating their ability to help themselves. Finally, radiotherapy, chemotherapy, and surgery have prominent roles in the palliation and control of certain diseases. Specifics in this area are beyond the scope of this work.

Control of Other Symptoms

Strategies to support adequate nutrition are important in terminal care. (4, 16)

There are a number of factors other than pain *per se* that strongly influence the quality of life of terminally ill patients during the phase of gradual decline. A major symptom of many malignancies is the *loss of a desire to eat.* Anorexia may stem from many causes, including nausea, constipation or depression. Its result is often a nutritionally related acceleration of the dying process beyond the rate dictated by the disease itself. The refusal to eat is also fraught with psychological implications for patients and families, and may become the focus of much conflict. Thus, it is vital that this issue be carefully considered.

The issue of monitoring weight is often complex. Although it is important that professionals keep generally aware of their patients' weight changes and diets, focus on this issue may be disturbing to patients and families. This is particularly true given that weight loss and anorexia accompany most terminal illnesses, and that they are often refractory to medical intervention. In many instances, concern about diet can best be focused as follows:

1. working with the family to avoid badgering or infantilizing the patient about food;
2. helping patients and families to understand that taste often changes with illness, and that sick bodies frequently do not ask to be fed;
3. promoting understanding that there are other ways to show caring and nurturance than through food; and
4. helping patients to change attitudes about food from something that is taken in for pleasure to something that is taken in as a medicine intended to help one feel better.

Management of bowel and bladder problems is of extreme importance. (4)

Careful monitoring of nausea and constipation should be initiated early in the course of the disease, and control instituted when indicated. Assistance in control of bowel and bladder function is also important to the quality of life of the dying. The humiliation and unpleasantness associated with the loss of sphincter control is profoundly disturbing to most persons. Professionals should be particularly sensitive to this issue and should attempt early to work out an acceptable means for managing this problem. The advisability of the use of diapers should be approached directly but sensitively when such measures are deemed appropriate. A gentle but matter of fact approach may allow patients to accept diapers with minimal humiliation or embarrassment, and may avoid dependency conflicts. The early institution of urinary catheters for bedridden and semiconscious patients often is most helpful.

Shortness of breath can be a most frightening symptom with profound destructive effects on the quality of life of the dying. The end stages of many fatal illnesses involve severe pulmonary complications. Administering narcotics or benzodiazepines can be particularly problematic because of respiratory depression. Low flow oxygen via nasal prongs often can provide some relief of dyspnea without reducing respiratory drive. Vigorous pulmonary toilet can avert many of these problems before they become serious. Judicious use of expectorants and antihistamines on a prophylactic basis often is helpful, as is mild diuresis if respiratory secretions are excessive. In patients with tracheostomies, careful hygiene can reduce problems with drainage and odor that may be profoundly disturbing for patients and families.

Skin care becomes critical for those who are confined to beds or wheelchairs. Decubitus ulcers can make life miserable for individuals who might otherwise be relatively pain-free, and are also frustrating to treat in permanently bedridden patients. They can be avoided in many cases by adequate skin care from the onset of a terminal disease. This should include the use of eggcrate foam pads, sheepskins, water or air pillows, or other measures designed to distribute body weight away from pressure points. Frequent changes of body position should be encouraged as permitted by the physical realities of the disease. Pillows should be placed routinely between the knees of patients resting on their sides. Daily massages with skin creams or alcohol-based body rubs as well as frequent baths are encouraged. These last measures may be of particular value, given the psychological comfort afforded by the touch of a caring hand.

In our experience, many dying patients seem to suffer from *touch deprivation*. This may stem from unconscious withdrawal or revulsion on the part of those who are not ill. Alternatively, it may be because of the dying patient's increased need for physical contact as a result of the common regression to a more childlike state. Further, the transition to institutional settings as death draws near often isolates patients from human contact. In any case, many dying patients seem to derive great solace from a loving touch.

Finally, because many of the above measures are likely to be instituted at home, it is important to *support and instruct family members* regarding their roles in the treatment team. Regular encouragement and frequent chances to ventilate stress-related emotions may prove vital to insuring optimal home care. Periodic visits by qualified nursing personnel to home care situations are invaluable in helping families to adapt general techniques to their specific situations.

Respiratory complications can greatly harm the quality of life.

Clinicians should attend early to preventing bedsores.

Behaviors Related to Stress

Prevention of Stress-Related Symptoms

During the course of a chronic illness, patients and families are likely to manifest various symptoms and behaviors related to long-term stress. These manifestations range from somatic complaints such as headaches or gastrointestinal problems to more overtly emotional reactions such as irritability and depression. Additional commonly encountered responses to the frustration inherent in this situation include manipulative, demanding, or inappropriately dependent behavior toward health care personnel.

Chronic stress reactions can be averted by timely intervention during earlier crises. (21)

Although we will deal with the specific management of some maladaptive stress-related behaviors individually, we emphasize that they are often preventable. The key to avoiding these problems is the early formation of a relationship that will provide those coping with a chronic disease with encouragement and a safe environment in which to express their feelings. In the rush of a busy clinic or hospital day, it may be easy to ignore the subtle signs of strain in our patients and their loved ones. If we can remain alert to early signs of problems in coping, however, much future trouble may be averted.

Knowing full well how overwhelmed with work clinicians are likely to be, patients and families often are reluctant to bring up apparently trivial strains. Because adequate information is central to timely intervention, professionals must make a point of encouraging patients and families to speak out. Statements such as, "Many people in your position feel pretty overwhelmed. I wonder if this could be the case for you?" can serve to open the floodgates.

Achieving contact, Boiling down the problem, and Challenging creative coping are the steps in a model for crisis intervention.

At this juncture, the *ABC* crisis intervention model described by Jones (1968) usually can be applied easily and effectively. Basically, the model consists of the following three steps:

A. Achieve contact with the individual.

B. Boil down the problem to its essentials.

C. Challenge creative coping via an inventory of the individual's problem-solving experiences to evolve an active program toward a solution.

Once contact is achieved by opening the floodgates as described, the communication skills presented in Chapter 2 are employed to effect steps B and C of the model. When this process is used before the reactions to stress became magnified and chronically entrenched, the latter can be significantly averted.

This model also has proven useful in working with terminally ill patients and their families during the many other crises that they face—both before and after the death.

Depression

It is vital to distinguish between a simple *depressed mood* and a clinically significant depression. (2)

Depression frequently affects those coping with terminal illness. In many ways, this emotion constitutes a natural and appropriate response to the existential plight and unrelieved stress that can plague a final illness. There is, however, an important distinction between a *clinically significant depression* and a more *simple depressed mood*. Few of us encounter difficulty in recognizing a depressed mood. Most often, there is little indication for special intercession with this simple feeling of sadness. This is particularly so if an emotionally open and supportive relationship already exists between patients, families, and health care professionals.

The following symptoms, however, should prompt further investigation and possible clinical intervention. The first of these is a *dysphoric mood*, often described as "very down," or "not caring anymore." This is often accompanied by a loss of interest or pleasure in life. Frequently, patients will *withdraw* from relationships or activities that previously were pleasurable. *Appetite disturbances* are common, with accompanying fluctuations in body weight. *Sleep disorders* often are present, with insomnia being more common than hypersomnia. *Psychomotor agitation or retardation* frequently occur as well, with patients either pointlessly active or displaying a marked decrease in movements and speech. A *lower energy level* is almost inevitable, with frequent complaints of fatigue and inability to complete even the simplest of tasks. Depressed patients commonly feel *inadequate* or *guilty,* and they may have thoughts of death or suicide. *Thought impairment* may be present, manifested by difficulty concentrating and making decisions. This disorder of thinking may assume psychotic proportions, including full-blown hallucinations and delusions.

Clinical depression is frequently unaccompanied by conscious feelings of sadness.

All too often in patients who have a clinically significant depression, there is no direct manifestation of sadness. Psychic manifestations of despair and dejection may be hidden completely or at most appear transiently so that only physical complaints are presented to the observer. These masked or covert depressions, or *depressive equivalents,* constitute a significant and often misunderstood problem of the dying and grieving. The depressive equivalents are at times difficult to separate from unwelcome painful interludes occasioned by various therapies. Surgical or other lesions are particularly damaging to self-esteem, and this loss is often the source of depression. The physical complaints most commonly presented are fatigue and weakness, along with muscle aches, headaches, and other pains. Such complaints in the setting of terminal illness or grief warrant investigating a possible clinically significant depression.

In any event, when more than a few of the above symptoms are noted, the possible existence of all of the others should be explored.

When to refer.

If more than four or five symptoms are present, the diagnosis of major depressive disorder is likely, and treatment should be undertaken. This usually consists of supportive psychotherapy combined with antidepressant medication. If the clinician already involved with the case is equipped to provide these, then there are distinct advantages to handling the problem within the context of an established relationship. If not, a referral should be made to a psychiatrist.

Dependency

Inappropriate dependency is a frequent problem during terminal illnesses.

Prominent among behavioral problems that arise in the context of terminal illness are reactions of dependency, both within families and toward professionals. As a terminal disease progresses, it is usually realistic and appropriate for patients to become more dependent on those who care for them. This easily can become a problem for family members who may already feel overextended and who are, in addition, trying to cope with their own threatened losses. When such issues arise, clinicians initially should encourage ventilation in private. Once again, emphasis should be placed on likely underlying feelings of abandonment and of need for nurturance rather than on the overt content of dependent behavior. An opportunity to blow off steam often enables all parties to sit down with professionals and work out practical means of dealing with problems of dependency.

There also are likely to be times when clinicians feel that patients and families are becoming too dependent on them. Once again, it is important for the involved caretakers to talk it out among themselves before addressing these issues directly. This process shields patients and families from inappropriate reactions based on the needs of professionals to withdraw. If there is any doubt about the validity of the concerns of key health care team members regarding inappropriate dependency, psychiatric consultation may provide clarification.

When to consult.

Passive-Aggressive Behavior

Passive-aggressive behavior is another problem that arises frequently during chronic illnesses. Passive-aggression may be viewed as the *indirect expression of hostility through noncooperative behavior.* The sense that patients or family members are withdrawn and noncommunicative because of some underlying resentment is often upsetting to clinicians. The resultant lack of active partnership in treatment makes provision of optimal care more difficult. It is not always easy, however, to be certain when one is encountering passive-aggression in this setting. It is at times difficult to differentiate such behavior from the predictable withdrawal of the seriously ill.

Passive-aggression should be addressed directly.

Passive-aggressive reactions from patients or family members can be addressed directly by professionals when they encounter them. Nonaccusatory statements such as the following may be useful: "I wonder if you can help me? You seem to be withdrawn, and I'm not certain if there is something I have said or done that has made you pull away, or perhaps even made you angry. Can you tell me what's going on?" If a satisfactory foundation for an open relationship between the involved parties has been laid down, such an opening should begin to reveal the underlying problems. If not, continued gentle exploration and reassurance that the sharing even of negative feelings is welcome may be useful. When persistent passive-aggressive behav-ior is resistant to such measures and begins to impair the ability of clinicians to provide optimal care, psychiatric consultation may be appropriate.

When to consult.

Manipulation

Manipulative behavior often is used to gain substitute rewards when more basic emotional needs are not being met.

Many professionals find it disturbing when they realize that those for whom they are providing care are relating to them in a manipulative fashion. When this is suspected, it is important first of all to verify individual impressions in conference with others involved in the case. If a consensus emerges that patients or families are being manipula-tive, clinicians should examine the possible motives underlying the attempted manipulation. Many times, those whose emotional needs are not met will resort to manipulative behavior in order to achieve various "secondary gains." These substitute rewards range broadly from the additional support and attention of authority figures to pun-ishment for past sins, either real or imagined. These issues can be very complex, and often are approachable only with great care by experienced psychotherapists. The overt problems generated, how-ever, can be handled constructively by clinicians in many instances. Here are a few guidelines.

First, a direct presentation of the particular problems stemming from their behavior should be made to manipulative persons in as nonjudgmental a manner as possible. Needs that are not being met should be sought and, if they are found, fully explored. The involved parties can attempt to work out ways of addressing these needs. Many times, however, such a resolution will be precluded by the funda-mental personality problems that underlie the manipulative behavior. Counseling referral should be made for such persons whenever pos-sible. In any case, clear limits should be worked out among health care team members and stated explicitly to the person in question.

When to refer.

Setting clear and consistently enforced limits on acceptable behavior that are clearly understood by all parties is vital in managing manipulative behavior.

The most important way in which professionals can protect the interests of everyone involved in manipulative behavior is by main-taining very clear communication among themselves. In this way, the

splitting of health care team members into warring factions by manipulative patients or family members is more likely to be averted.

One final word of caution is in order. Manipulators in terminal
care situations may turn out to be family members or even colleagues
on the professional staff. This represents one of the unfortunate reactions to the stresses of caring for the terminally ill. Thus, involved
personnel may need psychological support themselves, not only in
coping with difficult individuals, but also for their own stress-induced
manipulative behaviors.

References

Fagerhaugh, S. and Strauss, A. 1977. *Politics of Pain Management: Staff–
Patient Interaction.* Menlo Park, California: Addison-Wesley Publishing
Co., Inc.
Built upon theoretical constructs of the 1960's, this book represents
the findings of two years of observations in various medical settings.
It is worthwhile reading for all who work with patients in pain. The
three major themes developed are: (1) organizational settings affect
pain behavior, (2) political processes influence pain management, and
(3) the acute care model is inadequate for the management of chronic
pain. There is a good balance between theoretical constructs and clinical illustrations.

Finer, B. 1979. Hypnotherapy in the pain of advanced cancer. *Advances
in Pain Research and Treatment.* 2:223–229.

Forrest, W. M., Brown, B. W., Brown, C.R. *et al.* 1977. Dextroam-
phetamine and morphine for the treatment of postoperative pain.
New Engl. J. Med. 296:712–715.

Forrest, W. M., Jr. 1980. Orally administered zomepirac and parenter-
ally administered morphine. *JAMA* 244:2298–2302.

Gershon, S. 1981. Evaluation of trazodone. *Drugs.* 21:401.

Glaser, B. G. and Strauss, A. L. 1968. *Time for Dying.* Chicago: Aldine
Publishing Co.

Gonda, T. A. 1962. Some remarks on pain. *Bulletin of the British Psychological Society.* 47:1–7.

Jones, W. L. 1968. The ABC method of crisis management. *Mental
Hygiene.* 52:87–89.

Moos, R. H. ed. 1977. *Coping with Physical Illness.* New York: Plenum
Publishing Corp.

This well edited, multiauthored book emphasizes coping with two sets of crises: those of illness and those of treatment. A wide spectrum of illnesses and highly stressful treatment environments is discussed. Stresses on patients, families, and staff members are explored. Although the material on death and dying is a bit weak, it constitutes a small portion of the volume, and the remainder is very worthwhile for all who deal professionally with illness.

Noyes, R. 1981. Treatment of cancer pain. *Psychosomatic Medicine.* 43: 57–70.

Saunders, C. ed. 1978. *The Management of Terminal Disease.* London:Edward Arnold.

Edited by a person at the head of the current hospice movement, this multiauthored book focuses on cancer. Medical treatment issues are emphasized and well presented, and ethical, legal, psychological, and philosophical concerns are also addressed. A major shortcoming for American readers is that the social context of the work is strictly the British National Health Service. Notwithstanding, the book presents useful theoretical and practical insights on patient care.

Schoenberg, B., Carr, A. C., Peretz, D. and Kutscher, A. H. eds. 1972. *Psychosocial Aspects of Terminal Care.* New York: Columbia University Press.

This is one of several multiauthored books edited by the same Columbia University Medical Group. It includes a good mix of original and review articles of very high quality, and these bear on a host of psychosocial considerations in terminal care. It is an excellent introductory overview for beginners in the field.

Turk, J. and Rennert, O. 1981. Pain and the terminally ill cancer patient. In: Sobel, H. J. ed. *Behavior Therapy in Terminal Care.* Cambridge, Massachusetts: Ballinger Publishing Co.

Ward, N. G., Bloom, V. L. and Friedel, R. O. 1979. Effectiveness of tricyclic antidepressants in treating pain and concurrent depression. *Pain.* 7:331–341.

Young, E. W. D. 1976. Reflections on life and death. *Stanford MD.* 15:20–24.

7 As Death Draws Near: Supporting the Dying Patient

Overview

The phase of chronic illness in the course of a terminal disease reaches its close with the exhaustion of the ability to maintain metabolic homeostasis in the face of increasing challenges and dwindling reserves. Once this threshold is crossed, the irreversible slide toward death begins, and is likely to proceed inexorably in spite of any measures taken. Although absolute certainty is seldom possible in such complex situations, astute clinicians often are aware when the time remaining changes from months to weeks, days, or hours. When the endpoint has thus been identified, the tasks for clinicians often become equally better defined.

In this chapter we reconsider the issue of extension of dying versus prolongation of life in the stark light of imminent death. Then we look at some common reactions encountered during this period in patients and families.

These are closely related to both their previous patterns of stress response and to the chronicity of the illness. Management of family reactions includes measured support, sorting out the desires of the patient from those of family members, and dealing with inappropriate behaviors. As death draws near, the impetus toward resolving unfinished emotional business often reaches its peak. We end the chapter by looking at some implications of this phenomenon.

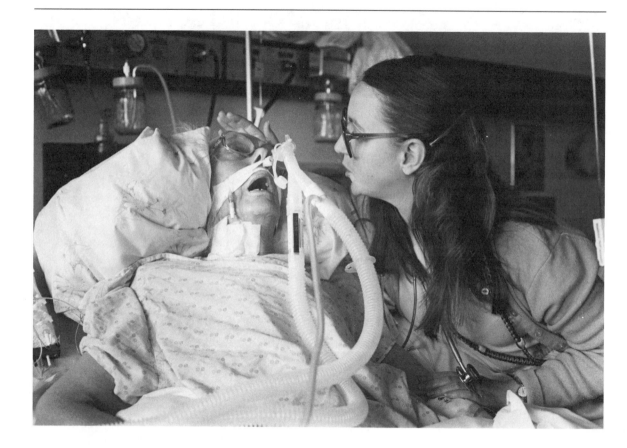

Extension of Living Versus Prolongation of Dying

Reconsideration of Parameters

In Chapter 6, we questioned the validity of medical interventions not focused on promoting an optimal quality of life. In the context of imminent death, a different set of circumstances may come into play.

When death is near, even basic medical interventions merit careful consideration. (13)

At times, even the most basic of treatments, such as the placement of intravenous lines to support adequate fluid intake, are questionable as well. Such therapies may relieve an acute crisis, but may force patients and families to endure days or weeks of additional suffering that they may not have chosen had the implications of treatment been made clear. On the other hand, the maintenance of a level of analgesia which results in freedom from pain may require a marked degree of sedation as an inevitable side-effect. Patients and families may feel that this prevents the kind of communication that they would have preferred had the implications of this intervention been explored fully with them. Further, they may not be aware that respiratory depression related to their analgesic medication may be hastening death.

Our point is that no simple ministration is either right or wrong in any general sense in the context of imminent death. We advocate a heightened awareness of the implications of each medical intervention in this setting. The delicate balance between patient comfort and optimal medical care can be struck only in close collaboration with patients and families. This requires a clear and simple explanation of the consequences, both negative and positive, of all significant medical interventions.

Natural Death Act *directives allow the terminally ill to instruct physicians not to extend the process of dying via artificial means.*

Additional problems can arise when, as is often the case, the mental status of patients deteriorates to the point that their ability to give informed consent is questionable. In this circumstance, a previously written directive from the patient to the physician, sometimes called a Living Will, may come into play. Authority for such directives comes from various state *Natural Death Acts,* beginning with that of California (1976). In essence, and with certain time limitations, the directive indicates patients' wishes about their treatment after they may have reached the point when they no longer can communicate these directly. The document is similar in format to a Last Testament; hence the catchy misnomer *Living Will.* Responsible physicians must discuss carefully all of the implications of the directive as set forth in state legal guidelines. Clear understanding should be established with patients, family members, and other involved professionals as to what kinds of interventions (artificial methods of prolonging life) are appropriate under a variety of circumstances. Time taken to discuss these difficult and painful issues before the fact can spare everyone much trauma when acute situations arise.

Decisions not to use artificial methods should be reviewed periodically.

It is important to review these decisions periodically with patients and family members during the course of an illness. This helps to obviate the possibility of momentary depressions or losses of heart resulting in actions that may later cause regret. Participation by the patient's family in these choices will facilitate carrying out patient's wishes in the event that they lose mental competence.

Communication among caretakers regarding such decisions is critical. Sometimes, families and clinicians come to a painstakingly derived

It is vital that all clinicians who could possibly initiate means of prolonging life be clearly informed as to any limitations desired by the patient.

consensus with patients concerning institution of life-support measures, but fail to communicate them clearly to the bedside staff. As a result, despite an important decision to the contrary, the night relief team may respond to a respiratory arrest by initiating life support. This then presents those responsible with the miserable choice of prolonging the dying process or actively discontinuing life-preserving measures. This situation usually can be avoided by leaving clearly written instructions for all those who could possibly initiate artificial means of support.

Resuscitation and "Pulling the Plug"

Negative results of initiating life-support measures during the phase of imminent death usually outweigh positive ones.

Initiating life-support measures is often problematic in the setting of chronic terminal disease. It is even more dubious during the phase of imminent death. The health care team should actively discuss these issues for each patient in order to clarify the choices available.

For one person, for example, respiratory support to get past an acute pneumonia in order to have a few more weeks of life might be desirable. For another, it might just prolong the agony of dying. This problem is even more difficult when the issue of whether or not to treat an infection is involved. Institution of antibiotic therapy is much easier and less intrusive than, say, starting a respirator. Further, health care team members tend to be more resistant to abandoning such simple measures that are considered to be a part of rudimentary medical care. A similar problem may arise when intravenous steroids are used to reduce acute cerebral edema, or when other easily administered life-extending or demise-prolonging interventions are employed. If such possibilities are talked over in advance, many problems can be averted. Unfortunately, there are many instances in which terminally ill patients are rushed to emergency rooms in acute distress. Clinicians who are unfamiliar with the case may quite appropriately respond to the obvious medical emergency by instituting life-support measures.

Even when a Natural Death Act directive is in force, there may arise daunting ethical and medico-legal issues in withdrawing life-support measures.

When the situation is finally clarified, it may be discovered to the dismay of all involved that the patient had specifically proscribed such interventions. Those involved must then cope with the decision to withdraw therapy that is clearly extending life. The situation is changed profoundly; now, in order to meet the patient's underlying desires, someone has to perform a positive act that may well result in a death. Clearly, ending a life by an act of commission is more ethically and morally difficult than allowing someone to drift off without interference.

The ethical and medico-legal aspects of this situation are extensive and daunting, even when patients have been restored to a sufficient level of consciousness and mental clarity to make their wishes clear. Although patients may have given directives to avoid life-support measures in the past, the actual choice to "pull the plug" on themselves may be difficult or even impossible. Further, the question of how competent anyone can be after a few days of intubation and four-point restraints in an intensive care setting is knotty in itself. Regardless of how much time and energy is devoted to painstaking exploration of options and emotions with the patient, these efforts may be inadequate. In whatever manner such a decision is reached, the more that family members are involved in this process, the less likely they will be to undermine the conclusions that finally emerge.

If the patient's consciousness is never fully restored, a new set of problems arise. The question of who can appropriately exercise authority for the patient in the matter of life-support withdrawal becomes central. Ideally, professionals can rely on carefully cultivated relationships with families to arrive at reasonable decisions with relative grace. Unfortunately, this is often not the case. There are many instances in which family members are divided in their opinions as to the proper course of action. If measures by clinicians and consultants to resolve such conflicts are unsuccessful, and a workable consensus never is reached, the final decisions may be left to the legal system.

Emotional support groups can be helpful for staff members in coping with these difficult situations.

The effect of these situations on members of the care team is often profound. The resultant stress on intensive and terminal care personnel is certainly one reason to provide regular emotional support for them. Ongoing groups may create the kind of supportive working environment that is conducive to fluent expression of feelings and resolution of problems surrounding these situations. These groups tend to work best when conducted by someone outside of the power hierarchy of the unit in question. Distance seems to be helpful in minimizing the choosing of sides that often occurs in such instances.

Reactions of Patients and Families to Imminent Death

Determinants of Acute Reactions

Intensity of reaction to imminent death is inversely related to the chronicity of the terminal illness.

In general, the longer people have to come to terms with an imminent death, the more likely they are to have a relatively modulated reaction. There are, however, important exceptions to this generalization. There are many instances when an individual family member has not been physically present during the course of a final illness. When such persons arrive on the scene as death nears, they may well find themselves out of synchronization with those who have had longer to resolve their feelings. This may happen in spite of the fact that the newcomers have been kept adequately informed during the entire course of the illness. Another situation occurs when loved ones have in some way held themselves back from allowing the emotions necessary for graceful reconciliation to emerge. These persons really have not been fully *present* to work through their feelings.

Professionals should be alerted to expect stronger reactions from those who suddenly confront the reality of the situation. Family members who have been present throughout may have difficulty supporting the newcomers, partly because the latters' responses can be at odds with the climate that has evolved over time. The support of an empathic and understanding clinician can prove invaluable at this stage, both by helping the individual in question, and by preventing conflicts and alienations.

Intensity of reaction to imminent death is proportional to the suddenness of the emotional confrontation with death's reality.

The reaction among family members to the strain of an imminent death is likely to reflect the patterns of stress response that are characteristic of that family. Professionals who are well acquainted with an entire family are at a distinct advantage in anticipating reactions and preparing themselves to provide optimal support. Conversely, those who have never observed the family in stressful situations are largely in the dark as to what responses are likely.

Acute reactions to imminent death tend to follow previous patterns of stress response.

Anticipatory Grief

Anticipatory grief constitutes a common and often fortunate means of coping with a long-foreseen loss. Particularly when the period of chronic illness has been extended and grueling, and when the outcome has been fairly certain for some time, patients and loved ones are likely to *grieve in anticipation of their impending losses.* This mechanism often allows for a more graceful acceptance of the death when it arrives. This is accomplished through facilitation of a sense of relative tranquillity in the face of imminent death. Clinicians who have encouraged an open climate of communication and sharing of both data and emotions will have tacitly supported this kind of coping throughout the course of a final illness.

Anticipatory grief is somewhat predictable, and is similar in form to grief after a loss.

There are, however, situations in which this coping mechanism may lead to problems, especially when anticipatory grieving goes too far and extends into the completion of the work of mourning. A major part of reconciling a loss involves withdrawing attachment to the lost object (see Chapter 1). If this takes place with a loved one before that individual has actually died, unnecessary trauma may be sustained. The last thing that someone facing the ultimate alienation of death needs is the sense that they are already sundered from key fellow humans before this is necessary.

Problems may arise if anticipatory grieving results in untimely withdrawal from the dying person.

Before professionals can address problems of emotional withdrawal, they must make some important differentiations. When withdrawal is apparent in the dying person, it is not necessarily a function of grief work. The systemic effects of advanced illness often physically impair brain function and level of consciousness. Thus, withdrawal might be more related to the waning of energy and metabolic encephalopathy that so often presage death. Simple and unobtrusive examinations of mental status aimed at assessing orientation and memory may be useful in making this distinction.

CASE ILLUSTRATION

A family physician was called into the hospital to assess the mental status of a patient with widespread atherosclerotic vascular disease who might have had a slight stroke. The patient happened to live near the doctor, who began the interview with a casual conversation concerning neighborhood affairs and the impending harvest. During the course of this chat, the intactness of the patient's temporospatial orientation and recent and distant memories was amply demonstrated. After completing this unobtrusive and quite intentional mental status exam, the doctor proceeded with the remainder of his neurological evaluation.

If encephalopathy is revealed, professionals must consider carefully before instituting medical measures that may prolong the process of dying while improving the patient's lucidity. If mental status is relatively intact, then the observation that the patient seems withdrawn may be communicated directly in a gentle fashion, followed by inquiries into the possible source of this reaction.

Protective withdrawal can be distinguished from overzealous anticipatory grief.

When this premature detachment of emotional ties appears in family members, another differentiation needs to be made. Many times, loved ones isolate themselves as death approaches because they have feelings that they cannot bear. These persons may not have been recognizably grieving, but may suddenly withdraw as death draws near. This should be distinguished from disengagement resulting from overzealous anticipatory grief (see Davidson's [1975] description of the "waiting vulture syndrome"). Such distinction is made most easily by someone who has had contact with the individual in question over the course of the illness. A gentle exploration of the feelings behind such retreat usually enables the individual in question to reestablish contact. If not, referral for brief psychotherapy may be indicated.

When to refer.

Management of Family Reactions

Close involvement of loved ones in almost every phase of care can be particularly rewarding to many families in the presence of imminent death. Performing concrete services for the dying often allays some

Staff support of family involvement in care as death draws near should be guided primarily by the patient's desires. (12)

of the helpless feelings that inevitably arise in this setting. There are families, however, for whom this is not the case. Further, some patients feel humiliated by receiving physical care from their loved ones.

Although it is reasonable for clinicians to encourage family involvement during this period, it is important to consider the desires of each individual. This often is done best in private, so that no one makes commitments with which they are uncomfortable just to avoid hurting someone else's feelings. Private exploration of these issues can serve as an entrée to probing the feelings that may be distancing loved ones at this time when support and intimacy are so vital. After thorough inquiry and ventilation with each party separately, direct contact and communication between those involved can be gently encouraged. Before this is done, however, professionals must be certain that they are not imposing their own ideals on patients or families whose lifelong patterns proscribe such contact. If there is any suggestion of this possibility, conference among involved staff members often resolves ambiguities.

Patient-Family Conflicts

The values and desires of patients must be sorted out from those of family members. (6)

Another important consideration in the management of family reactions involves distinguishing the values and desires of patients from those of family members and loved ones. Often, patients become less able to stand up for their own wishes against the pressures of loved ones who may advocate choices that are contrary to the patients' desires. As we have stated, many families react to their sense of guilt and helplessness by pushing for maximal medical intervention until the bitter end. This often results in patients whose fires have burned too low to resist persuasion accepting treatments that they never would have chosen if left to themselves. Such a course may allow families to postpone their loss for a short time, but at a high cost to the dying person. Further, the time thereby mortgaged is seldom of sufficient quality to justify its prolongation. In the end, death often is rendered even less dignified than it need have been.

Treatment rationales and plans should be reviewed frequently with patients and families.

A reasonable way to avoid such destructive conflicts is to work out in advance the rationale for the boundaries and trade-offs of particular medical interventions that will be undertaken under specific circumstances. Again, the more that patients and key loved ones are involved in this process, the less likely they are to attempt to sabotage its results at a later time. Also, the atmosphere in which these important decisions are made is considerably less strained if conclusions are reached before an actual crisis has developed. Professionals should emphasize that plans are not chiseled in stone, but will be reevaluated whenever the situation takes an unexpected turn.

Clinicians should take their own biases into account when presenting treatment options.

It is difficult for clinicians to facilitate this process if they are not clear as to the biases they bring to the choices at hand. We recommend review of each situation with this issue specifically in mind. This is best done in staff conferences designed to allow the consideration of various viewpoints. In any case, it should be done before final presentation of the major options is made.

When conflicts between patients and loved ones arise over decisions concerning treatment options, it is important for professionals to attempt a resolution first by nonjudgmental exploration of the alternative viewpoints. Once people feel as though they have been heard, they are often able to compromise much more gracefully than otherwise would have been the case. It is particularly vital to allow for full examination of the feelings underlying strongly held opinions. Ideally, this should take place in the presence of all involved parties. Often, however, full expression is difficult for individuals in such highly charged situations, and an initial chance to explore feelings in private with a sympathetic clinician can prove valuable. If conflicts are not resolvable by counseling intervention, a difficult situation is presented. Although such irreconcilable differences seldom occur when clinicians have been careful in laying the foundations of a solid relationship with key parties, they do crop up periodically. In the end, the interests of the patient have to take precedence.

Irreconcilable conflicts over treatment options should be resolved in favor of the patient whenever possible.

Inappropriate behavior is encountered more often as death nears.

Professionals may at times encounter apparently inappropriate communications or behavior on the part of loved ones. Understandably, the incidence of these increases in rough proportion to the stress present. It is not surprising that the period of imminent death is marked by a particular tendency toward such expressions. They may range from histrionic outbursts to sullen withdrawal, and may be directed toward virtually anyone. Because these reactions can have profound adverse effects on the experience of those involved during this critical period, it is important that professionals be prepared to deal with them as fluently as possible.

When clinicians observe inappropriate, destructive behavior they should first try to size up the situation. This moment of thought before action may prove invaluable in promoting a reasoned and effective response. If an intensely emotional conflict is in progress, immediate exploration of the feelings involved may not be feasible. In this case, if possible, trusted health care team members should attempt to talk separately with those at odds. This should be handled as gently and nonjudgmentally as possible, in order to reduce defensiveness to a manageable level.

After exploration of the feelings and behaviors that precipitated the crisis, a facilitated meeting between those in conflict can be most valuable. The goal of this confrontation should be clearly defined as the evolution of a less problematic way of handling the underlying

When to refer.

emotions. Professionals should take special pains to ensure that no party ends up feeling like the villain, because such an outcome often sabotages the entire effort. Although this strategy generally will suffice to resolve issues surrounding inappropriate behavior, psychiatric consultation may be necessary in particularly difficult cases. If that is of no avail, clear limit setting as to what is acceptable may be the only recourse.

CASE ILLUSTRATION

A young man who was an adherent of a far Eastern religion was very near death from lymphoma. His wife and the religious community to which they belonged were intimately and gracefully involved in creating a bedside atmosphere that clearly gave him great peace. A long-estranged brother burst suddenly upon the scene, full of proselytizing fervor. He was bent upon reclaiming his brother's soul to the religion of their childhood while there was still time. A heated argument ensued between the brother and the dismayed wife, with no potential for a calm resolution. In a momentary lull, a wise chaplain intervened to draw the brother aside, encouraging him to express feelings of helplessness and grief. After a time, the brother agreed to remain in prayer with the chaplain, and the patient died peacefully in his wife's arms, surrounded by the rituals of his adopted faith.

Splitting

Splitting *behavior is a common occurrence in the highly charged settings surrounding an imminent death.*

Splitting behavior arises from *the tendency of individuals to see others as either heroes or villains,* rather than as single entities possessed of both positive and negative qualities. It is especially common in those who are possessed of strong, unintegrated ambiguous feelings. These conflicting emotions are particularly prone to arise in coping with imminent death. The reasons for this are many. Loved ones often have endured a long and arduous siege in which they have assumed sizable burdens to support patients who are progressively less able to be supportive in return. Contemplation of an imminent loss may prompt both withdrawal and clinging, sometimes simultaneously. The imminent death may trigger recall of instances in which we may have wished that person ill or treated them poorly: fertile soil for paralyzing guilt. All of these may combine with other factors to create situations in which another's death is longed for while it is feared, and in which intense resentment and profound love go hand-in-hand.

Probably the most common way that this splitting becomes apparent in terminal care settings is through the externalization or projection of these conflicts onto various staff members. Thus, for example, a particularly brisk doctor may become the "villain," and a more accessible nurse may assume the mantle of the "heroine." It is remarkable that certain individuals seem to possess a gift for subtly influencing staff members to play the actual roles into which they have been projected. What is astounding is that, in some instances, this has resulted in entire hospital units being reduced to warring camps. The effect of this phenomenon on the quality of terminal care is profound, and can become ruinous.

Clear communication within the team is the key to avoiding conflicts surrounding splitting.

The best way to avoid problems with splitting behavior is to maintain clear and open channels of communication among the health care team. All major decisions should be discussed with everyone centrally involved in implementing them before they are instituted. Communications from patients and family members should be shared among team members as much as possible, so that secret alliances are not perpetuated. If any individuals feel uncomfortable with their roles or with the roles they perceive others playing, this should be discussed openly and in a timely fashion. Another useful tactic in coping with splitters is to designate a single professional as the official *communicator* with the person in question. This eliminates some of the potential for ambiguity. If the staff presents a united and supportive front to patients and families, problems of this sort are less likely to occur.

When to consult.

When difficulties do arise to a significant degree, however, outside consultation almost inevitably is needed for resolution of the very complicated situations that tend to develop within a surprisingly brief period.

Resolution of Unfinished Emotional Business

Role of the Clinician

The drive to resolve unfinished business often increases as death draws near.

During this final phase of a terminal illness, the impetus toward seeking resolution of unfinished emotional business often reaches a peak. It may be tempting for health care professionals to promote actively the final addressing of profound emotional concerns regardless of the desires of those involved. In truth, the clinician's work is particularly satisfying if the patient dies following a moving and significant exchange that resolves long-standing problems. Professionals must be constantly aware of their hopes for such outcomes if they are to modulate their overt expression of these expectations. Of course, they will be likely to convey their wishes on some level in any case. The major difficulty occurs when clinicians are unaware of the strength of their agenda, which they may then communicate powerfully. This can have serious adverse effects on patients and families, as well as on their relationship with professionals. Patients and families may feel pres-

Professionals should temper their expectations regarding resolution of unfinished business.

sured, for example, into encounters that are exceedingly uncomfortable for them. These interchanges are unlikely to be fruitful. Indeed, the dying and their loved ones may experience a subtle sense that they have failed to meet the expectations and earn the approval of their caretakers.

In our experience, people's deaths tend to reflect their lives. If one has lived vibrantly and openly, one's death is likely to mirror these characteristics. If one has been inward with feelings and expression throughout life, then death may well be equally solitary. We do not imply that growth and change cannot take place in this context. Rather, we mean that major breakthroughs in the direction of the clinician's value system are not necessarily the hallmark of optimal terminal care.

Effects on Survivors

Successful communications during this period can avert future problems for survivors. (3)

Knowing that one has fully expressed one's love and sense of gratitude for a shared lifetime can be of extreme comfort after the death of a loved one. Conversely, the awareness that one failed to communicate these feelings can gnaw at one's vitals for years. Apologizing for past wrongs and conflicts, particularly if it results in resolution or forgiveness on all sides, can be of equal value in easing the mourning process. Exploring unresolved incidents or feelings can settle doubts or uncertainties that never can be fully reconciled once death has intervened. If this communication fails to occur, working through the resulting feelings can become complex enough to challenge experienced psychotherapists.

The principal manner in which clinicians can assist resolution of unfinished emotional matters is by creating supportive and sensitive terminal care environments where open communication is clearly welcome. Health care team members can set an example for patients and families by maintaining an atmosphere of open communication among themselves.

When to refer.

When clinicians suspect patients or families have unresolved emotions, tentative and gentle reflection in private of this impression may be appropriate. If this tactic fails to elicit a response, it may be that the issue cannot be resolved. On the other hand, the reflection that unresolved feelings may exist conveys in itself the tacit message that the clinician regards the feelings as acceptable; it may open the path to exploration at a future time. Often, however, the chance to ventilate such feelings will be seized upon with vigor. Once this process is complete, the practicality of bringing the issue up with all involved parties can be approached and an attempt can be made to work the problem through. If clinicians feel unequal to this task, consultation with an outside therapist may be of value.

References

Brody, H. 1976. *Ethical Decisions in Medicine*. Boston: Little, Brown, & Co.

Books on medical ethics are beginning to come into their own. To date, this one leads the field because of its clarity, organization, and relevance to practical issues surrounding chronic and terminal disease. This book is a must for practitioners who have not been exposed recently to a systematic examination of ethics in medicine.

California Natural Death Act (1976). State of California Health and Safety Code. Division 7, Part 1, Chapter 3.9, Section 7185.

Davidson, G. W. "The Waiting Vulture Syndrome." In Schoenberg, B. et al. eds. 1975. *Bereavement: Its Psychosocial Aspects*. New York: Columbia University Press

Schoenberg, B., Carr, A. C., Peretz, D. and Kutscher, A. H. eds. 1974. *Anticipatory Grief*. New York: Columbia University Press.

Although generally valuable, this is probably the weakest of the several multiauthored books edited by the Columbia group. Its weakness is largely a product of redundancy, with reproduction of the introductory content in nearly all of the 41 chapters. However, for those willing to wade through the same basic concepts as applied to many different disciplinary contexts, this book contains many practical suggestions for management of anticipatory grief problems. The few mediocre essays (such as that on LSD therapy) are easy to spot.

8 At Life's End

Overview

Anyone who has witnessed a death is likely to recall the momentous nature of that encounter with inescapable finality. This instant has always taken on a particular significance for Western civilization, and as such should be handled thoughtfully and sensitively. In our discussion of care issues at life's end we will first consider the importance of the setting in which death occurs, and in which loved ones first confront the concrete reality of their loss. We then turn to suggestions for effective professional management of immediate family reactions, including special problems associated with sudden or unexpected death. Finally, some pertinent concerns not directly related to patient care are addressed.

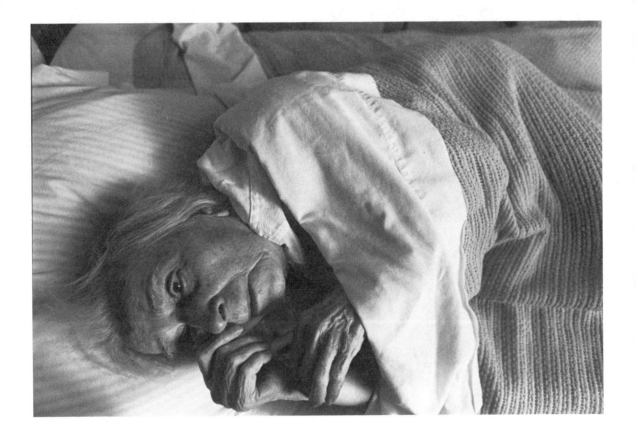

Importance of the Setting

General Concerns

Even in a terminal care setting, breaking the news of a death remains a very delicate and sensitive transaction, and one to which few pro-

The person breaking the news should have time to provide immediate emotional support. (13)

fessionals look forward. Whenever possible, the clinicians with whom the bereaved have the closest relationship should inform the family. Most information the family desires immediately usually can be provided by them. Generally, it is more important that the person undertaking this task be the one with whom family members feel least inhibited in their expression of acute grief. This person should be prepared to spend time providing emotional support. In our experience, support most often consists of caring involvement. In such settings, the appropriate motto once again is, *Don't just do something, sit there!* Band-aid platitudes do not deal effectively either with the professional's own discomfort or with the pain of loss in the bereaved.

We have heard more than one clinician take family members aside after a death and say, "Don't go in there; you really don't want to see that." This behavior is more likely to reflect the professional's discomfort than to result from a careful assessment of the best interests of the bereaved. Further, the resulting vague, negative fantasies about the death setting usually are far more difficult to deal with than the stark reality.

The setting for the initial contact with the body may affect the bereaved for some time to come.

The setting and manner in which family members first observe the body of their lost loved one is likely to remain burned into their memories for years. Because this can profoundly influence their grief and mourning process as well as their future attitude toward the health care system, particular sensitivity is in order. As peaceful a scene as possible should be created in the room where the body is to be seen. This involves removal of any apparent blood or secretions, as well as all extraneous lines and tubes unless they must be left in place for pathological examination. At times, endotracheal tubes or indwelling catheters must not be removed, because their placement may be a key pathological observation.

Someone should disconnect, turn off, and if possible remove all monitoring equipment; complicated technology may be distracting or even intimidating to family members. We have seen a number of cases where a flat line on a monitor or an incessantly beeping alarm is the strongest memory taken away from the deathbed by the bereaved.

Depersonalization of the deathbed scene should be avoided.

Insofar as possible, depersonalization of the deathbed setting is to be avoided. Loved ones who arrive at a deathbed to discover the belongings of the deceased packed into a box at the bedside often feel offended or hurt by the cavalier implication that the dead no longer matter. It is advisable to leave these small reminders of the personality of the deceased in their accustomed places. When the time comes for the body to be removed, family members will often take the initiative to pack the effects. If this is not the case, they can be asked gently if they wish to do so themselves or if they would prefer that health care team members help.

There is seldom such a demand for bed space that the body needs to be whisked out of sight as soon as possible. We suspect that the tendency to do this reflects the discomfort we all may feel around corpses. However, there is seldom much to be gained by hurrying family members along. Rather, within realistic limits, they should be given as much time and privacy with the deceased as they wish. The presence of a well known and trusted professional may be of positive value here, but a direct inquiry as to the wishes of those grieving regarding such attendance always is appropriate.

Special Problems

Resuscitation creates special problems in managing the deathbed setting.

Of the special problems that arise in the period immediately surrounding a death, perhaps the most difficult concern resuscitation. As we have pointed out, resuscitation always is questionable in the setting of terminal disease unless the patient has unequivocally indicated that it is desired. Unfortunately, ambiguous circumstances arise wherein resuscitation is undertaken. When it is deemed that resuscitation should be attempted, it is important to escort family members from the room, and provide them with staff support if possible. Health care personnel often seem to forget how violent a process a full resuscitation can appear, particularly as perceived by the uninitiated. Yet, instances occur in which neglected family members cower helplessly in the background as various bloody and undignified procedures are performed on their inert loved ones. The occasional family member who reacts so violently as to require restraint in such situations may reflect a depth of feeling being controlled by those who remain calm on the surface. Once enough personnel are on the scene to proceed with resuscitation, late arrivals may be diverted to taking care of family members. This also serves to reduce crowding at the bedside.

Failed resuscitation efforts can deprive family members of important final moments with the deceased.

Another consideration before undertaking a resuscitation in this setting is that often the attempt will be unsuccessful. If it is, family members are likely to be deprived of final precious moments with their loved one. Further, if an unsuccessful resuscitation is initiated while the patient is still conscious, any hope of a peaceful death for that individual is likely to be destroyed. Although no controlled studies have demonstrated a negative effect of this on unaware family members, we nevertheless feel compelled to hold these last moments of life sacred. If it is possible, those who have suffered a chronic terminal illness ought at least to have earned the right to a peaceful and dignified death if they wish it.

Brain death presents special problems.

Irreversible cessation of all brain functions (see Chapter 15) in patients whose cardiorespiratory activities are being artificially supported presents special problems in informing loved ones. In approaching families it is important to *avoid* asking whether or not they will permit life support to be removed. Rather, families should be notified that death has occurred, and that cardiorespiratory supports should now be discontinued.

If family members ask how professionals can be certain that death has occurred, it is usually appropriate to review the steps taken both to establish the cause of coma and to exclude the possibility of recovery. This nearly always suffices to enable families to accept the medical assessment of death. Most bereaved can then accept death without the added burden of guilt over decisions regarding turning off life-support machines. A preferable course is open communication in advance with the family when this problem is foreseen.

Critical care settings are likely to be intimidating to most nonprofessionals.

Whether we like it or not, death often takes place in critical care units. Professionals should be aware of the intimidating nature of this setting for most patients and families. Critical care units of necessity are designed for optimal use of highly technological interventions, often resulting in the creation of a physical environment that is perceived as threatening and inhuman. There are some measures that can be taken by clinicians to blunt the negative effects of these settings. Warmth and understanding can go a long way toward balancing even the most forbidding of contexts.

Health care professionals should recall that empathic relationships with loved ones as well as patients can make their own jobs more pleasant. Also, well thought out bending of regulations regarding visiting hours, the presence of children, and even patient belongings can serve to brighten and humanize critical care units. When one is focused on the complex and difficult technical aspects of critical care, it is often too easy to dismiss human concerns. Clinicians need to recall that a fundamental purpose of critical care units is caring, and that this function needs to be exercised on a number of levels.

Management of Immediate Reactions

Reactions of the Bereaved

Professionals should support the expression of grief. (20)

Expression of strong emotions most often is a healthy and appropriate reaction of grief. This holds in spite of the culturally inspired personal discomfort with public displays of vulnerability that is so characteristic among Americans. *Requirements* for expression of powerful feelings, however, are as injudicious as the more common encouragements toward stoicism. Health care professionals should be prepared to provide support for the bereaved regardless of the mode in which their grief is expressed.

One area of particular concern is the influence that emotional outbursts of the bereaved may have on the unit atmosphere and upon other patients. This can be averted to some extent by the provision of an appropriate degree of privacy for family members. Unfortunately, this is not always possible.

If expressions of grief are loud but within broadly acceptable limits, it may be wise to allow them to go on regardless of the setting. Clinicians should take pains to talk with the patients who have overheard the commotion. Other patients' feelings about what is going on should be explored and dealt with as sensitively and completely as possible. Alternatively, immediate efforts can be made to provide privacy for the bereaved. Professionals can escort bystanders from the room if they are willing to leave, and close the door. If this is not possible, it may prove necessary to usher the bereaved gently into a more private setting until they are able to compose themselves. In all cases, clinicians must balance the interests of the bereaved with those of the other occupants of the unit.

When to refer.

There may be times when expressions of grief exceed the boundaries of acceptable behavior. Examples of this include a persistent unwillingness to let go of the body, uncontrollable outbursts of rage, and major self-destructive behavior. In such situations, firm but empathic verbal intervention should be attempted first. Professionals should attempt to reflect the feelings expressed in the inappropriate behavior. If this fails, compassionate physical restraint may prove necessary. Psychiatric consultation often proves useful or even necessary if matters remain at a frenetic level for more than several hours.

Professionals can often support the bereaved by a carefully modulated sharing of their own feelings.

Another particularly useful way in which clinicians can show support is by sharing their own feelings with the bereaved. These communications need to be carefully modulated in order not to shift the focus of caretaking from grieving loved ones to professionals. Further, it is vital that any emotions expressed be absolutely genuine! Families are bound to sense and be disturbed if professionals mouth words without substance. It is most reasonable for clinicians to permit themselves this freedom to share feelings when relationships and emotional intimacy are well established. After all, there are many instances in which professionals find themselves caring for close friends, or developing strong emotional bonds during a terminal illness. In such instances, we have observed some beautifully tender exchanges that have been remembered as deeply significant by all involved. If there is any doubt as to the appropriateness of an expression of powerful feelings by health care professionals, it is probably best for them to deal with these emotions in private with colleagues. There are likely to be appropriate future opportunities to convey to the bereaved that one was touched. It is hard to go wrong if clinicians keep in mind that the primary purpose of relationships between health care team members and patients or family members is caregiving.

Grief-Related Anger

Health care personnel are often handy targets for grief-related anger. (16)

As we have discussed, anger is a common response to feelings of helplessness and abandonment that are evoked by the death of someone close. Health care personnel are particularly handy targets for expression of this free-floating hostility, in part because of their implied failure to save the patient. In many instances, professionals can serve the interests of the bereaved best by allowing such expressions to take place. Ideally, they should respond with a nondefensive reflection of the angry feelings, followed by a declaration of willingness to explore the basis of these emotions. During this process, grieving loved ones almost invariably become sufficiently relieved to reveal the underlying despair that prompted their inappropriate behavior. The key is to remain nonjudgmental and to avoid defensiveness as much as possible. By addressing these underlying feelings before turning to the specific content of angry expressions, clinicians can often defuse the situation to such an extent that no further intervention is necessary.

The key to useful intervention is to remain nonjudgmental and to avoid undue defensiveness.

If the bereaved persist in this behavior, the next step may be for professionals to admit frankly their own discomfort with being the target of such feelings. By admitting discomfort and possible bewilderment about what is going on, clinicians may give the angry person a sense of power and control in helping to clear up the confusion. If these measures are not effective within a reasonable period, then setting clear limits may prove helpful. If anger persists and is accompanied by other symptoms of pathological grief (see Chapter 9), psychiatric consultation may be necessary.

When to refer.

Clinicians who are the targets of irrational anger need a forum in which resultant feelings may be worked through.

The one major problem with allowing oneself to be the target for these expressions is the serious emotional toll that can be exacted. For that reason, it is important for the clinician who has been the target of an outburst to find some forum in which any resulting sense of violation can be worked through. Ideally, this could be undertaken with other members of the terminal care staff who are familiar with the situation. Any other colleagues who are likely to be empathic and supportive also can help in dealing with these feelings. If this is not attended to, the result can be resentment of patients, reduction in effectiveness of caretaking, and eventual burnout.

Medical Therapy in Acute Bereavement

There are selective indications for the use of medication in the management of acute grief.

It is somewhat traditional to provide the bereaved with considerable doses of sedatives or tranquilizers. We suspect that this may have as much to do with the need of nonplussed clinicians to be doing something concrete as it does with safeguarding of the welfare of the bereaved. This is not to say that there is no place for skilled and appropriate use of medications in supporting loved ones through the difficult period of acute grief. We contend, however, that the indications

Temporary support of sleep with short-acting benzodiazepines may be appropriate.

for daytime sedation in this context are the same as in any other. They include anxiety so crippling as to prevent the grieving person from conducting necessary business, and overtly psychotic symptoms or behavior. Anxiety is appropriately addressed with small doses of one of the benzodiazepines, and psychotic manifestations with adequate antipsychotic medication. We emphasize, however, that certain transient psychotic symptoms are a common part of acute grief (see Chapter 9). Only when relatively florid psychotic manifestations are present is antipsychotic medication indicated. Pharmacologic interventions should be initiated following a reasonable trial of the first line therapy—namely, skilled crisis intervention counseling.

Temporary support of sleep is the one fairly routine and reasonable indication for prescription of medication during acute bereavement. Many grieving individuals experience serious disruption of their sleep. Such insomnia can prove quite debilitating and may even interfere with the resolution of the emotions of acute grief. We recommend the prescription of a short-acting benzodiazepine such as oxazepam or temazepam in order to aid such persons in falling asleep during the first few days after their loss.

Reactions of the Health Care Team

Clinicians often become acutely depressed following a long-term effort ending in death. (16)

The reactions of health care professionals when death has finally taken place are, of course, as variable between individuals as are the reactions of loved ones. Nonetheless, there are some patterns that are sufficiently prevalent to warrant specific mention. The first of these is the tendency to become depressed. It is not difficult to understand how clinicians might feel downtrodden following the death of a patient. For one thing, persons who are sensitive enough to choose to work in such settings are bound to form personal attachments. This attachment is accentuated when the deceased has been a personal friend as well as a patient, as is frequently the case in smaller communities. As a result, the tasks of grief and mourning may be as necessary for involved professionals as for, say, friends of the family.

A related issue is that a death in a medical setting usually follows a major effort on the part of everyone involved. It is usual to feel let down following such an intense exertion of energy. This tendency can only be accentuated by the fact that the endpoint is in itself a sad and existentially disturbing event. In acute care settings, the sense of failure often experienced by health care professionals on the death of a patient may contribute even more significantly to the likelihood of depression.

Given the direction of the above forces, it becomes clear that professionals can expect to feel depressed once a death has taken place.

Professionals who lose a patient may need to engage in a mourning process as well.

Clinicians most effectively resolve losses, whether of relationship or self-esteem, through the same grief and mourning processes occurring in bereaved loved ones. To facilitate this resolution, we strongly recommend that health care team members regularly set aside some time with each other after a death has occurred in order to work through the strong emotions that are bound to be present. There may be times when clinicians may feel moved to share some of these feelings with the family of the deceased. If the precautions characterized earlier in this chapter are taken to insure that such sharing is appropriate, it may be of great mutual value.

If there are no recognized provisions for ventilation of feelings and mutual support among professionals in terminal care settings, morale is likely to suffer. Our culture provides little in the way of traditions or other everyday community-based conventional mechanisms of support through sharing of emotions. While some outlets are present in, for example, various religious practices, these are often insufficient. As a result, the families and friends of health care personnel can be overtaxed with making up for the support that should be available in the professional setting. This further contributes to the stresses on clinicians, and adds to the tension already present in the terminal care setting. In turn, this is likely to have a negative influence on the experiences of other patients, or anyone else involved.

Skilled psychological counseling for terminal care team members can be beneficial by (1) facilitating better patient care, (2) increasing staff morale, and (3) lowering burnout and turnover rates.

Therefore, we recommend that institutions involved in terminal or critical care assume the responsibility of providing skilled professional counseling for staff members. This can take place either on an individual or a group basis, although there are certain advantages to the latter. These include the more efficient use of time and the chance to deal directly with problems involving more than one professional. In addition, the *esprit de corps* generated by effective regular meetings among all key team members can enhance the atmosphere of the terminal care setting. Further, such meetings can serve to break down hierarchically based communication difficulties, thereby permitting more efficient flow of vital information. The institution stands to benefit highly from this investment in terms of better patient care, higher staff morale, lower burnout rates, and reduced need to train new staff members for these difficult jobs.

Allegations Between Clinicians

Allegations of professional culpability arise at times in these settings, often without basis in reality.

There are likely to be instances in critical or terminal care facilities when allegations of suboptimal professional performance are raised following a death, often without clear basis. Given the volatile nature of these situations, such accusations can generate very potent emotions on all sides, and even can cause serious rifts among colleagues.

Whether these allegations originate from the bereaved or from other clinicians, they should be dealt with as promptly and openly as possible. The usual institutional procedures of investigation should proceed in parallel to the process detailed below. The following is aimed more at early resolution of accusations stemming from grief rather than actual malpractice.

When an allegation is made that professional performance was inadequate, the first step should be a nondefensive exploration with a colleague or group of peers of the feelings and data presented by the accuser. Once it is clear that the issue has been explored fully and that ample opportunity for ventilation has been allowed, it is important to get the involved parties together. A mutually recognized mediator who can intercede effectively if necessary should be an integral part of these sessions. The role of this individual is to make the situation as safe as possible for all those involved to express their feelings and viewpoints. If anyone becomes defensive, it is important to point this out and to inquire as to the feelings underlying this reaction. Both accused and accuser should be offered a full opportunity to voice the thoughts and perceptions that prompted the behavior and allegations. Many times, this procedure will sufficiently defuse the situation so that no further steps are necessary.

If doubts and accusations still persist or if culpability on the part of accused staff members remains apparent to colleagues after careful exploration by all involved, the sessions should be suspended. Institutional procedures, which should have been proceeding in parallel, should take precedence. Of course, the final arbiter is the legal system.

When Death Occurs Suddenly

Introduction

Many of the points we have made about death in chronic settings apply to unexpected death as well. In part this is because death almost always seems sudden and shocking to those close to the deceased, often regardless of their conscious expectations of its inevitability. Professionals should expect to see a broad spectrum of reactions depending on the situation. There are, however, significant differences in reactions of the bereaved and in the nature of optimal professional intervention when death is unexpected.

Breaking the News

One way in which unexpected death differs significantly from death in the setting of chronic illness is in the difficulty of breaking the news. Professionals who must bear such tidings understandably feel highly

The setting in which the news is broken is important in shaping reactions of the bereaved.

uncomfortable conveying information that may drastically change the lives of those receiving it. We can offer no pat solutions for making this task simple, but we have a few suggestions that may prove helpful.

The *setting* in which such news is imparted is of great importance in shaping the reactions that follow. We recommend strongly against use of the telephone to report a sudden death to a loved one. Ideally, the clinician should be present to assess needed support and provide appropriate professional intervention. It also should be borne in mind that there is a hazard inherent in having a deeply shocked person arrange transportation to a place of death. In instances of sudden and unexpected death in which the family member is not known to the informant, it is probably best to indicate only that there is a grave medical problem involving the deceased, and that the presence of the family as soon as possible is advisable. If the persons contacted inquire directly as to the state of the patient, it may be reasonable to say only that the situation is critical and that appropriate measures have been taken.

Every effort should be made to reach the family physician of a patient who dies in the emergency room or who arrives in the hospital or morgue already dead. It is often appropriate to delay contacting the family until the personal physician is reached and consulted on how to proceed. Because personal physicians have at least some degree of familiarity with the family and with the deceased, they are likely to be of more comfort to the bereaved as the bearer of these tidings.

A clinician who is familiar to the family should break the news whenever possible. (13)

Regarding breaking the news *per se*, the *words employed* are much less important than the choice of a setting that allows for the private expression of powerful feelings. Indeed, the actual language used for the communication itself is so contingent on the styles and relationships of those involved that generalizations are not likely to be useful. The clinician involved, however, should be prepared to take *time* to support the bereaved as they attempt to reconcile themselves to their loss.

Unfinished Business

Sudden death is more likely to result in significant unfinished business.

Most of us do not have our lives in such order that if we were to die suddenly our business and personal affairs would be resolved simply. This perhaps reflects the extent to which we chronically deny the ever present reality of our own mortality. Loved ones who are in deep shock can find themselves facing complex business affairs with which they may be totally unfamiliar. This situation can prove highly disturbing and frustrating, and also may become a major distraction from the work of mourning. When death is unexpected, there has seldom been the opportunity afforded by an anticipated death to settle unfinished emotional affairs. Resultant unresolved feelings often further complicate the difficult processes of grief and mourning.

Implications for Professionals

Survivors of unexpected death have longer and stronger grief reactions that are more likely to require assistance.

The emotions of grief and mourning are likely to be expressed with greater intensity and for a longer time in cases of unexpected death. This is partly explained by the fact that there is simply more with which to cope in a relatively shorter period. Problems also derive from the absence of the opportunity for anticipatory grief.

Another reason for this increase in the magnitude of reactions following an unexpected death is that the cause of death is more likely to involve violence or mutilation. In addition, because of the prevalence of accidental deaths, suicides, and homicides among younger age groups, sudden deaths are more likely to be untimely. These factors tend to make it much more difficult to assimilate a loss, and may lead to more feelings of guilt or blame.

Clearly, bereaved loved ones are apt to require more help from professionals in coping with an unexpected death than they might have if their loss had been anticipated. Increased need for help is likely during both the periods of acute grief and of chronic mourning. Once again, the manner in which these more intense reactions are best managed involves increased professional sensitivity, supportiveness, and availability.

Concerns Less Directly Related to Patient Care

Death Certification

Declaration of death is of great symbolic significance to the bereaved, and provides key opportunities for support and counsel. (13)

In most terminal care settings, certification of death will not be a legal issue. This is because the death will have been anticipated and professionals will likely have been recently involved. However, the signature of a physician will be necessary on the death certificate, and this will require an examination to ensure that death is indeed present. The act of placing the imprimatur of the clinician on a death is one of great symbolic significance for the bereaved, and often provides an important opportunity for support and counsel.

Although there are few terminal care settings in which more than simple confirmation by physical examination is necessary, ambiguities arise more often with unexpected death or in acute care contexts. For example, if the patient has drowned in cold water, particularly if he or she is a young child, electroencephalography may be necessary to insure that neocortical function is absent. The same may be the case with certain drug overdoses, such as those involving barbiturates. Also, if organ donation is involved there may be specific local regulations that need to be observed. The local medical examiner or district attorney's office should be consulted if clinicians have any doubts about specifics.

Autopsies

Laws prescribe the conditions under which an autopsy must be performed. (5)

Another concern that arises frequently following a death involves autopsies. Many laypersons have a strong and understandable aversion to this disturbance of the remains of their dead loved ones. In most regions of the United States, however, a post-mortem examination is required in a number of circumstances, regardless of the desires of the family. The specific laws governing this requirement differ in detail. They generally state, however, that anyone not seen by a physician within a brief period before the death must undergo post-mortem examination to determine cause of death. This usually requires at least a partial autopsy. Of course, if there is any suspicion of foul play, the medical examiner's services will be required. For local requirements beyond these, clinicians should contact their medical examiner or coroner.

When autopsies are desired for educational purposes only, this should be explained clearly.

The question of autopsies often arises for other than legal reasons. This is particularly true for patients who die in the hospital, where clinicians may have an understandable educational interest in pathological findings. Instances in which pressure is placed on family members for permission when autopsy is for this purpose alone often constitute taking unfair advantage of distraught persons. If an autopsy is desired by the attending clinicians, a clear and sensitive request should be made by that individual to the family. Emphasis may be placed on the educational purposes that can contribute to better understanding and hence potentially to better care for future patients. If families remain resistant, however, the issue should be dropped.

Tissue and Organ Donation

Tissue and organ donations are increasingly common as medical technology advances. Even the most ravaged individuals often can provide concrete assistance to others by donating corneas, middle ears, skin, or other tissues that remain viable. Further, many people derive comfort from the knowledge that their remains might prove useful to new generations of clinicians in anatomy laboratories. Many states have passed laws facilitating the donation of body parts after death. The pre-mortem arrangement is simple and straightforward.

In the case of major organ transplantation, the deaths that provide these life-saving gifts are most often unexpected. Great care must be taken in such situations that families are not put under pressure to agree to donation. Probably the most effective tactic to secure appropriate consent is to emphasize the magnitude of this final offering of the deceased to the world.

Embalming and the Funeral Industry

Expenses of and fallacies regarding funeral services can be useful information for the bereaved. (6)

While we discuss funeral costs in some detail in Chapter 15, a few points about the funeral industry are worth reviewing here. The majority of funeral directors provide a necessary service at a reasonable price. The vulnerability of the bereaved, however, does open possibilities for exploitation. Family members often turn to health care professionals in terminal care settings for advice regarding these issues. Clinicians frequently can help by knowing the availability and cost of local funeral services.

There are some specific notions worth clarification here. First, *no state requires embalming before a burial or cremation that takes place within 24 hours of death* except in cases involving communicable diseases. There are legal requirements that remains be embalmed before being transported over state lines by common carriers, or across certain regional boundaries, but these affect fairly few individuals. Most funeral homes, however, include the cost of embalming as a part of their services whether or not it is performed. Some will waive this charge if specifically requested.

Another belief is that there are techniques for preserving corpses indefinitely. *Length of preservation depends upon the type of soil, vault, coffin, and embalming procedure.* Decomposition will take its course, usually in less than 50 years, or somewhat longer in dry or cold climates.

An additional common concern regards disposal of ashes after a cremation. *Ashes do not have to be placed in a cemetery columbarium.* In most of the United States, they may be buried in or scattered on private property with the permission of the owner. Disposal of ashes at sea is also generally unregulated. Many localities, however, prohibit scattering on public land.

Memorial societies are nonprofit consumer-oriented organizations that assist members to make prearrangements for death. They are a good source of information concerning alternatives to the conventional service. These societies currently have about a million members, and information about them is available from: The Continental Association of Funeral and Memorial Societies, 1828 L Street NW, Washington, DC 20036.

References

Lindemann, E. 1944. Symptomatology and management of acute grief. *Am. J. Psychiat.* 101:141–148.

This is the seminal paper in the area of acute grief and its management. The setting is the tragic Cocoanut Grove fire and its aftermath. Examples of acute grief symptomatology and crisis intervention techniques are succinctly presented. For clinical information, if not for historical interest alone, this brief article is a must for all clinicians.

Schoenberg, B., Carr, A. C., Peretz, D. and Kutscher, A. H. eds. 1970. *Loss and Grief: Psychological Management in Medical Practice.* New York: Columbia University Press.

This is probably the best of the several multiauthored books edited by the Columbia medical group with support from the Foundation of Thanatology. It shines in distinction of contributors, high quality of authorship, editorial excellence, and range of situations addressed. Humanistic and psychological concepts central to loss and grief are presented from a number of viewpoints. A brief annotated bibliography highlights well selected contributions from the 1950 to 1970 period. The book is a benchmark in the art of psychological management of loss and grief in the 1960s, and much of it remains applicable in current medical practice.

9 The Aftermath: Grief and Mourning

Brief Contents

Overview

The final chapter in our practical approach to terminal care concerns the period of bereavement. We begin by reviewing the reactions and problems clinicians are likely to encounter after a death. Health care professionals often are the targets of the reactions of the bereaved, so they must understand and be able to deal with them. We present strategies for dealing with these reactions as well as some specific means whereby the grief and mourning processes can be supported. Finally, we look at a variety of manifestations of pathological grief, and make some suggestions as to their management.

What to Expect: Clinical Aspects of Bereavement

Review of Pertinent Studies

Many studies demonstrate an increase in ill health for the bereaved. (11)

In Chapter 1, we discussed a series of key studies by Bowlby and Parkes concerning patterns in grief and mourning and the medical aftereffects of a recent loss. Findings in these and other studies support the clinical and popular observation that *bereavement has the potential for devastating effect on health.*

Young et al. (1963) followed a group of nearly 4500 widowers during the year after the death of their wives, and compared their death rates to an age matched cohort. They observed a 40% increase in death rate above the married, nonbereaved control group in the first six months, followed by a rapid reversion to about the same death rate as the married controls. In support of Parkes' (1972) *"broken heart"* phenomenon, about three-quarters of this increase was attributable to heart disease. Rees and Lutkins (1967) reported a survey of about one thousand close relatives of persons who died between 1960 and 1965 in Wales. They found that 4.8% of their study group died during this period, as compared to 0.7% of an age-matched control group from the same region.

Common responses during bereavement include denial, somatic complaints, withdrawal, and anger.

Nonfatal medical problems also follow the loss of someone close. Parkes observed a 63% increase in the number of widows who consulted their family physician within 6 months of their loss. The main complaints were anxiety, depression, and insomnia. Consultations for physical symptoms also increased, particularly those relating to arthritic complaints. A comprehensive study involving about 350 American and Australian widows was reported by Maddison and Viola (1968). They followed this cohort (all of whom were less than 60 years old) for 13 months. About 30% of the widows experienced a marked deterioration in health after their loss, as compared to less than 5% of the matched, married control group. Common symptoms, in addition to those found by Parkes, included nightmares, trembling, appetite disorders, weight loss, and fatigue. All of these often are associated with grief. Somatic complaints such as headaches, dizziness, fainting, blurred vision, skin rashes, excessive sweating, indigestion, problems with swallowing, vomiting, menstrual disturbances, palpitations, chest pain, shortness of breath, infection, and myalgias all were significantly increased in the study group. More recent studies of younger widows and widowers in the Boston area by Glick (1974) showed they had less somatic complaints than did the older groups studied, but similar depressive symptoms. Further, four times as many people from this study group than from the control group were hospitalized in the year following their loss.

The conclusions are that widows and widowers are more likely to seek medical help, and that they are at greater risk for physical illness during the year following their loss. Not surprisingly, many studies support the contention that the bereaved also are at a markedly increased risk for psychiatric illness, both short- and long-term.

Emotional Reactions During Bereavement

Engagement in grief and mourning is vital in assimilating a loss. (9)

Because the feelings associated with the difficult healing processes of grief and mourning can be agonizing, many of us resist them strongly. These blocks are broadly reinforced by societal discomfort with public expression of emotions. Clinicians should make a special effort to support the sharing of the difficult feelings that usually arise. The persistence of denial, somatization, withdrawal, or anger is evidence that problems are being encountered.

Periodic expressions of denial may simply signal the need for a respite. (13)

There are likely to be many times during the course of grief and mourning when patients will demonstrate varying degrees of denial of their situation. Often, such episodes arise when the individual simply feels unable to cope with the unpleasant reality. Periodic occurrences of denial are not in themselves indicative of pathological grief, but may signal a simple need for a momentary respite. Demonstrations of denial do not need to be challenged overtly in early bereavement as long as they are not causing problems. When denial is more strongly manifest, it may be appropriate to explore gently for the existence of feelings of being overwhelmed that often underly this phenomenon.

CASE ILLUSTRATION

A 70-year-old widower was brought to his family physician's office by his son-in-law, who had become concerned about the old man's behavior. At times, the widower would hold long conversations with his recently departed wife, and would even serve a meal for her at dinner. The doctor began by inquiring as to how the patient was holding up. The response of "Just fine," was followed by a long silence. The doctor gently recalled her experience that those who had lost someone dear often felt so overwhelmed that sometimes they just didn't want to believe what had happened. This seemed to break the deadlock, and the rest of the interview was poignant and productive from everyone's perspective.

In our experience, many people, bereaved or otherwise, find it much easier to seek professional help for *physical* than for emotional problems. Sometimes grief even is manifested by physical symptoms

The bereaved commonly manifest their anguish in somatic complaints.

similar to those of the deceased. When patients present with bodily complaints following a significant loss, an evaluation of the psychosocial situation should assume as prominent a place in the workup as a thorough medical investigation. Explaining that minds and bodies are inextricably linked, and that problems with feelings often present on a physical level, frequently suffices in itself to produce some relief. If such somatic complaints persist, they often represent pathological mourning.

Withdrawal by the bereaved may be quite jolting to those who have formed intimate partnerships with the family of the deceased in the

Withdrawal often is displayed by the bereaved.

mutual effort to care for the deceased patient. This reaction may arise from the association by the bereaved of medical professionals with agony and loss. There need be few, if any, negative consequences to this sort of avoidance, particularly if the bereaved are receiving adequate medical and emotional support elsewhere. Unfortunately, this is often not the case. Additional problems arise when the primary care physician is the target of such avoidance. Accordingly, clinicians need to develop strategies for ensuring that the interests of bereaved family members are protected.

The bereaved may react strongly toward professionals. (3, 11, 16)

Angry *blaming of others* is a common reaction during the course of grief and mourning. It is commonly directed toward clinicians, who are perceived, in a primitive sense, to have *failed* to prevent a loss. Health care personnel may be the handiest targets for feelings of rage that arise so often in the bereaved.

CASE ILLUSTRATION

A primary care practitioner had followed to the letter the provisions of a patient's Natural Death Act directive that was well known to the family. He thereby allowed an elderly patient a peaceful and relatively pain-free death. Soon thereafter, the physician became the target of a great deal of anger from the bereaved family. They condemned him for not doing his utmost to preserve the life of their lost loved one. He listened quietly to their protestations, drawing them out to further express their sense of loss and regret. As the intensity of their emotions subsided, some family members spontaneously began to present the doctor's side of the case. By the end of the hour, they parted company on much better terms. The family went on to resolve their loss appropriately, and the physician felt better after a hard game of squash that evening.

We submit that this doctor probably did this family a considerable service by his nondefensive acceptance of the rage and guilt for which the bereaved so desperately needed to find a target. In general, we encourage clinicians to follow this example when they are faced with similar expressions by the bereaved.

By now, it should be very clear that in the context of the aftermath of a death, strong reactions toward medical personnel often are expressed by the bereaved. These are frequently disturbing and confusing, especially for those who have done their utmost to provide the best possible care. There may be times when grieving loved ones are unable to relate objectively to even caring professionals with whom they have had an intense and intimate involvement during a difficult time. Rather, they may react to their own intensely subjective associations of that individual with a traumatic loss. If professionals are able to recognize when they have become symbols of pain and abandonment to the bereaved, many problems may be averted. Although this knowledge may not make it easy to be on the receiving end of unpleasant expressions, it may stay the clinician's hand from thoughtlessly defensive reactions that are likely only to escalate matters.

Strategies for Supporting Mourning

General Considerations: Prevention of Pathology

Many times, the caregiver of the deceased is not that of the bereaved. Even so, the former can play a vital role by virtue of the relationship established during the terminal illness. First, as a wise clinician advised a younger colleague, "Be sure you always write a letter of condolence to the families of patients of yours who die." This preferably is done in longhand on high quality paper. Such a message may include a statement of personal respect for the manner in which the patient met the trials of the fatal illness. It also might remark upon the conduct of and support and care rendered by the family.

Clinicians should consider preventive issues when dealing with the bereaved. (8)

Further, the physician—knowing the risks of physical and emotional morbidity during bereavement—has the opportunity to acquaint the family with community resources for assistance. This may even extend to putting relatives in touch with appropriate agencies.

The patient's doctor also can, given consent, alert a relative's physician to the situation and share information as to potential problems in coping. It is often appropriate to suggest that relatives schedule a visit with their own physician shortly after the death.

When the bereaved relative is also the patient of the doctor of the deceased, the physician's obligation to act in a preventive role is even greater. For example, the common reaction of withdrawal may be averted by addressing the issue directly, even in the first few contacts after a death has taken place. The primary care physician responsible for the family should make an appointment to see each bereaved person within a week or two of the death. This visit serves two functions: to avert the medical problems discussed earlier, and to assess the status of the

Grieving patients should routinely be evaluated by a health care professional soon after their loss. (11)

grief process. At this initial visit, it is usually a helpful preventive measure to address openly the issue of withdrawal with a statement such as: "I can understand how you might want to avoid even the thought of the medical world after what you and————[name of deceased] have been through. It wouldn't surprise me if you would rather not recall the memories and associations that my presence might bring back. I just want you to know that I still care about what is going on with you, and that I think it is important for us to get together now and then over the next few months if you feel any need to at all."

This sort of communication can accomplish a number of purposes. It tacitly gives the bereaved the permission to have the desire to withdraw. This can be helpful because they may not understand such feelings, and in fact may judge themselves harshly for their apparently unseemly urge. It assures patients that whatever their emotions toward the clinician may be, they will not be abandoned. This fear of abandonment may be related to the urge to withdraw in the first place. The bereaved often feel that medical personnel will lose interest in them once their loved one has died. Assurance that caring and involvement will not be interrupted can be of great comfort.

Medical Therapy

Medication is over-used in "treating" the symptoms of grief. (14)

Of the various strategies that clinicians can employ to support the grief process, in our view medication constitutes the most inappropriately over-used therapeutic tool. All too often, professionals uneasy with the emotional expressions central to the mourning process will opt for the prescription pad. Perhaps this allows them to feel as though they are doing something.

During mourning, as in any setting, drugs should be used to treat demonstrable psychopathology only.

We do not mean that use of prescription drugs is never appropriate in the context of mourning. Our point is rather that the indications for their use do not include grief, sadness, or even emotional pain that is less than extremely debilitating. The specific instances in which the use of medication is advisable in this context center around the presence of demonstrable psychopathology that would generally warrant chemical intervention. Thus, crippling anxiety that is refractory to counseling might justify the use of benzodiazepines or small doses of neuroleptics for a brief period. Psychotic symptoms beyond those described in Chapter 1 as ordinary concomitants of grief may be addressed with antipsychotic agents or brief hospitalization. Severe depression may warrant use of tricyclic antidepressants, monoamine oxidase inhibitors, or even electroconvulsive therapy in refractory cases, as well as hospitalization. When there is any uncertainty as to diagnosis or treatment in these situations, psychiatric referral is advisable.

When to refer.

Insomnia often presents as a part of the symptom complex of depression. If, however, it exists as an isolated symptom that is refractory to counseling, the temporary use of short-acting benzodiazepines to counteract debilitating loss of sleep may be warranted.

Nonindicated drugs reinforce the belief that the bereaved are incapable of managing their own lives.

The bottom line is that there are no studies supporting the efficacy of chemical intervention beyond the instances just presented. Further, prescribing drugs that are not medically indicated is likely to reinforce any conviction of the bereaved that they are incapable of managing their own lives. This can undermine the process of restructuring a satisfying life after a serious loss.

Ventilation of Emotions

Talking it through is the principal tool for assisting the grief process. (9, 14)

The principal recommended strategy for professionals to support the grief process is to encourage ventilation and working through. This may require a considerable investment of time, energy, and patience. The payoffs, however, generally are more than worth the cost.

No magic! Just supportive discussion of worrisome feelings from time to time. (17)

Overt support of the feelings and reactions of the bereaved underlines the conviction that the ultimate power to heal the psychic wound occasioned by a loss resides within the individual. Often, grieving individuals may think that they are going crazy as they are assaulted by a barrage of conflicting and misunderstood feelings. If such persons have a respected professional with whom they can discuss their reactions, they may be reassured. As mourning progresses, the bereaved should evolve increased trust in their own feelings and become less dependent on outsiders to support the resolution of their loss. Clinicians need to remember that their most appropriate role in supporting the grief process is to work themselves out of a job, rather than to foster dependency that will eventuate in everyone's discomfort.

Clinicians should foster support and communication within bereaved families.

Communication among family members also is very important during this period when a sense of alienation, isolation, and abandonment may be so prominent. Clinicians should watch carefully for signs that this mutual support is not taking place. When this is suspected, it is best to begin by addressing family members separately before attempting a mutual resolution. In this way, the chance of defensive and unproductive encounters is diminished by ventilation, exploration, and clarification of key issues.

Ongoing Contact

Clear opportunities for ongoing support should be provided.

Providing opportunities for continued contact with the bereaved is a key responsibility of clinicians attempting to ensure ongoing support. Clinicians should go out of their way to communicate that they are interested in and deeply committed to seeing their patients through this difficult time. The simple statement that a call is welcome at any hour if a moment of desperation arises is not only immediately reassuring, but can continue to be of great comfort even if this option is never exercised. The sense of being overwhelmed in such situations can be markedly alleviated if the patient knows that there is someone else to fall back on. Further, as we have noted earlier, maintenance of regular contacts between primary health care provider and patient during the mourning period also is an important means for early detection of medical and emotional complications.

Alternate Sources of Support

Alternative arrangements for support often can be made available.

When to refer.

If the primary health care provider feels uneasy about handling such calls or is unable to supply the requisite level of support, alternative arrangements should be made for continuing contacts. A thoughtful referral to another health care professional may be in order. Some clinicians make such referrals as a preventive tactic prior to the death. For families involved in hospices, followup during the bereavement period is usual (see Chapter 12). Another possibility for continuing supportive contact that is often of value is group therapy with others who have similar problems. Supervised self-help groups usually can be located by consulting the local chapter of the American Cancer Society or local information and referral services. The chance to share one's experiences and concerns with others enduring similar problems can be extremely valuable to the grieving. In part, this derives from realizing that one may not be entirely alone or alienated from the rest of the human race. Support groups also can form an important stepping stone back into life by providing the bereaved with a pathway out of the house and by opening the door for new social contacts.

Group therapy may be of value. (14)

Supportive counseling is often helpful. (9)

When to refer.

Another resource for one-to-one support lies in volunteer peer counseling organizations that have sprung up in many communities. Most of these groups consist of professionally supervised volunteers who work with problems surrounding death at no charge to the dying or bereaved. Finally, when professionals feel over their heads in dealing with more complicated individual or family psychodynamics, early referral to a trusted psychiatric consultant can be of great value.

Recognition and Management of Grief Pathology

Absence of Grief

Absence of grief may be a serious problem. (14)

The absence of mourning may constitute a serious problem. Depending on the profundity of the loss for the bereaved individual, the failure of the grief process may prevent a healthy assimilation of the loss and thereby delay a return to satisfying living. If professionals sense, after a few weeks have passed since a death, that a bereaved patient is not demonstrating any usual manifestations of mourning, investigation is in order. Clearly, the way in which individuals show these feelings varies widely, as does their comfort in revealing them to others. It is unwise to assume that the patient is not grieving simply because the clinician or family member is not party to that grief.

There are ways of uncovering grief that is present but not apparent.

One direct and effective way of uncovering hidden grief is to make the statement: "I understand that you may not feel at ease sharing your grief with me, but I am also aware of the importance of these feelings in allowing people to recover from losses such as yours. It would ease my mind to know that you are unburdening yourself with someone. If you are not, I would be glad to help you to find someone with whom you might feel comfortable in doing so." Many times, the floodgates will be unlocked by this demonstration of professional concern and availability.

When to refer.

If this approach does not elicit emotional expression, clinicians should begin careful exploration to uncover any underlying feelings that the agony of grief would be overwhelming if it were allowed to emerge. If this process does not overcome resistance to mourning, clinicians may need to bide their time. While doing so, it will be important to keep close contact to ensure that nothing more serious begins to develop. If similar overtures remain ineffective after a few weeks, or if the primary coping mechanism continues to be a denial of psychotic proportions, referral for psychiatric consultation is advisable.

Merry Widow Equivalents

The manic escape is another form of grief pathology.

Another common manifestation of grief pathology might most aptly be termed the *"manic escape."* This behavior is characterized by frenzied activity often accompanied by an inappropriately cheerful demeanor. This flight into *busy-ness* is yet another defense: a way of avoiding the feelings of loss and helplessness engendered by the death of someone close.

We do not imply that some degree of losing oneself in activities is a bad thing in and of itself. Indeed, there are bound to be times in which great relief can be found in occupying one's mind with chores or details in order to gain a respite from confronting a loss. Rather, it is the quality of compulsion and desperation that most clearly distinguishes the pathological manifestations of this common escape mechanism.

Gentle investigation is in order when patients maintain brittle, cheerful, or frenetically active fronts. The examination can begin with simple inquiries as to how the person is doing. If the response is consistent with the initial presentation, the observation can be made that while clinicians appreciate the effort being made to cope, they wonder about what may be going on underneath. Possible feelings of helplessness or fears of inability to cope may be tentatively reflected. If such reflection fails to elicit a reduction of this defense, all that may be necessary is an assurance that the professional will be glad to listen if such emotions do come up. If this defense persists for more than a week, or if it begins to cause problems with other family members, a more direct expression of concern may be in order. Once again, when clinicians begin to feel at a loss after attempting such interventions, psychiatric referral often is advisable.

When to refer.

Yet another *merry widow*-like manifestation of problems with grief or mourning is characterized by sudden decisions to make drastic alterations in one's life. The psychological drive for this reaction to a loss is probably the urge to flee the situation entirely, and thereby to leave behind the old life that seems to be so shattered. Unfortunately, the judgment necessary to make major decisions is often impaired following a traumatic loss. Further, these actions can easily lead to isolation of the bereaved from the kinship support system that normally plays an important part in reconstructing a life.

Drastic life changes soon after a loss may represent grief pathology.

When bereaved patients present such decisions, professionals probably should avoid directly challenging them at the outset. Rather, they should encourage nonjudgmental exploration of the feelings underlying these ideas. Often, this alone is sufficient to restore better judgment. If the resolve to act on questionable decisions persists, the direct declaration may be made that in the clinician's experience it is unwise to make major moves under circumstances of bereavement. Careful and gentle reasoning may be ventured as to why actions on such impulses should be postponed until the life situation becomes more settled. If this still does not suffice to forestall rash decisions, referral for counseling may be the only viable alternative.

When to refer.

Dysfunctional Hostility

Grief pathology may become evident in extreme or apparently irrational hostility. This can be particularly problematic in the situation of acute loss because it enhances the sense of isolation and alienation that the bereaved are likely to feel. As we have seen, it also creates stress for professionals, who are likely to be the targets of such hostility.

Dysfunctional hostility often constitutes a manifestation of grief pathology.

Rage often elicits angry reactions from others in the support system of the enraged person, and the reverberations may crescendo to the detriment of everyone involved. The likelihood of reinforcement of the sense of isolation, helplessness, loss, and abandonment that first prompted the angry response tends to perpetuate the whole cycle.

Once again, we advise against early direct confrontation of such behavior unless it is so flagrant that there are fears for the personal safety of anyone involved. We recommend the usual course of non-defensive exploration of underlying feelings and thoughts, followed by specific discussions of the behavior in question. It is at times helpful to communicate in a nonbelligerent manner the effect that these expressions of rage have on the clinician. This not only makes the discussion more personal, but also can serve as a model for constructive coping with expression of anger. It also might illustrate in a reasoned manner how this behavior could be affecting others in the life of the bereaved. A search for alternative modes of displaying the underlying feelings often can be undertaken at that point.

CASE ILLUSTRATION

An elderly woman had been living with her daughter in the six months since the death of her husband of 50 years. She was initially withdrawn and silent, then increasingly demanding and critical of her daughter. By the time the situation came to the attention of the family physician, anger and distance were destroying the home atmosphere and endangering the daughter's marriage. The doctor began by talking to the daughter and mother separately, encouraging each to express their emotions freely. On the next visit, all of the parties met together to talk through their differences. Once lines of communication and understanding were reestablished, it became clear that the mother was feeling unconscious jealousness of her daughter's marriage and position in the prime of life. The expression of these feelings led to a rapid correction of the situation.

When to refer.

Family members may be involved in working through these feelings once the situation is defused. Once again, the key to facilitating group discussions is to make one's primary concern the assurance of safe passage for everyone involved. Call a halt whenever it seems that someone is being pointlessly attacked, and redirect the focus to the feelings prompting the assault. If the clinician feels at any point that this process is too complex or too time consuming, referral should be made for psychiatric counseling.

Clinical Depression

Clinical depression is more common among the elderly bereaved.

The final expression of grief pathology that we shall address in this chapter is clinical depression. This response to the loss of someone important is particularly common in the elderly. If clinical depression is not recognized and treated appropriately, it can indeed prove fatal as the bereaved spirals downward emotionally and physically to fatal illness or suicide. To review, the manifestations of a clinically serious depression are most commonly aberrations of those psychophysiological functions designed to maintain homeostasis (see Table 9-1). Thus, disturbances in sleep, eating, energy level, sexual interest, ability to experience pleasure, and ability to think are characteristic of serious depression. Gastrointestinal function may be drastically impaired, anxiety may be prominent, and psychomotor retardation or agitation may be present.

When to refer.

To assist clinicians in evaluating depression, Hamilton (1960, 1980) has developed a simple, 17-symptom test. The instrument consists of 21 items, each rated on a three to five point scale. This test is administered by a physician or a trained technician in a brief interview, and is scored on the basis of both clinical observations and answers given by the patient. If there is some question as to the existence of serious depression, the Hamilton Scale can be administered weekly or more often as indicated. Scores over 20 justify concern, and those over 30 indicate a high probability of serious depression warranting prompt intervention including psychiatric referral.

Hospitalization is advisable if there is any doubt as to suicide potential.

If the clinician is satisfied that a severe depression is present, it is first necessary to assess suicidal potential (see Chapter 11). If there is any doubt, hospitalization is recommended. If there is no immediate risk of suicide, it may be reasonable to undertake treatment of the depression on an outpatient basis. This usually consists of a combination of supportive psychotherapy and antidepressant medication.

Patients should be informed that the effects of antidepressants cannot be assessed for some weeks after therapeutic doses are reached. Great caution should be used in the prescription of tricyclic antidepressants, as they have potentially serious cardiac and anticholinergic

Table 9-1:   Common Symptoms of Clinical Depression

Symptom	Definitions
Depressed Mood	Sad, hopeless, helpless, worthless
Anxiety	Fearfulness, with physiologic symptoms
Insomnia	Early, middle, or late in sleep cycle
Work	Reduction in activity and interest
Suicide	Thoughts of death, wishes, plans, attempts
Insight	Denial of being ill, suspiciousness
Somatic	Aches and pains, constipation, decreased libido
Guilt	Self-reproach, deprecatory hallucinations

There may be increased risk of suicide as a depression begins to lift.

side-effects. These medications can be given primarily at bedtime to take advantage of sedative side-effects and to minimize unpleasant anticholinergic symptoms. Treatment should be initiated gradually with these agents, in order to avoid cardiac instability, and periodic electrocardiograms are recommended. Further, because they constitute potent suicide weapons, they should be dispensed in quantities of less than one gram. The period of greatest risk of suicide for seriously depressed patients often occurs when antidepressants have reduced the physiological depression just enough so that the energy to act on suicidal impulses is present. If clinicians in any way feel uncomfort-

When to refer.

able in managing potentially suicidally depressed patients, psychiatric referral is strongly encouraged (see Chapter 11).

References

Glick, I. O. 1974. *The First Year of Bereavement*. New York: John Wiley & Sons, Inc.

Hamilton, M. 1960. A rating scale for depression. *J. Neurol. Neurosurg. Psychiat.* 23:56–62.

Hamilton, M. 1980. Rating depressive patients. *J. Clin. Psychiat.* 41:21–24.

Maddison, D. and Viola, A. 1968. The health of widows in the year following bereavement. *J. Psychosomatic Res.* 12:297–306.

Parkes, C. M. 1972. *Bereavement*. New York: International Universities Press.

A significant scholarly work on adult grief. It explores bereavements with respect to the risks they pose, including abnormal grief reactions and reactive illnesses such as the "broken heart" syndrome. Implications for the care of the bereaved are discussed.

Pincus, L. 1974. *Death and the Family: The Importance of Mourning*. New York: Pantheon Books.

The author was an experienced social worker who was 75 years old when she undertook this project. The book focuses on the more immediate reactions during bereavement of surviving family members. The likely family dynamics underlying the various reactions are formulated with great understanding and are plausible as well as sensitively presented. The brief chapter on helping the bereaved centers on short-term therapy, and is by itself worth twice the price of the 1976 paperback edition.

Rees, W. D. and Lutkins, S. G. 1967. Mortality of Bereavement. *Brit. Med. J.* 4:13.

Schoenberg, B., Carr, A. C., Peretz, D. and Kutscher, A. H. eds. 1975. *Bereavement: Its Psychological Aspects.* New York: Columbia University Press.

Yet another of the multi-authored Columbia group works. The kaleidoscopic view that is presented represents differences of approach, philosophy, and state of development of various professions dealing with bereavement. Some conceptual editorial glue to bind the chips of content into a more coherent whole would have been helpful. Despite its unevenness, the reader is given a good taste of the breadth of the issues involved in understanding and managing bereavement problems. The usefulness of this volume is greatly enhanced when coupled with the Parkes and Pincus works.

Young, M., Benjamin, B. and Wallis, C. 1963. Mortality of Widowers. *Lancet*, 2:454.

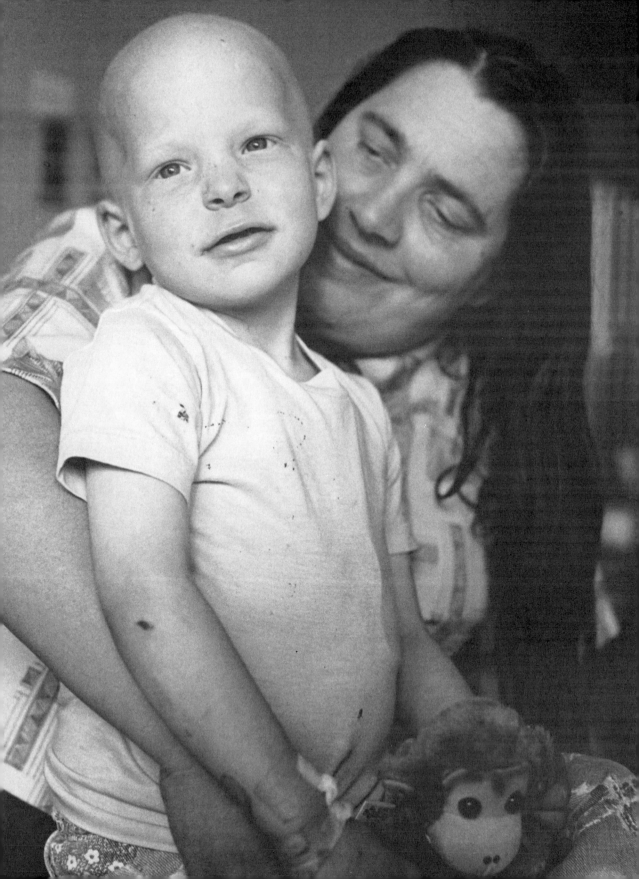

PART 4

Special Clinical Topics

In Part III we addressed a number of specific problems related to the care of the dying and their loved ones in roughly the sequence that one might expect to encounter them in clinical situations. In Part IV we turn to three special death-related topics that warrant a more detailed examination. They are death and children, suicide, *and the hospice.*

10 Death and Children

Overview

Knowledge about the evolution of children's concepts concerning death is central to a clear understanding of the principles guiding care of the dying child. Such information also is crucial in dealing with the reactions of children to the deaths of others. Thus, we look first at the developmental aspects of children's concepts of death. These concepts are applied to the care of the dying child, including the child's role in medical decision-making. We also explore the reactions of parents and health care professionals to the dying child. Finally, we discuss the effects of parental death on children.

Children's Concepts of Death

Developmental Aspects

Children's concepts concerning death evolve at widely varying rates. However, three loosely age-related stages in the child's view of death can be characterized as (1) *prelanguage,* (2) *preschool,* and (3) *preadolescent.* These milestones correlate roughly with the child's mastery of certain essential sensorimotor and cognitive tasks.

To be sure, there are other possible classifications. Students of child development have advanced various theories of personality development and have used differing terminologies according to the needs of their analysis. Agreement does exist, however, on the occurrence of stages, with wide individual disparities in timing. We will now describe this developmental process in a way that is consistent with our own experience.

Prelanguage Stage

Although children have no clear understanding of death in the prelanguage stage, they have intense reactions to separation.

During the first 18 months of life, children face developmental tasks that are primarily sensorimotor. Through mastery of these hurdles in creative interaction with their environments, youngsters evolve a basic sense of trust in others and confidence in the world. On the other hand, reactions of intense fear and anxiety to separation from key figures in the infant's environment are observed nearly universally.

There is no evidence that children of this age group have any understanding of death. Throughout their preverbal stage of cognitive development, it is questionable whether children have the capacity to distinguish between the living and the dead. However, they clearly recognize the presence and absence of key caretakers, and frequently manifest strong emotional reactions to separation. The death of a parent during this period usually will have a strong influence on the developing child.

Preschool Stage

Rudimentary ideas and feelings about death take shape in the preschool stage.

From the eighteenth month to about the third year of life, the task of learning language is begun. By the age of three or four years most children have made sufficient progress to comprehend much of what they are told. During this same period, while children are finding their place in the family constellation and sometimes experiencing heightened separation anxieties, rudimentary ideas about death begin to form. A frequently observed example of this phenomenon is the child who steps on a bug, looks down on the crushed animal, and says, "All gone." Thus is expressed an important initial connection between death and the absence of mobility.

As reasoning develops between the second and fifth or sixth years, children evolve clearer senses of reality on many levels. They begin to grasp that dead organisms are immobile and that they disappear. Both disappearance and immobility therefore often are associated with unpleasant feelings, chiefly fear.

During this period, preschool children continue to struggle with the development of their identities and begin to deal with conflicts around autonomy and independent initiative. They often have serious concerns about their experience and existence, although these questions may not be clearly conceived or communicated. In fact, fantasy and reality intermingle freely in the minds of many children during this stage. It is not surprising that they often view death as related to sleep, as temporary, or as personified. Many times, youngsters of this age will see death as caused by a supernatural being (for example, *The Boogey Man*), and therefore amenable to being warded off by a rescuer.

During the preschool stage, death is viewed as sleep, as temporary, or as personified.

Preadolescent Stage

From as early as their fifth year children perceive many objects and events in their environment as associated with death. As a clearer sense of their own identity and awareness of their own existence develops, they begin to recognize that phenomena such as accidents and funerals are real possibilities that might even happen to them. There is great individual variation in this development depending on the child's abilities and experiences. It is likely, however, that sometime between the ages of seven and 13 years most children develop adult, abstract concepts of death.

Between ages seven and 13 years, most children come to regard death as universal and irreversible (Figure 10-1).

Age and cultural dependence notwithstanding, the principal characteristics of the adult concept of death are that it is *universal* and *irrevocable*. Some children show an awareness of this universality of death as early as the age of four years (Childers and Wimmer, 1971). Rochlin (1965) also demonstrated that increasing percentages of youngsters through age ten years respond positively to the question of the universality of death. By their thirteenth year, nearly all children in Western culture not only grasp this concept but actually believe in it. On the other hand, irreversibility of death, although understood as an idea by most early teenagers, is not a clear part of the belief system of any age group. This observation probably reflects the controversial nature of the concept of permanence of life in our prevailing culture.

Figure 10-1:   Development of Cognitive Potential in Children

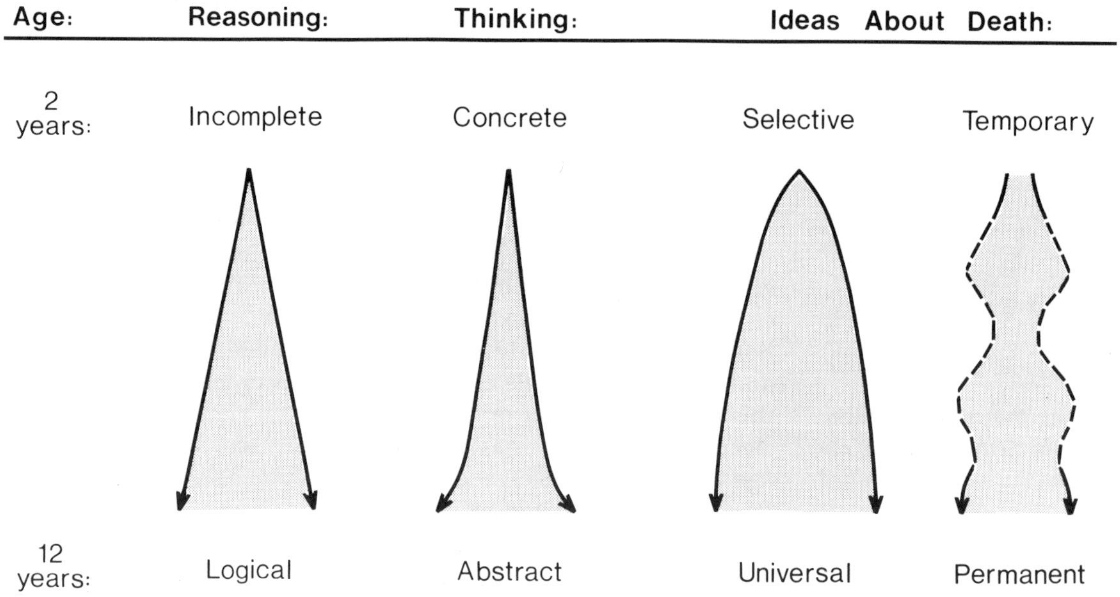

Age:	Reasoning:	Thinking:	Ideas About Death:	
2 years:	Incomplete	Concrete	Selective	Temporary

	Logical	Abstract	Universal	Permanent
12 years:				

Care of the Dying Child

Children's Reactions to Their Own Approaching Death

Children react to their own dying according to their stage of development.

There is no solid evidence that children under the age of two years are capable of knowing that they are dying. Notwithstanding this, if such toddlers are abandoned by key environmental figures during their illnesses, they probably will suffer significant separation anxieties. As we have pointed out, there is a gradual evolution of children's ideas about death from about the age of two years. The timing and specific nature of these developments is, however, an individual matter that is heavily influenced by the unique experiences of each child. Thus, what follows can serve as a rough guideline at best. Optimal application of these ideas is highly contingent on accurate observation of the youngster in question.

From the third to about the sixth year, youngsters often intermingle fantasy and reality. Children in this age group have only vague ideas about death. Those caring for the child must be willing and able to separate out and attempt to understand the meaning of death-related fantasies and symbols in the child's own world view. Because such material often is closely mixed with learned facts and social attitudes that may or may not be well integrated, this process requires patience and a nonjudgmental approach. If the preschool child's symbolic language about death is deciphered successfully, vital information about what is going on may become accessible.

CASE ILLUSTRATION

A four-year-old girl was suffering her third relapse of leukemia. When she was hospitalized for chemotherapy, the staff noticed a striking difference in her personality from previous visits. This usually lively child had become withdrawn and uncommunicative, clearly evidencing signs of depression. A play therapist was called in and noted that when playing house, the child would begin each game by deliberately picking up the father doll and hiding it. On inquiry with the child's mother, it emerged that the father had in fact been subtly withdrawing since the most recent relapse. These issues were addressed directly during family sessions, and the child's depression lifted after she received consistent and concrete reassurances that she would not be abandoned.

After the age of five or six years, children begin to accommodate themselves to the fact that death is universal and thus applicable to them. By their tenth year, youngsters generally have an increasingly realistic understanding of death. By adolescence, their thoughts and feelings have been shown to match well with those of their family and of the broader culture, even though these may be in conflict. In fact, these ambiguities may be acted out rather graphically in various manifestations of the adolescent preoccupation with death.

To what extent should children be informed of and included in decision-making regarding their own terminal illnesses? This question is often difficult and controversial. The first step is to ascertain the nature of each child's understanding of both death in general and the nature of his or her own situation. Often, this exploration can be accomplished in a much more straightforward manner with children than with adults. The clinician with whom the child is most comfortable usually is best suited to this role, and such discussions can be more fruitful in the absence of parents.

Very ill children often develop an early understanding of the seriousness of the signs and symptoms that they experience. Concomitantly, they may begin to organize and express their thoughts about their illness, albeit on a symbolic level. Consciousness of being seriously ill is frequently the first step toward awareness that the disease and resultant weakening of the body may lead to death. In fact, children as young as three years demonstrate awareness that bodily decay is an aspect of death.

Communication with the Dying Child

Children's ability to convey directly their thoughts about dying may be limited by their stage of conceptual maturation, by overwhelming anxiety, or even by their desire to protect others from knowing these concerns. There often develops what has been termed by Glaser and Strauss (1965) a game of *"mutual pretense."* When this occurs, terminally ill children and those in their environment adhere to safe topics and above all avoid discussions of the future.

Games of mutual pretense are likely to be harmful in the long run. (11)

Mutual pretense usually is based upon a desire on all sides to be protective. On the part of the adults, it usually stems from the rationalization that young children do not have adequate coping mechanisms. Often, this rationale is based upon adult projections of uncomfortable and helpless feelings onto the child. In other instances, it may result from denial by the parents, who in turn bolster any denial present in the child.

This deception tends to culminate in poor communication and uneasy feelings on all sides. Though it is intended to shield children from anxiety, pain, and frightening news, the strain of carrying on this charade encourages emotional withdrawal at an inopportune time. As children's illnesses progress, the likelihood of their discovery of the truth steadily increases. Consequently, loss of trust and credibility between deceived children and their caretakers may occur just when these are most crucial.

CASE ILLUSTRATION

An 8-year-old boy was readmitted to the hospital when his bone cancer recurred at multiple sites only months after aggressive initial therapy. His parents understood the dire implications of his condition, but it was not clear whether he did. His pediatrician approached the issue starting with a casual conversation in which she sat on his bed and asked him what he thought was going on. He paled, but replied that the cancer had come back. She then inquired as to what he thought was going to happen. He replied that he didn't know, and that he couldn't think about that right now. She respected his wishes, and after assuring him that she wouldn't mind talking to him about this when he wanted to, switched the topic to the plans for the present visit. Over the next few weeks, all gradually acknowledged that he was dying, and he participated in making some realistic choices regarding the transition from aggressive to supportive therapy.

If honest and open communication is generally preferable to paternalistic protection, how should this difficult information best be shared with the dying child? Because of the differences in rate of development among children, our guiding principle is to *avoid lying*. Additionally, we observe two other principles: let the child tell you how much to say at any particular moment, and tailor what you say as closely as possible to your assessment of the child's conception of death.

To meet the goals implicit in the above guidelines, past methods by which terminally ill children have coped with crises, including the nature of the child's regression when placed under stress, must be explored. This can be done with parents in the absence of the child as well as with the child directly.

Clinicians must approach children sensitively and supportively. They must be careful to encourage each youngster to express and elaborate ideas and feelings concerning the current situation. The specific language used to express these central issues is of particular importance, in that it is likely to be most useful in future communication. It is vital, however, that the meanings of key terms be clearly elucidated before they are included in a mutual vocabulary.

If attempts to communicate with children through talk are unproductive, various nonverbal techniques are available. These include play therapy and interpretation by children of their own drawings (see Adams, 1982).

During these discussions, it is likely that clinicians will become aware of the nature of each child's concerns and how much that child wishes to know at any particular moment. In fact, if a child is truly comfortable with a questioner, any session that goes on too long or becomes too uncomfortable is likely to be ended rather concisely by the child. This is demonstrated in the first doctor–patient conversation in the last case illustration.

If children are comfortably accepted on the health care team, they usually take on a self-measured role in decision-making.

Once the above determinations are complete, it may be possible to ascertain the extent to which children can participate in decisions regarding the course of their medical care. If given the chance, children generally will take the lead in letting caretakers know the role they wish to have in the decision-making process. This will happen, however, only if everyone involved is comfortable in including sick children in the health care team. Children are likely to be acutely aware of the presence of anxiety in their caretakers and to shy away from discussion of sensitive issues when they sense that adults are uneasy.

It is also reassuring to know that children most often will protect themselves from finding out information or engaging in decisions when they feel unprepared to cope. Given a secure and astute professional who is sensitive to signals from the child, clarification of the appropriate approach to decision-making will be facilitated by gentle probing. Pressure is seldom in the best interest of the child. The key here, as we have noted in many other situations involving terminally ill care, is exploration of and responsiveness to the individual needs of each patient at any specific moment. Attempts to be prescriptive without the awareness obtained in this process are unlikely to eventuate in optimal care.

Family Reactions to the Dying Child

Parents have extreme reactions to the impending death of a child.

Although parental reactions to the impending death of a child vary widely with such circumstances as the child's age, the cause, and the suddenness of death, the feelings engendered ordinarily are extreme. Untimely death awakens most people's dread of dying before their life goals have been fulfilled, and prompts such diverse feelings as compassion, anguish, and guilt. When death is sudden, shock, numbness, anger, guilt, and anxiety are prominent. In instances where the terminal illness is extended, anticipatory grief work frequently takes place. This process is usually characterized by alternating feelings of hope and despair. Anticipatory grief also is likely to be accompanied at times by significant anxiety, anger, and guilt. As parents gradually withdraw their emotional attachment, they often begin to accept that death is inevitable.

Parents should be informed of the gravity of the situation as soon as the diagnosis is certain.

Clinicians usually can best facilitate effective resolution of these painful processes by communicating the grave nature of the situation as soon as the diagnosis is certain. As with adults, this should be accomplished in a setting as conducive as possible to support of emotional responses that are bound to arise in the face of life-threatening illness. Initially, explanations should be offered in as much detail as is necessary to convey the basics. The facts leading to the diagnosis should be presented in a clear and straightforward manner. The issue of the cause of the illness should be addressed as soon as possible to deal with the guilt feelings that parents usually have. The communication skills outlined throughout this book may promote clarity of interchange about these crucial issues. Within realistic limits, clinicians should help parents to maintain hope for a positive outcome.

As reality permits, professionals should help parents to maintain hope.

These steps are particularly important during the early stages of diagnosis and treatment in order to form a caretaking alliance between professionals and parents in support of the child.

As time passes, specific attention should be directed toward assisting parents in dealing with their anger, assuaging their guilt, and alleviating their anxieties. Open discussion of these emotions, including direct questioning as to their existence, is the key to supporting family members during this trying period. These feelings may be even more exaggerated when a child dies unexpectedly, and hence must be addressed with some urgency. Clinicians should strive to maintain close, supportive contact with families, guided by the limits set by parents. In this framework, professionals can help parents to manage their reactions optimally.

Clinicians' Reactions

Clinicians have strong feelings that may impact on their care of dying children.

The role of clinicians includes anticipation of as well as direct coping with the specific reactions of family members. This extremely difficult task is likely to be complicated by the feelings of frustration, anger, and guilt awakened in health care professionals. Such emotions are likely to be even more prominent when one works with dying children than in adult terminal care settings. We have suggested a number of techniques for dealing with these reactions in previous chapters. It is worth emphasizing that the greater the degree of self-awareness and integration of the feelings of professionals, the better prepared they will be to provide optimal care and support. This is particularly true as regards mastery of the common overwhelming sense of helplessness that assaults those who must watch the life of a child melt away in spite of their efforts.

As a rule of thumb, clinicians should maintain honest and supportive working relationships with youngsters and their parents when guiding them through this period. But exactly what professionals should say, and in what manner, must be highly individualized. As we have stated, the child's wishes and level of understanding are important. In addition, the wishes of and psychodynamics within each family contribute strongly to their style of communication and problem solving.

An important limiting factor in the closeness of the relationship with child and family is the degree of anxiety experienced by the professional when difficult issues must be discussed. This anxiety may be substantial, and may persist even after a few contacts. It is then incumbent on the clinician to seek resolution for this unease before it further jeopardizes relationships upon which optimal care depends.

When to consult.

We advise that professionals refrain from emotional discussions with family members until these feelings can be worked through with a colleague or consultant.

Effect of Children's Deaths on Families

After a child's death, bereaved families need substantial support. (6)

Following the death of a child, the emotions of sadness, anger, and anxiety are likely to persist in the survivors for varying periods of time. Clearly, family members need continuing support as they deal with their conviction that life has been fundamentally unfair, and that only someone who has also lost a child could possibly understand. They feel alone, alienated, and, frequently, fearful regarding their future. It is during this period that emotional support and eventual gentle channeling back into the mainstream of life may be of great assistance.

More often than not, however, bereaved parents tend to live in the past rather than turning to the future. By placing blame on each other, they may accentuate the negative feelings that they already have.

The common result of this is *family breakup*, which constitutes an appallingly common aftereffect of the death of a child. Kaplan et al (1976) found in the case of deaths of leukemic children, almost 90% of families evidenced severe emotional pathology. Another unhealthy reaction is to bring a *replacement* child into the family. The burden placed on the new child almost from birth is not likely to contribute to healthy psychological development.

One way clinicians can help to prevent grief pathology, family disruptions, and similar adverse reactions is to assist family members to communicate openly with each other. The ability to share what is going on within the family circle has been shown by Kaplan (1976) to predict significantly families who are likely to weather this storm while remaining relatively intact. Professionals can play an important modeling role in this regard, listening attentively, providing support at appropriate intervals, and even sharing their own feelings when this seems the right thing to do. Telephoning families at times when they may be particularly vulnerable, such as anniversaries, birthdays, and holidays, frequently provides much needed reassurance.

Siblings of dying children should be kept informed, and often need specific reassurances that they are not responsible for the death.

When a dying child has siblings, clinicians should be aware that these children are particularly vulnerable. Generally, brothers and sisters should be included in information about and care of their dying sibling to a degree indicated in private conversation with them. Above all, they need specific support and reassurance that any previous hostile thoughts and feelings toward their sibling were not magically responsible for the illness. Issues of overprotection and favoritism are likely to be prominent, and should be inquired after in private conversations with each family member in as gentle a manner as possible.

When a child has died, the family must adapt to a new reality.

After a child has died, families engage in various dynamics with surviving siblings. The effects of the death can include (a) a *haunted* child who is reacting to a conspiracy of silence and guilt, (b) a *bound* child who is overprotected by parents who feel the preciousness of surviving children, and (c) a *resurrected* child who plays the role of substitute for the lost child. These are succinctly described by Krell and Rabkin (1979). Such untoward effects may be mitigated by management techniques described throughout this chapter.

Children's Reactions to the Deaths of Others

Developmental Correlations

At any stage of development, children tend to regress when their caretakers become ill or die.

The reactions of children to the death of another depends largely upon their cognitive maturation, similarly to their response to their own approaching death. In the period prior to their development of the ability to grasp abstract concepts, they may have special difficulty coping with serious parental illness and death. Under such circumstances, children are likely to regress to more primitive coping mechanisms characteristic of an earlier stage of development. This may be true even in adolescents, whose capacity for abstract thinking is likely to be fully developed: the ability to think as an adult does not imply an adult level of differentiation from parents. When dealing with children about the deaths of their parents, clinicians must take into account both their baseline capacity for conceptual thought and their present degree of emotional regression.

Specific Reactions to Approaching Parental Death

Children whose parents are dying usually fear abandonment.

The primordial fear of abandonment will be present and potentially prominent in a child of any age whose parent becomes ill. This reaction to the loss of the attention of the ill parent demands prompt resolution, especially when other caretakers are not present to ease the deprivation of usual sources of emotional and physical nurturance. Strategies for promoting reassurance must be geared to the stage of maturation of the child in question. Initially, there should be reassurance that the ill parent is *somewhere*. This may entail a visit to the hospital and an explanation, at an appropriate level of complexity, of the gist of what is going on. It also should include acknowledging and sharing, within the child's ability, of the feelings generated by the parental illness. When feasible, a known and trusted temporary caretaker should be introduced into the situation as early as possible, if the remaining parent is absent or otherwise unable to provide the extra nurturance that the child needs.

Children frequently feel responsible and guilty when parents become ill.

In cases of serious parental illness, children usually experience extreme stress. Particularly when the illness is chronic, the child's amplified sense of powerlessness often engenders strong feelings of *guilt*. These feelings are particularly prominent during developmental stages when fears of retaliation for intense aggressive or sexual impulses toward parents ordinarily are present. In any case, clinicians should be very supportive of the child. After a full exploration of guilty feelings, one should offer concrete reassurance that any such magical thoughts are unreal, although understandable. It is vital that clinicians be on the lookout for these emotions even when they are not overtly manifested. If left uncorrected, such beliefs frequently develop into pathology following the death of the parent.

Effects of Parental Death

Children have a wide variety of reactions to the death of a parent. These may range from behaving as though nothing unusual has happened to intensely displaying emotions. As we have noted, some amount of regressive behavior can be expected. Whatever the response, it is vital for caretakers to deal nonjudgmentally with the child's behavior, questions, and perceptions. Further, they should pay specific attention to clear reassurance that loving warmth will be continued. Both may be difficult because of the intense feelings of family members and the tumult that often surrounds a death.

Including children in mourning is an important preventive measure.

The bereaved child is likely to experience more relief than discomfort from participating in the family's sorrow as well as its happiness. The greatest fear arising in children following a death is that the remainder of the family may abandon them too. Including children in the family mourning process communicates that they are valued enough to be part of this difficult family transition. Adults and children should cry together if possible. Mutual silence (to a point) also is acceptable. Much has been made of the need to protect children from uncontrolled displays of emotion. In fact, any effects on children of witnessing strong expressions of emotion are not likely to be adverse if stable adults are present, or if such displays are their cultural norm. Children who express the wish should be given the opportunity to participate in family death ceremonials.

It is vital to be alert to any weakening in the child's remaining support system.

Thus, professionals can be of direct assistance to children coping with their own internal reactions; they also have the equally important role of shoring up the strength of the child's remaining support structure. This is especially true when the surviving parent becomes emotionally dependent on a child. In such cases, especially with adolescents, the healthy separation from a parent that marks transition into adulthood may be sabotaged. Because of the complexity of the dynamics in such situations, it is usually advisable to refer the family to a psychiatric consultant.

When to refer.

Explaining Parental Death to Children

As we have discussed, direct and open communication usually is preferable when discussing death with children. Concealing feelings, excluding children from participation in funerals, and concocting stories to explain the loss are examples of behaviors fraught with potential harm to the child. Rather than *sparing* children, these actions are likely to cause confusion, anxiety, and a sense of isolation and abandonment.

Explanations about the death of parents should be direct.

Therefore, explanations regarding parental death should be direct. Professionals should explain the cause of death in words appropriate to the child's level of development. It will be helpful to differentiate clearly between deaths related to accident, illness, homicide, and even suicide. Clear and accurate information about the irreversibility of the event, within the culturally determined parameters of the family's belief system, is vital. When children ask specific questions, as: *Has life stopped? Will the dead person return? What will happen to the body?,* professionals should answer specifically and honestly.

CASE ILLUSTRATION

The father of three young children died at home after a long struggle with testicular cancer. The family physician was called in to pronounce the death, and afterward was offered some coffee in the kitchen. The children were called in by the mother, and it became clear that she expected some help in explaining things to them. The doctor began by asking what they thought had happened, and the eldest (age 11 years) responded rather disdainfully, "Daddy is dead!" Each of the youngsters was then asked what that meant, and their responses opened a rather wide-ranging discussion of life and death. Because the family had strong religious beliefs about an afterlife, the doctor focused on the irreversibility of the death on a practical level only. The discussion ended with concrete reassurances that both the mother and the doctor would be there to take care of the children and to answer any more questions that they might have.

Specific, direct supportive measures and honest reassurances are helpful. (20)

It usually is helpful if these explanations are accompanied by overt verbal and physical assurances that there are survivors who will support and care for the child. Indeed, specific knowledge of which individuals will perform particular caretaking tasks, as well as of who would take over if the surviving parent left, is likely to be of great relief to the child. Extreme care must be taken to address the child's freedom from responsibility for the death, even when the issue is not raised directly by bereaved children. Furthermore, unless bereaved children are also dangerously ill, it may be very supportive to provide reassurance that they may expect a long and full life. This should be attempted only after the fears of the child regarding the future have been explored fully.

The overriding principle in dealing with children who experience parental death is that *whereas avoidance increases distress and anxiety, accurate information and direct clarification of childhood fantasies provides support.* The child's imagined monster in the dark almost invariably is more frightening than reality as explained by a supportive and loving caretaker. The bottom line is that, above all, *children need honesty!*

References

Adams, P. 1982. *Primer of Child Psychotherapy.* Boston: Little, Brown & Company.

Anthony, E. J. and Koupernik, C. 1973. *The Child and His Family: Impact of Disease and Death.* New York: John Wiley & Sons, Inc.

This is the second volume of the Yearbook of the International Association for Child Psychiatry and Allied Professions. Seventy of the first 100 pages deal with the effect of disease on children, and the remaining 400 examine death in the context of the child. The majority of this multiauthored (53 contributors) yearbook are from the United States, although there are a few authors from other countries. As a reference text for those dealing with ill or dying children, this book presents valuable, albeit dated, basic concepts.

Bowlby, J. 1977. *Attachment and Loss.* (Two volumes). New York: Basic Books, Inc., Publishers.

Childers, P. and Wimmer, M. 1971. The concept of death in early childhood. *Child Devel.* 42:1299–1301.

Glaser, B. G. and Strauss, A. L. 1965. *Awareness of Dying.* Chicago: Aldine Publishing Co.

Kaplan, D. M., Grobstein, R. and Smith, A. 1976. Predicting the impact of severe illness in families. *Health and Social Work* 1:72–82.

Krell, R. and Rabkin, L. 1979. The effects of sibling death on a surviving child: a family perspective. *Family Process* 18:471–477.

Rochlin, G. 1965. *Griefs and Discontents.* Boston: Little, Brown & Company.

Wolf, A. M. 1973. *Helping Your Children to Understand Death.* New York: Child Study Press.

This tiny (less than 65 pages), reasonably priced paperback straightforwardly addresses frequently asked questions concerning death. The author's commonsense approach is based on sound theoretical constructs, and can be useful to most adults in discussing death with children. For professionals and parents both, this book is worthwhile reading.

11 Suicide

Overview

Self-inflicted death probably has occurred as long as there have been thinking humans. Cultural attitudes toward suicide and the methods employed in committing the act, however, have varied widely through the ages. Today, suicide is regarded under most circumstances as a stigmatic act that insults humanity.

In this chapter we examine suicide, a phenomenon accounting for over 25,000 deaths annually in the United States. We present major risk factors, including certain demographic characteristics, alienation from social supports, tendency to direct aggression inward, and severe depression. Later we discuss some modes of useful intervention. We end by examining the nature and management of the emotional responses of survivors.

Demographic Factors

Extent of the Problem

In spite of the current cultural antipathy to suicide, more than 100,000 Americans attempt to take their own lives annually. The fact that at least one-quarter of them do so successfully points up the magnitude of the suicide problem in this country.

Suicide is self-inflicted and self-intentioned death.

We shall look upon suicide as *self-inflicted and self-intentioned death.* While willfulness always is present to some degree by definition, clearly some suicides are less deliberate than others. The many complexities and subtleties characterizing suicidal events make it difficult to determine their incidence and the risk factors that contribute to them. Such information is central to the development of effective strategies for professional intervention both before and after an attempt at self-murder.

Acute suicide probably is the fourth leading cause of death in the United States.

As we point out in Chapter 15, reported suicides account for some 25,000 deaths in the United States each year. This figure must be interpreted in light of the social and religious stigmata attached to the act of killing oneself, as well as of the difficulty in assessing the presence or absence of intent. Given these factors, the actual number of suicides in this country usually is estimated to be at least twice the official figure (Farberow et al. 1977). Thus, suicide may constitute the fourth leading cause of death in the United States.

Self-destructive behavior probably is the third leading cause of death in America.

It is important to remember that these figures reflect only *acute* suicides, or direct consequences of specific and identifiable individual acts. There are a large variety of methods available for *chronic* or *slow* suicide. These include alcoholism, drug abuse, and conscious refusal to cooperate with life-saving medical regimens as, for example, in patients with diabetes or hypertension. Further, there are even less well defined types of self-destructive behavior ranging from reckless driving to cigarette smoking that may reflect unconscious or partially conscious suicidal urges. Although this sort of suicide would be difficult to include in the above statistics, self-destructive behavior of all sorts probably ranks as the third leading cause of death in America, secondary to only cardiovascular disease and cancer.

Historically, the suicide rate in the United States has varied widely since 1900, when it was 10.2 per 100,000 (as opposed to the 1979 rate of 11.7).* There were peaks of 16.2 during World War I and 17.4 after the stock market crash of 1929. Since World War II, the rate has fluctuated between 10 and 13, with some inverse correlation to economic fortunes.

The methods employed for successful suicides also vary considerably. In 1975, firearms accounted for 55% of self-murders, followed

*Note: all subsequent statistics in this Chapter are from Frederick (1978), except when otherwise indicated.

Firearms are used in over one-half of self-murders in America, in sharp contrast to the rest of the world.

by ingestions (14%), and hanging or strangulation (13%). Poisoning by gases comprised 10%, followed by jumping (3%), drowning (2%), and cutting or piercing (1%). The inadequacy of these figures is demonstrated by the absence of motor vehicle suicides; many experts estimate that at least 20% of single vehicle fatalities are suicides. The percentage of successful suicides employing firearms has increased during this century in proportion to the availability of guns. This is in sharp contrast to the rest of the world, where guns generally are less available and suicides by gunshot are relatively rare.

Internationally, there seems to be a *suicide belt* of countries including the Scandinavian nations, West Germany, Switzerland, Austria, Eastern Europe, and Japan. Although there is some controversy over accuracy of reporting, these lands have an average official suicide rate of at least twice that in the United States, where the rate is in the midrange of countries. Spain and Italy have the lowest suicide rates internationally, at less than 10 per 100,000 population. Various explanations have been invoked to account for these differences, including religion, climate, social norms and pressures, and rate of cultural change.

Specific Correlates

Male suicide attempts are about ten times as lethal as those of females.

Males of all ages are about three times as likely as females to succeed in taking their own lives. Women, however, are about three times as likely as men to make a suicide attempt. The striking conclusion from these figures is that male suicide attempts are about a full order of magnitude more lethal than those of women. Another interesting correlation with gender is that since 1900 the suicide rate among women has fluctuated far less than that among men. The difference between the highest and lowest annual rates over this period is about 4 per 100,000 for women, as opposed to 15 per 100,000 for men. Finally, there is a clear sex difference in methods. In 1975, 82% of suicides employing firearms, 74% using cutting or piercing, and 62% from jumping occurred among men. On the other hand, 88% of suicides by ingestion occurred among women.

There has been a dramatic increase in suicide among the young.

Age and suicide also are strongly correlated (Figure 11-1). Until the mid-1950s, there seemed to be a relatively linear increase in rate of suicides from the age of 10 to about 60 years, after which point the rate remained fairly constant. By 1975, however, a disturbing trend among the young was established, with a drastic increase in reported suicides among those aged 10 to 24 years. Of particular concern among males 20 to 24 years old is a rate increase from under 10 per 100,000 in 1955 to nearly 30 in 1975, with a parallel jump for females in the same age group. The prevalence of suicide among the elderly is underscored by the fact that 25% of all suicides occur in those over 65, although this group makes up only 10% of the population.

The elderly still are the most likely to commit suicide.

Figure 11-1:   Age-Specific Suicide Rates in the United States for 1955, 1965, and 1975

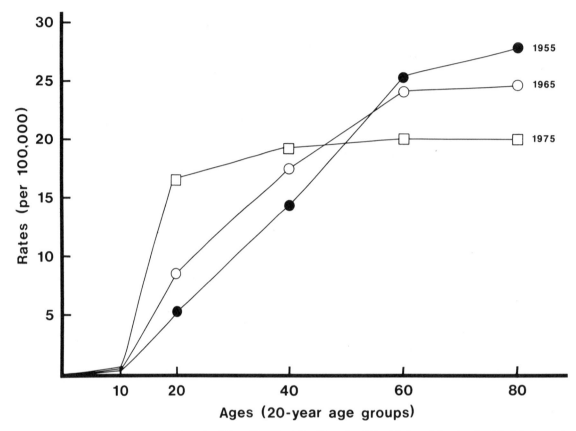

From the Mortality Statistics Branch of the National Center for Health Statistics.

Excepting Native Americans, whites are twice as likely as nonwhites to suicide.

In general, white Americans are about twice as likely as nonwhites to take their own lives. There are, however, some significant exceptions to this finding. For example, the suicide rate among Native Americans is about twice that for the nation overall, and among those aged 15 to 24 years it is almost four times that for this age group nationally. These figures parallel a difference of a factor of two to five in the death rate by alcoholic cirrhosis among Native Americans as compared with the national average. There is a definite trend over the past decade for other nonwhite groups to move fairly rapidly toward the higher suicide rate of the white population.

Persons who have never been married show a suicide rate double the national average, and slightly lower than the 24 per 100,000 rate

Divorced men are six times as likely to kill themselves as age-matched cohorts.

Health care professionals are at greater risk of suicide than the general population.

Those who commit suicide are likely to have seen a doctor within their last month.

for those who have been widowed. In 1975, divorced women committed suicide at a rate of 18 per 100,000, whereas divorced men killed themselves at an astonishing clip of 69 per 100,000, or about six times the national average. Correlations to occupation are less clearly significant, but health care professionals commit suicide at somewhat less than twice the national rate, with psychiatrists being at greatest risk.

Seventy percent of suicide victims were found by Dorpat et al. (1968) to have an active (usually chronic) illness at death. The authors found this to be a contributing factor to the suicide in 41% of the total. Loss of function or mobility, disfigurement, and pain were found to contribute significantly in many cases, as did secondary effects of illness including problems with jobs and relationships. Of successful suicides, 7% saw a doctor on the day of their attempt, another 23% within a week, and a further 27% within 30 days. This yields a total of over 50% of suicides who sought medical help in the last month of their lives. These visits usually were related to the somatic symptoms of depression, and a large percentage of the deaths resulted from overdose of prescribed medication.

Evaluation of Suicide Risk

Risk Profile

Demographic information points toward a suicide profile. (14) See Table 11-1.

The psychosocial context is vital in assessing suicide risk.

The demographic correlations we have presented point to a profile of an individual who is more likely to commit suicide. As we have outlined in Table 11-1, an older (greater than 45 years), white, widowed (or divorced or separated), unemployed (or retired) male in poor health falls into the category of highest risk. Although such information is useful in understanding suicidal risk in the population at large, certainly only a small percentage of those fitting this description actually commit suicide. Further, many of those at low risk still kill themselves.

Clearly, in evaluating suicide risk we must also consider its psychosocial framework, in terms of the existing emotional, social, and behavioral contexts (see Table 11-1). Thus, when we are faced with individuals who feel worthless, helpless, and hopeless, who find life meaningless, and who feel powerless to do anything about it, we must be alert to the risk of suicide. If such persons are living alone, have had a recent loss, and are not integrated into any social group, concern should rise even higher. If inwardly aggressive behaviors such as alcoholism and prior suicide attempts are present, especially if previous attempts were of high lethality or involved a suicide note, investigation of suicidal potential becomes even more urgent.

Table 11-1   High Risk Factors for Suicide: This table highlights the risk factors for suicide. The bottom line represents a summation of the factors in each category.

Demographic Data	Social Context	Behavioral Context	Emotional Context
• Gender: male • Age: over 45 years • Race: white • Marital status: single widowed divorced separated • Occupation: unemployed • Health: poor	• Not integrated into social group • Living alone • Recent loss	• Alcoholism • Prior suicide attempt of high lethality • Suicide note	• Helplessness • Hopelessness • Meaninglessness • Worthlessness • Impotence
Individual characteristics	*Alienated from social supports*	*Directs aggression inward*	*Depressed*

Young Adults and Teenagers

Outwardly aggressive behavior may be a prelude to suicide in teenagers.

A special word is in order about young adults and teenagers of both sexes. These groups have shown a recent dramatic threefold increase in suicide rates. Many of these young persons display evidence of outwardly directed aggression before their deaths. Their behaviors include hostile, assaultive, and antisocial activity, as well as sexual promiscuity and unusually serious risk-taking. Such acts may represent behaviors aimed at countering an underlying depression, or attempts to seek a social support system. It could be that when such activities fail to generate a sense of belonging, aggression turns inward in the form of self-murder.

Clinical Assessment

Many depressed persons seek help through suicidal behavior.

The first step in assessing suicidal risk is knowing what kinds of information are relevant, as summarized above. However, the meaning of such material in any individual case must be evaluated thoroughly during a detailed clinical examination. Professionals must bear in mind that suicide threats and attempts frequently are a patient's way of asking for help.

All individuals who express suicidal thoughts must be taken seriously, whether or not they rate highly with respect to the outlined risk factors. Certainly, most people who threaten suicide do not attempt it. On the other hand, about 80% of those who make an attempt have made such remarks. If patients express suicidal thoughts ruminatively, and if they have made actual plans or preparations for death, immediate intervention is called for. Professionals also should be aware that persons in constant pain and those who believe they have incurable illnesses frequently consider suicide as a means of escape from suffering.

On a more impulsive level, individuals who are in situations of extreme frustration or disappointment may be moved to seek this route of release as well. Examples of the former are persons, particularly among the elderly, who take significant amounts of medication and whose medical prognoses are poor. Anorexia or marked reduction in the normal activities of life in such individuals should alert professionals to investigate the potential for suicide. The same is true of younger people who become overly concerned about someone else's death or who voice exaggerated disappointment about their failures in life. Clinicians should ask such persons directly if they sometimes feel that life is just not worth living. This sort of inquiry can open the door to revelation of a serious risk.

Direct inquiry about suicidal intention may stem a suicidal tide.

Intervention

Investigation as Intervention

A supportive, concerned, and reassuring stance becomes a vital therapeutic ingredient.

The process of assessing suicide risk has the potential of being a therapeutic intervention in itself. Alternatively, a poorly performed investigation may add to a troubled person's sense of guilt, and may even confirm his or her feelings that no one really understands or cares. Thus, it is particularly important, both while taking the initial history and during subsequent examination, that clinicians take positive steps to engender a therapeutic alliance with the patient (see Chapter 3).

It is vital that professionals assume a supportive, concerned, and reassuring stance. Nonverbal cues from patients such as sad or immobile facial expressions, or motor retardation or agitation, are ominous hints of the possible presence of suicidal thoughts. If patients respond to the clinician's encouragements to speak with slow, quiet, monotonous answers, suspicions should be further alerted.

It is best to direct questions toward identifying the nature and source of the difficulty that prompted the individual to seek medical attention. Patients of primary care physicians often display their distress in somatic symptoms, frequently of a neurovegetative nature.

Anorexia, insomnia with early awakening, and fatigue or listlessness are common manifestations of underlying depression, even in the absence of an overtly sad mood. Whether or not these symptoms are associated with loss of interest in work, sex, or other previously pleasurable activities, they should alert professionals to the risk of suicide.

Facilitating Discussion

Suspicions concerning suicide should be investigated rapidly.

If clinicians suspect suicidal potential, they should test the validity of their concern as early as possible. At the first appropriate moment in the course of the interaction, patients should be asked directly if they have thoughts of suicide. The specific words employed are not as important as the manner of asking, which must be concerned, supportive, and nonaccusatory. Some professionals feel comfortable inquiring directly whether their patients have now or in the past experienced any thought of doing away with themselves. Others prefer to approach the issue in stages, beginning with the comment, "You appear troubled. Can you tell me about it?" This can be followed with questions such as, "Has it ever been so bad that you have felt like hurting yourself?", or, "Have you ever felt so troubled that you felt like ending it all?"

Invitations to talk about suicidal intent can reassure patients.

Regardless of the words employed, invitations to talk about one's self-destructive impulses frequently are reassuring. They demonstrate that the clinician is taking the individual seriously and is trying to understand the latter's feelings in the current crisis. Subsequent questioning can be directed toward ascertaining the origins of these frightening emotions. Clinicians must walk a careful path, avoiding glib reassurances based upon inadequate data while stating supportively that, with appropriate help, the troubled person can feel differently in the future. Finally, there is absolutely no evidence to support the popular misconception that an inquiry about suicide may "put ideas into someone's head" when they are not already present.

Often, after a careful evaluation, including assessment of the nature of the precipitating crisis and the social, behavioral, and emotional contexts, professionals may conclude that the risk of suicide is low. If clinicians form therapeutic alliances with their patients to address the problem, they can take various directly supportive measures to aid the suicidal person. Attempts at resolution of the acute stress may include open discussion with patients and their key supporting figures, and gradual evolution of appropriate environmental changes. If primary care physicians feel unable or unwilling to work through these issues with patients, referral should be made to other suitable professionals.

When to refer.

Patients at High Risk

Patients at high risk should be referred for psychotherapy.

If clinicians assess that significant suicide risk is present, *psychiatric referral should be made.* Individuals with active suicide potential, particularly if under the influence of alcohol or drugs, must be kept under close watch until transfer of care is complete.

After psychiatric referral, primary care physicians should follow through as part of a continuing support system. An important function for them at this stage is to assist family and friends of potentially suicidal patients in improving their interpersonal environment and understanding. Clinicians should be open about the nature of suicide, direct concerning the warning signs, and candid as to the importance of loving support. Although compassion and love can reduce the risk of self-destruction, they are inadequate tools to combat it unless reinforced with adequate information about and understanding of suicide.

Reactions of Survivors

Emotional Responses

Survivor–victims often experience intensely ambivalent feelings toward the deceased.

The term *"survivor–victim"* frequently is applied to those left behind after a suicide. This is often appropriate, because the bereaved in such cases are deeply wounded by the violent and personal final statement of a suicide. Those who remain frequently voice self-blame for either causing or failing to prevent the final act. Remorse may be coupled with intense ambivalence reflected in feelings of rage toward the dead person. This often is accentuated when the dead person had a history of suicide threats or attempts. Survivors may feel both a sense of relief and strong emotions of anger and recrimination over having been subjected to such misery.

Partly as a result of the shame and anger generated by a self-murder, families are likely to hide the fact that suicide was the cause of death. This may be aided by sympathetic physicians whose sense of duty to report an accurate cause of death is compromised by ambivalent feelings similar to those of the family. Anyone in the interpersonal constellation of a suicide will find it difficult to escape some sense of responsibility and failure.

Grief pathology is likely to be present.

The long-term emotional impact of suicide can be devastating to survivor–victims. Too often, they are not able to complete the grieving process. Untoward sequelae include a characteristic unremitting depression with ongoing self-blame, or the inward direction of the anger described above. The latter may be manifested by stress-related medical complaints or by some variety of self-destructive behavior ranging from trivial actions to suicide itself.

Postvention

Postvention is the care of the survivor–victims.

About a decade ago, Shneidman (1971) introduced the term *"postvention"* for the management and care of the aftereffects of a suicide attempt, whether or not it succeeded. Any overt act of self-destruction calls into question our presumed love of life and fear of death. It also brings home the distressing fact that one can die by one's own hand. The ensuing existential crisis is likely to accentuate even further the feelings of guilt and anger engendered in the survivor–victims.

The primary immediate task in postvention is management of the survivor–victim's acute grief, which is likely to be complicated by extreme ambivalence. The latter is manifested by simultaneous or alternating conflicted feelings, or by powerful expressions of guilt and anger. The general principles for care in these settings are similar to those outlined above for management of grief (see Chapter 9). Early followup discussions with key survivor–victims are advisable. Frequently, an office visit or telephone call timed to coincide with the anniversary date of the suicide can be helpful. Clinicians should take pains to anticipate complications in the completion of the grief process, which are more likely to arise in this setting. Professionals should make a prompt referral to a psychiatrist if they detect signs pointing toward serious grief pathology.

When to refer.

Professionals whose patients have committed suicide encounter problems in helping survivors.

Professionals whose patients have committed suicide are more likely to experience guilt, anger, and generalized distress added to their personal sense of loss than they are when a patient dies by another cause. This frequently has an adverse effect on the clinician's ability to be of assistance to other survivor–victims. As a rule, we recommend that professionals discuss their feelings with experienced and sympathetic colleagues or knowledgeable friends. This chance to ventilate usually provides sufficient resolution for clinicians to resume adequate performance of caretaking tasks. If feelings of rage and depression persist, consultation with an experienced counselor may be helpful.

Postvention is crucial in suicide attempts of the young.

Once again, we call special attention to the suicide of an adolescent or young adult. The effects on survivor–victims are likely to be very marked, and the need for active postvention is nearly universal. Most readily apparent is the bewilderment of the key survivors, especially when the suicide is that of a college student (a greatly overrepresented group). Parents, siblings, and other relatives often show an inability to reconcile the discrepancy between youth, intelligence, opportunity, and the act of self-murder. This problem is likely to further accentuate the guilt and anger of the survivor–victims. They may require extra attention and sensitive, understanding support from professionals if they are to manage the situation satisfactorily.

References

Dorpat, T. L., Anderson, W. F., and Ripley, H. S. "The relationship of physical illness to suicide." In Resnick, H. L. ed. 1968. *Suicidal Behavior*. Boston: Little, Brown, & Co. p 209–219.

Farberow, N. L., MacKinnon, D. R., and Nelson, F. L. 1977. Suicide: who's counting? *Public Health Reports* 92:223–232.

Frederick, C. J. 1978. Current trends in suicidal behavior in the United States. *Am. J. Psychotherapy* 32:172–200.

Hatton, C. L., Valente, S. M., and Reink, R. eds. 1977. *Suicide Assessment and Intervention*. New York: Appleton-Century-Crofts.

Shneidman labels this work as the *Suicidology Desk Reference* in his foreword, although we dispute this assessment. Rather, this volume is a basic practical text on diagnostic techniques and assessment of findings, with some helpful interventions. Until a future edition comes along that is better organized as a practical desk reference, this book will serve as a very good basic text for those learning to deal with suicidal persons.

Shneidman, E. and Farberow, N. eds. 1957. *Clues to Suicide*. New York: McGraw-Hill Books, Inc.

A seminal book, comparable in suicidology to Durkheim's early treatise. It remains important largely for historical reasons. It is well written, with many scholarly authors, several of whom pioneered the suicide prevention movement. The book remains interesting and thought provoking.

Shneidman, E. 1971. Prevention, intervention, and postvention of suicide. *Ann. Intern. Med.* 75:453–458.

Shneidman, E. ed. 1976. *Suicidology: Contemporary Developments*. New York: Grune & Stratton, Inc.

This work is essentially a 20-year update and elaboration (largely by different authors) of the classic *Clues to Suicide*. Concepts are reconsidered in light of more recently developed methods and findings. Perspective is added by preceding each chapter with historical excerpts dating as far back as the seventeenth century. Nearly 600 pages long, this book is an excellent current compendium of suicidology. Unfortunately, it contains few practical guidelines for clinicians.

12 The Hospice

Overview

Although its institutional roots in Europe extend back to about the fifth century in the form of way stations for ill, dying, or merely roadworn and weary pilgrims, the modern hospice movement is a product of this century. St. Christopher's Hospice in Sydenham, England represents the immediate forerunner of today's hospices in this country, and is now almost 20 years old. In a look at the contemporary British scene, Hinton (1979) concluded that persons dying in hospices were less depressed and anxious than a similar sample dying on acute hospital wards.

Only in the last decade has hospice care become a major factor in American medicine. Its principal function is to help patients die in a manner closer to what they would choose—with a degree of comfort and dignity. In this chapter, we discuss the characteristics of an operational hospice that fulfills these functions and meets related needs of families and hospice staff members as well.

Development of a Sensible Alternative for Terminal Care

The Hospice Explosion

In the mid 1970's, Gonda (coauthor of this book) undertook an informal survey to ascertain the importance of the hospice concept to a group of colleagues interested in the care of the dying. His question to them was: "If you were writing a 100-page book on death and dying, how many pages would you devote to the hospice?" Answers ranged from "a paragraph or two" (from an oncologist) to "over 50 pages" (from a member of the board of directors of a developing hospice). Perhaps it should not have been surprising that several physicians queried were unaware of what the word "hospice" meant.

Only three years later, the situation had changed significantly. Hospices, practically unheard of in this country a few years earlier, had become a fast growing phenomenon. The National Hospice Organization held its first annual meeting in 1978. In late 1979, Sylvia Porter devoted five daily columns to the hospice in her syndicated series, *Your Money. The Hospice Story in California*, compiled by the Committee on Evolving Trends in Society of the California Medical Association in July, 1978, contained information about twelve developing hospices. The latest edition (August, 1980) listed over fifty operational programs. By the time this book is published, every state in America will have at least one functioning hospice, with a national total of over a thousand. Clearly, the hospice movement no longer can be considered a mere fad.

Reasons for the Growth of the Hospice Movement

The mainstream medical establishment is often ill-prepared to meet the needs of the dying. (15)

Why has the hospice movement shown this phenomenal growth? The histories of various hospices appear to have a common thread: hospices were founded to address unmet patient needs. Although the specifics vary between communities, in each instance an important motive for establishing a hospice was that some elements of terminal care were found wanting. Vital psychological counseling, spiritual support, social services, or provisions for respite care were missing or inadequate in conventional settings (see Chapter 14). Such shortcomings particularly affected people for whom physical recovery from a life-threatening illness no longer was a realistic goal (see Chapter 7).

By maintaining its diversity, the hospice has met disparate terminal care needs and has proven useful in many settings. Clearly, it deserves the community support that it has gathered during its formative stages. However, as with many institutions that have experi-

A diversity of forms enables hospices to meet disparate needs.

enced rapid growth, the potential for problems is ever present. It is notable that as of 1983, Medicare provides some payment for hospice services. Will a hospice bureaucracy develop? Will standardization reduce the effectiveness of this concept in meeting local needs, and result in a more impersonal institutional model? Will the profit motive prompt the commercial exploitation of patient needs? Will the majority of the dying, for whom an inpatient hospice may have some disadvantages, be forced by economic considerations to seek hospice care? Let us hope that the answers to these questions are *"No!"*, and that the hospice concept will continue to form a philosophical basis for a variety of humane alternatives to the care offered the dying by conventional institutions.

Characteristics of an Operational Hospice

Central Concepts of Hospice Care

Hospices are dedicated to the humanization of terminal care. (6)

The primary mission embodied in the hospice concept is *to assist patients and families to meet with dignity the burdens and trauma of dying.* To this end, patients are given the opportunity to live each remaining day in a manner as personally satisfying as can be achieved.

In order to reach these goals, patients are given as much *control* as they wish over their own destinies. Whenever feasible, *the patient's family serves as the primary support structure.* Members of the staff turn their technical skills from curative interventions toward palliation of physical symptoms, of psychosocial distress, and of spiritual anguish. The exercise of *compassion,* always a cornerstone of health care, takes on even greater importance here. In addition to direct services provided while the patient is alive, staff members help to arrange for support of family members during grief and mourning.

Any community which recognizes and is concerned over a lack of available support for the dying and their loved ones may develop an organized hospice care program. The specific form that a program takes, its criteria for admission, and the precise services provided will depend on the needs and resources present in the community.

Form of the Hospice

Hospices can coordinate various service agencies that contribute to the care of the dying. (16)

Most hospices are private, nonprofit organizations with community-based boards of directors and advisory committees, and both paid and volunteer staff representing many health care disciplines. The majority of hospices in this country offer predominantly home care, though institutional care may be provided in general hospitals, nursing homes, or free-standing, independent facilities. Often the hospice acts as a coordinator for other service agencies such as departments of social service, visiting nurse associations, and homemaking services. It is the combination of these and other equally vital offerings that can make someone's last days as comfortable, peaceful, and meaningful as possible.

Functional Elements of Hospice Care

Although there is no universal agreement as to what constitute the basic elements of hospice care, there is consensus that a well rounded hospice program should have at least the following functional characteristics:

1. The patient and family comprise the unit of care.
2. Home care services in collaboration with inpatient backup facilities are available and are coordinated by a central agency.
3. Care is provided by a multidisciplinary team with special expertise in symptom control, on which medical, nursing, social, chaplaincy, and volunteer services are represented.
4. Skills of the multidisciplinary group are available on a 24-hours-per-day, seven-days-per-week basis with provisions for on-call coverage.
5. Followup care for key loved ones extends through the mourning period.
6. Ongoing emotional support is provided for all hospice personnel on a systematic basis.

Hospice concepts can be successfully applied in almost every community. (5)

Even in relatively isolated areas, a physician working with a visiting nurse can organize home-based terminal care providing most, if not all, of the above elements. In such settings, hospice programs might consist of a consortium of well intentioned, well trained people—visiting nurses, social workers, volunteers, pastors, and physicians—who can meet the needs of patients and families.

Services to Patients, Families, and Staff

Admission Criteria

Typical criteria for admission to hospice care include the following. Potential patients must have a *terminal illness with a relatively short prognosis,* usually less than six months. This must be coupled with a perceived *need for and consent to hospice care* on the part of the patient, family, and attending physician. A family member or other responsible person must be *available to take care of the patient's basic needs at home*, or arrangements must be made for this coverage.

A pathway must be kept open between the cure system of the hospital and the care system of the hospice.

Less frequently seen criteria for admission are geographic accessibility and the requirement that all involved accept basically palliative care strategies. It is best to heed Saunders' (1978) admonition to keep an open pathway between "the cure system of the hospital and the care system of the hospice." This insures that no one becomes locked into either alternative.

An admission issue receiving much current attention is the financial failure of increasing numbers of hospices whose services were available regardless of ability to pay. There already is a serious question whether hospices can meet their patients' needs without significant volunteer involvement and private medical insurance reimbursement. It is argued that too much concern for reimbursement could well weaken public and volunteer support that is now enjoyed in abundance by the entire movement. Two major factors that could result in this weakening are the proliferation of a hospice bureaucracy and a new public perception of hospices as profit seeking institutions.

Meeting Patient Needs

A primary goal of hospice care includes *helping the dying to live as fully as they are able*. This aim can be achieved only if efforts are tailored to meet the needs and personality of each individual patient. It follows that the specific nature of assistance, and the context in which it is offered, varies considerably from case to case. There are, however, some broad needs that all patients will have in common, stemming from the great regularity with which certain traumas present themselves in this setting. These include physical symptoms, psychological distress, environmental problems, and spiritual anguish.

Relief of physical symptoms is central to hospice care. (13)

Terminal illnesses often are accompanied by untoward *physical symptoms* such as pain, lack of appetite, nausea, and shortness of breath. Other common physical complaints are associated with treatment procedures and medications, and with the patient's status of nutrition, elimination, hydration, and skin integrity. Because nearly one-half of dying patients complain of severe chronic pain during the course of their illness, adequate pain control is central to hospice care. Understanding the complexities of pain complaints and their interrelation with anxiety and depression is essential in the often demanding and poignant tasks involved in the care of the terminally ill. Specific suggestions about dealing with physical symptoms may be found in Chapter 6.

Hospices must be organized to address the psychological needs of their clients.

We have discussed general principles and specific techniques for dealing with *psychological distress* in the setting of life-threatening disease throughout this book. A few points, however, are worth underlining here. Psychological distress in the dying and their loved ones is to be anticipated on a number of counts. In addition to the existential despair they may feel on confronting death, specific physical and functional losses cause great damage to patients' self-esteem. The hospice care structure as we have outlined it above lends itself readily to addressing these issues. Supportive emotional counseling often is available from a variety of staff members, ranging from lay volunteers to physicians. Further, effective participation of the family in both inpatient and outpatient care plays a key role in addressing issues of separation, isolation, and abandonment.

Families are a key resource in addressing environmental problems.

In helping to accomplish the tasks of everyday living, families are once again the primary resource in many hospice programs. They are expected to engage heavily in such diverse *environmental support* tasks as shopping, cooking, housekeeping, caring for pets, visiting and sitting with patients, providing entertainment by reading and playing games, caring for children, and driving patients to appointments. Outside the hospice setting, family members must often perform these tasks without support. When a patient is enrolled in a hospice program, many of these services can be performed by trained volunteers on a respite basis. Further, skilled professionals often are available to the hospice team for consultation on legal, funeral, or other environmental problems that may interfere with everyone's peace of mind.

Volunteer clergy are vital in relieving the spiritual anguish of patients and families.

Spiritual anguish is as varied among patients and families as are their belief systems and religious practices. Spiritual support should be aimed to meet the expressed needs of patients enrolled in a hospice program as much as possible. Most hospices have volunteer clergy on their multidisciplinary care teams. When feasible, however, it is preferable to seek clergy known to the patient and family, and of the latter's own denomination. It is important that hospice staff not have any spiritual axe to grind with patients and families.

Meeting Family Needs

Families are as likely to be deeply disturbed as are patients.

As we have seen, patients and their families comprise the basic unit of hospice care. The nature of the support and the reactions to their illnesses received by patients from family members will have a profound impact on each terminally ill patient's response to care. Indeed, patient–family interactions during the dying process will be a primary determinant of how comfortable, peaceful, and meaningful the last days of the patient's life turn out to be.

During this period, the rest of the family can be as deeply disturbed by the events as the patient. As we have pointed out, among the most difficult tasks faced by family members in interacting with the one who is dying is that of dealing with their own emotions. At times, even giving patients an opportunity to say what they need to can be a most painful and difficult experience for other family members.

In what ways can hospices serve to help this passage through the crisis of coping with the dying and death of a loved one? Mainly, this is accomplished through (a) *education* aimed to simplify the tasks to be faced, (b) *respite care* to give the full-time caretakers some peaceful moments, and (c) *emotional support* throughout the period of dying and grieving.

Education includes learning as much as one desires about the terminal illness of a family member. Additionally, it should include practical advice and training in such elementary skills as bathing, dressing, feeding, turning, and administering medications. Hospices commonly offer these services to the loved ones with whom they cooperate in providing terminal care.

Respite care includes periodic relief for the family from the watchful attention related to everyday living. At times, respite care can be performed at home by volunteers or by paid personnel who come in to take on these routine but taxing jobs for brief periods. When this is not feasible, such relief can be obtained by bringing the patient into the inpatient arm of the hospice for care. Even a few hours off can work wonders in terms of restoring one's energy and ability to provide loving, supportive care.

Finally, *emotional support* is made continuously accessible to family members on request. This usually includes availability of a bereavement support program for a year or so following a death. Special attention is given to supportive assistance immediately after a death, including help with funeral arrangements if desired. This sort of outreach to survivors is provided by word of mouth before the death, and by cards, phone calls, and personal visits afterward.

Family needs are mainly met through education, respite care, and emotional support. (8)

Meeting Hospice Staff Needs

The stress faced by hospice staff members is a function of the intensity and constancy of traumatic emotions experienced in caring for the dying and their loved ones. As we discuss throughout this book, the responses to these demands are varied, but often manifest as anxiety, depression, and irritability. These reactions are understandable in the context of trauma occasioned by repeated loss, and by continual contact with sorrow and grief. Unfortunately, an additional factor often arises from the failure of the staff member's ordinary external emotional support system. That is, family and friends of terminal care clinicians are often reluctant and fearful to enter into discussions with them about the upsetting aspects of their hospice activity.

Systematic safeguards to relieve emotional pressures upon staff members are vital.

To maintain the equilibrium and performance levels of both paid and volunteer staff members, it is vital to provide several safeguards. Regularized continuing education, systematic personal supervision and feedback, frequent informal clinical conferences, and ongoing multidisciplinary support groups are mechanisms employed by many hospices to relieve emotional pressures. Some hospices also provide the opportunity for regular psychotherapeutic assistance for staff members who feel the need for more concentrated support. By making this a primary concern, well organized terminal care programs can avoid many problems arising from staff burnout, with its resultant high turnover rate and low morale.

References

California Medical Association Committee on Evolving Trends in Society. 1980. *The Hospice Story in California.* San Francisco: Sutter Press.

This book briefly describes over 50 hospices operating in California as of August, 1980. In addition to locations and key personnel, succinct data are presented concerning their various features. These include their background, structure, services provided, admission criteria and procedures, care plans, personnel, administrative policies, funding, evaluation activities, and future plans. A valuable document for those who intend to be involved with a hospice.

Cohen, K. P. 1979. *Hospice: Prescription for Terminal Care.* Germantown, Maryland: Aspen Systems.

A medically naive, otherwise down-to-earth book that considers the hospice care model within the framework of broader terminal care issues. There is some worthwhile nonmedical information for those seeking to establish a community-based hospice. For example, reimbursement methods, licensure requirements, relevant legislation, and potential roadblocks to the establishment of a hospice are discussed. A helpful glossary for the uninitiated contains about 100 terms. As far as clinical care is concerned, the book is a void, lacking in artful presentation and useful information.

Hinton, J. 1979. Comparison of places and policies for terminal care. *Lancet,* 2:29–32.

Saunders, C. ed. 1978. *The Management of Terminal Disease.* London: Edward Arnold.

Zimmerman, J. M. 1981. *Hospice: Complete Care for the Terminally Ill.* Baltimore, Maryland: Urban & Schwarzenburg, Inc.

This book is the best and most comprehensive clinically oriented account of hospice care to date. It is based pricipally on the Church Hospital hospice experience in Baltimore. The first third of the book describes hospice care. This is followed by an excellent chapter on practical medical measures in symptom control. Later chapters describe the hospice care team, outpatient hospice care, and the administration of a hospital-based program. A chapter entitled *Questions most commonly asked about hospice care* includes authoritative, straightforward, and understandable answers.

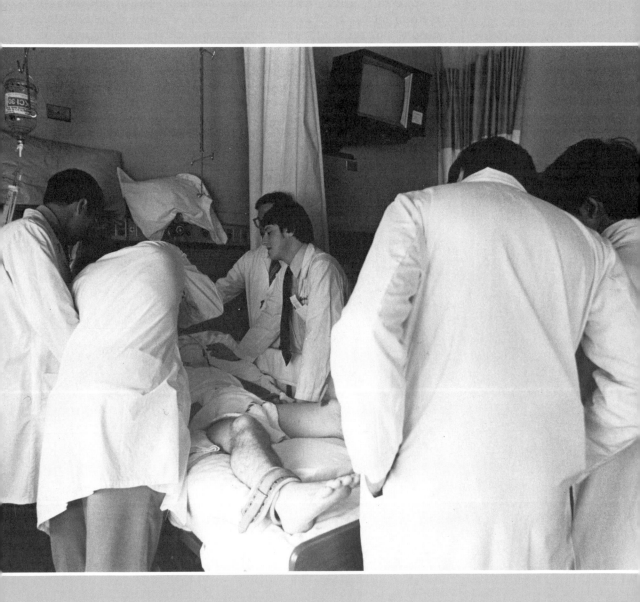

PART 5

Problems in the Care of the Terminally Ill

Problems in terminal care originate with the people involved and the environments in which they operate. The primary actors are dying patients, with a supporting cast of loved ones and health care professionals involved to varying degrees. Their stage is the modern health care system.

The medical profession has largely determined the structure and underlying scientific principles of the modern health care system; a system that has serious shortcomings as regards chronic and terminal care. In our exploration of the genesis of these problems, we have thus looked primarily at the field of medicine. In fact, many of the other health care professions may have evolved in response to the needs left unmet by medical doctors. As scientific and technical aspects of the newer health care callings increase, they too may fall heir to professional molding and practices that prepare physicians more to cure than to care.

The very presence of life-threatening illness works against a calm, supportive, low anxiety atmosphere even under the best of circumstances. Further complications arise from unrealistic expectations regarding the powers of scientific medicine. The frequently cold, impersonal settings of many hospitals figure strongly as well. Given these factors, it is not surprising that many untoward emotional reactions and interpersonal exchanges occur during the care of the dying.

In this section we explore some of the origins, nature, and negative consequences of problems in the management of terminal illness. Taken together, the two chapters that comprise this section aim to make explicit the need for this book.

13 Untoward Reactions During Terminal Care

Overview

We begin this chapter by outlining some parameters of ideal terminal care. Then we examine common untoward reactions arising from the experiences, expectations, practices, settings, roles, and relationships we will discuss in Chapter 14. Some of the feelings that commonly arise include anger, guilt, and emotional withdrawal. Important among the interpersonal responses often observed are avoidance, inappropriate persistence in efforts to cure, ineffective communication, and burnout. These sequelae frequently occur as a result of specific deficiencies in terminal care management. They also may derive from the tendency to equate the death of patients with personal failure. The presence of these phenomena commonly reinforces and amplifies the very problems from which they may have arisen. We conclude by looking at more remote negative consequences of poorly managed terminal disease.

Parameters of *Ideal* Terminal Care

Appropriate Death

Before we look at untoward reactions and their results in terminal care settings, it seems reasonable to examine some parameters of *ideal* care of the dying. Indeed, compelling humanitarian and ethical concerns alone require us to approximate goals toward which to aspire. This issue has been addressed succinctly and sensitively by Weisman (1972), who describes the conditions for what he characterizes as an *appropriate death*:

Someone who dies an appropriate death must be helped in the following ways: he should be relatively pain-free, his suffering reduced, and emotional and social impoverishments kept to a minimum. Within the limits of disability, he should operate on as high and effective a level as possible, even though only tokens of former fulfillments can be offered. He should also recognize and resolve residual conflicts, and satisfy whatever remaining wishes are consistent with his present plight and with his ego ideal. Finally, among his choices, he should be able to yield control to others in whom he has confidence. He also has the option of seeking or relinquishing key people.

As Weisman goes on to point out, few of us are likely to be fortunate enough to accomplish these goals in any aspect of our lives. This is particularly true for one for which we are so poorly schooled: death. We hope we can allow such ideals to inspire rather than daunt us. We emphasize the underlying values implied in this description. Most prominent among them is the *maintenance of human dignity*, and the avoidance of behaviors that would tend to diminish it. Next is *support of satisfying function*, on physical, emotional, and interpersonal levels. Finally, there is *caretaking that avoids arbitrary infantilization* by leaving the locus of *control* with patients to whatever degree they desire. It is vital to remember that these concepts are ideals toward which

Terminal care professionals should strive to maintain dignity, support satisfying function, and leave patients in control. (6, 12, 20)

professionals should strive, rather than goals that patients must achieve so that clinicians can congratulate themselves on another perfectly managed death.

Philosophical Considerations

Professionals should not expect to change lifelong patterns of coping and relating in terminal patients. (5)

It is unlikely that most terminal patients will achieve such an exemplary ending for their lives. In truth, the values reflected in one's manner of death usually mirror those characterized in one's way of living. This leads us to an important point that applies to all health care clinicians, regardless of how sensitive and skillful they may be. It is unreasonable to expect professional interventions easily to reverse deeply ingrained coping and communication patterns of terminally ill patients and their families. From our perspective, it would be presumptuous for anyone to assume that they could *teach* someone else how to die. For one thing, barring metaphysical considerations beyond the scope of this work, the experience required for an instructor's permit would seem to put the qualified teacher somewhat beyond our reach.

Dying can present an opportunity for change and growth.

This is not to say that health care professionals cannot have a significant influence on the quality of the experience of the dying and their loved ones; nor do we imply that the idea of death cannot be a positive and growth-promoting experience for both. As Yalom (1980) points out, the Chinese character for "crisis" is a combination of two characters: that for "danger," and that for "opportunity." Weisman (1972) also notes that the Greek word *kairos*, which he translates as "an auspicious moment that leads to a decisive change," also can be applied to the event of dying. Even if the meaning of our lives has remained obscure to us for decades, it is always possible to use the challenge presented by death as a motivation for change and growth. One of the cornerstones of modern existentialist philosophy is that we are best able to discover meaning in life when confronting the reality of death. One task for health care professionals in terminal care settings is to foster possibilities for patients and families to augment their lives' meaning. Clinicians should approach this without pressuring people to change if they do not desire to do so.

Common Untoward Reactions During Terminal Care

Anger

We are likely to become angry in situations in which we feel helpless, stressed, or powerless to achieve desired goals. According to The Oxford English Dictionary, the word "anger" has the same derivation as

Professionals must be aware of the permutations of anger felt by those intimately involved in a terminal illness. (17)

"anguish." Few situations in life are more likely to elicit feelings of anguish than participation in the process of dying. Feelings of anger are particularly prominent in all persons involved when dying is clearly a horrible experience for the patient.

Professionals who feel inadequate may tend to blame their patients unconsciously for the failure of medical measures to stave off the spread of disease. They rarely communicate such primitive and intellectually unacceptable feelings to patients directly. Nonetheless, we have at times seen these reactions revealed, for example, by a clinician's brusqueness or even overt hostility of manner or touch. More frequently, professionals manifest these reactions in more covert ways. Indirect expression of anger toward patients may be more apparent in what is not done, in the absence of gestures of warmth or caring. This, in turn, can compound the patient's sense of withdrawal and loss of human contact described later in this chapter.

Clinicians' anger at patients appears as the absence of warmth or caring gestures, or as derogatory humor in conversation with colleagues.

Quite commonly, a clinician's sense of resentment toward patients finds outlet in derogatory humorous asides. These interactions among professionals usually occur when patients are not present, and often constitute an acceptable and useful mechanism for blowing off steam in a harmless way. Nonetheless, this behavior should alert conscientious professionals to the possibility that their underlying anger also may be manifesting itself in less innocuous forms.

Patients and family members also commonly feel anger that arises from a sense of failure, either on their own parts or on the part of health care professionals. Their anger may be directed toward clinicians, family members, or patients themselves. No matter who is the object, such rage is often confusing and guilt-provoking to persons who experience it, particularly when they do not clearly understand its origins.

Patient and family frustration with a no win situation often is directed toward terminal care professionals. (13)

Often, anger reflecting frustration and dissatisfaction with a *no win* situation may be directed against professionals. In such cases, patients and families may feel guilty that they are not more supportive of those who are trying to help them. In turn, resultant demanding or passive-aggressive behavior on the part of patients or families may provoke an angry response from health care team members. Professionals generally feel extremely ill-at-ease with their reactive anger, and may be reluctant, even to themselves, to admit that they harbor such feelings. Basic societal prohibitions, particularly in mainstream American culture, operate to oppose air-clearing interchanges. The result can be an escalating series of covertly or even directly venomous exchanges that are most likely to result in further misery for all involved.

When the family's rage is directed toward patients, it may seem especially inappropriate in view of the traumas that already have been inflicted on the dying. Nonetheless, such anger is common in terminal care settings. It probably derives as much from loved ones' feelings of abandonment and helplessness as from actual behaviors and events in the course of dying.

Anger between patients and families is common and disturbing in terminal care settings.

Patients who are angry at family members may be bewildered by their negative feelings toward those for whom they usually care the most, and on whom they are most dependent. Many times, the dying even experience irrational anger toward themselves in response to their own sense of personal failure as they deteriorate. They may manifest such feelings in self-destructive behavior, either tacit or overt.

Guilt of Patients and Families

Anyone closely involved in terminal care settings, including patients, clinicians, and families, is likely to feel guilty at times. Patients commonly feel some sense of responsibility for the deterioration of their health. They frequently examine their lives quite meticulously to turn up some behavior that may have led to their predicament. Those who fail to find satisfactory answers may conclude that they are being punished in retribution for moral lapses. This can accentuate the feelings of powerlessness and the senselessness of the situation so often experienced by victims of catastrophic illness.

Guilt arises from many sources for all those involved in terminal care. (12, 16, 18)

Patients may feel guilty if they do not respond to treatment.

Patients may also feel guilty when they do not respond to treatment. Those who continue to deteriorate (or, in standard medical jargon, "to fail") in spite of medical treatments often think that they have let everyone down. Ironically, the efforts of medical professionals to foster hope by painting therapeutic opportunities in an optimistic light plays into this dynamic. When patients unrealistically assume that treatments are likely to succeed, they become especially prone to this kind of guilt. Their expectations prompt them to wonder why things did not work in their case. A particularly untoward consequence can be their reluctance to inform medical personnel of important symptoms promptly enough to permit optimal therapeutic intervention.

Other common sources of guilt in dying patients and their families are avoidance and inappropriate expression of anger. We have already seen some of the origins and effects of anger, and shortly we shall examine the phenomenon of avoidance. Suffice it to say that the dying and their loved ones often find themselves behaving angrily toward or avoiding each other at a time when closeness and support are most vital. When this occurs, they are likely to experience guilt. This is particularly problematic for survivors who look back with regret on their behavior toward the deceased. Finally, surviving family members may feel guilty about any sense of relief they may experience after the death of their loved one.

Guilt of Professionals

Professionals in terminal care settings often experience guilt.

Guilt may be particularly prominent for health care professionals, given the sense of responsibility that they are bound to feel. Their guilt often is a reaction to real or imagined expectations that medical intervention must result in a cure in order to be successful. By definition, this outcome never will take place in terminal care settings. However, involved clinicians are likely at some level to attribute the failure of medical measures to inadequacy of their own performance, regardless of the actual excellence of medical management.

A word of caution is in order regarding the expectations of well meaning colleagues. We have commonly observed direct or implied communication from those who regard themselves as more experienced regarding appropriate behavior toward dying patients and their families. Clearly, the wisdom of clinical experience can be of great value in providing guideposts in this complex area. This is especially true if it comes from individuals not deeply enmeshed in our cultural discomfort with death. Often, however, advice from colleagues regarding terminal care may reflect primarily the discomfort of the person passing it on. The underlying source of such communications always should be considered carefully; any discomfort or guilt in response to a colleague's expectations should be tempered in this light.

Too often, guilt among professionals stems from concrete contributions to poorly managed terminal disease. The specific failures giving rise to such feelings may become apparent when clinicians examine their own behavior and motives. For example, they may feel guilty upon realizing that they have inappropriately expressed anger toward their patients, or that they have withdrawn emotionally. Lack of understanding of the origins of our own guilt can only enhance the feelings underlying it.

Guilt can be provoked by a clinician's failure to meet legitimate expectations.

A related guilt-producing phenomenon comes from the clinician's failure to meet legitimate expectations of patients and their families. Prominent among these are their need to participate in their own care and their desire to have more open emotional communication with involved professionals. Few clinicians can avoid a nagging sense that something is not being done correctly when they fail to meet these needs. Often, the only clue they have is a feeling that management has gone astray in some ill-defined manner. Clearly, their uncertainty makes it difficult for them to address the underlying problems. Professionals may therefore find themselves in the painful and helpless position of feeling guilty over situations that are poorly defined and ill-understood.

Withdrawal

Those clinicians who equate death of patients with their own failure are more likely to manifest emotional withdrawal as death draws near. Such behavior is not difficult to understand in light of the pervasive urge for any organism to avoid situations that are painful. Acute sensitivity toward abandonment, however, is almost universal among those confronting death. Patients and families usually sense that such withdrawals have taken place, even though nothing may be said. Their awareness may be communicated by reactive withdrawal, demanding or passive-aggressive behavior, or even expression of overt hostility. The atmosphere in terminal care settings suffers greatly as a result of these dynamics.

Professionals tend to withdraw emotionally from the dying as death draws near. (16)

Emotional withdrawal by anyone involved in terminal care, unless openly resolved, can result in reactive distancing by others, including the health care team. Retreat may be seen as the only alternative available to protect against feelings of helplessness, anger, and guilt. This is particularly likely when caretakers sense little support among patients, families, or colleagues for the open resolution of this conflict. Patients and families may respond by emotionally retreating themselves, rendering resolution of problems even less likely. Alternatively, they may become more demanding or increasingly hostile, which can prompt further withdrawal by professionals, until the whole situation becomes untenable. In either case, the results of such self-reinforcing negative behaviors are likely to be disastrous.

Emotional withdrawal can trigger reactive distancing.

There may be times when clinicians or family members feel so uncomfortable with the dying patient that it is impractical for them to avoid withdrawing. Attempts to *stick it out* in spite of strong feelings to the contrary are likely to leave all parties feeling uncomfortable. In such cases, frank discussions with colleagues or other sympathetic listeners are the first alternative. If strong discomfort persists, professionals should seek psychiatric help to understand their reactions. When this fails to produce a lessening of tension, sympathetic referral to another caretaker, or some other means of gracefully retiring from the field should be undertaken. Frank discussion with patients about the problem, particularly when mediated by a wise consultant, is likely to be of use to all involved. Clinicians should bend over backwards to accept the responsibility for the failure of the caretaking relationship when they discuss with their patients the desire to make a referral.

When to refer.

Avoidance

There is ample documentation collected in general hospital settings that unresolved discomfort toward dying patients is translated into actual physical shunning of them (Glaser and Strauss, 1965). Patients

Physical avoidance is a characteristic reaction to unresolved emotional tension in terminal care settings. (17)

complain that friends and family members emotionally and physically withdraw as the seriousness of a terminal illness becomes more difficult to conceal. We reiterate that under most circumstances abandonment and isolation are perhaps the most fundamental terrors facing the dying and their loved ones. A more inopportune behavior on the part of key caretakers is hard to imagine.

To be sure, significant motivation for such avoidance derives from the existential discomfort elicited by a confrontation with death. Also, the desire of clinicians to minimize contact with those who remind them eloquently of the failure of their efforts must provide additional incentive to avoid dying patients.

Oversedation of dying patients may represent a means of avoiding them.

One particular manifestation of avoidance of the dying is the predilection to oversedate patients for whom cure is out of the question. This behavior is often cloaked in the ostensible aim to make the patient as comfortable as possible. We suspect, however, that clinicians often benefit most from overmedication, because it eases their emotional pain at this rude confrontation with their limits. Clearly, the oversedated patient is less likely to complain or demand attention from those who would prefer not to face the realities evoked by contact with the dying. We do not mean to minimize the vital role of adequate pain control as a central aspect of terminal care. High levels of sedation, however, render patients less accessible to communication during a period when clear interchanges may be crucial to them, and might avert future problems for surviving loved ones.

Inappropriate Persistence in Efforts to Cure

Inappropriate persistence in efforts to cure frequently is a problem in terminal care.

Professionals often persist in efforts to cure without full regard for the quality of the time that may be purchased at a high cost. Much ill-advised medical intervention probably derives from equating advancing disease with personal and professional failure. To be sure, not many of us find failure easy to accept under any circumstances. Thus, clinicians often resist acknowledging failures that have such striking existential implications as death. Health care professionals commonly experience strong internal pressure to fight harder when death inexorably gains the upper hand. This pressure not only derives from clinicians themselves, but may be externally applied by patients, family members, or colleagues.

Patients and families may pressure clinicians to make ill-advised efforts to cure.

Patients' desire to persist in therapy when the point of diminishing returns has been passed may arise from a number of sources. Basic fear of death may account for a significant portion of requests to persist. As we have repeatedly stressed, however, most people fear abandonment, humiliation, debility, loss of control, and pain more than they fear death itself. The side-effects of many therapies employed in patients who have advanced cancer, for example, easily can enhance such feelings. On the other hand, fear of failure as well as fear of death may prompt patients to press for persistence past the point where treatment seems medically sensible. This is corroborated by our experience that patients who apply this sort of pressure despite the resultant devastating effects on their quality of life tend to be driven and success-oriented people. Others who have not satisfactorily negotiated midlife developmental tasks or who have failed to achieve important goals also may push for poorly indicated persistence.

Family members consititute another prominent source of inappropriate demands for persistence in curative efforts. Often, the primary motivation for this pressure arises from feelings of attachment and a desire to resolve unfinished emotional business. Many families regard themselves as a team striving with the patient to defeat the illness which threatens their homeostasis. For such individuals, decline of the patient may represent failure of the whole group.

Closed Communication

Poor communication about stress-related issues commonly causes problems during terminal care. (7, 8)

Few working environments have a potential for higher levels of chronic stress than those involving terminal and intensive care. The issues that routinely surface in such contexts are among the most difficult any of us ever have to face. It is thus to be expected that those involved frequently will experience strong feelings and reactions. If these emotions are to be resolved creatively, clear and efficient communication within the entire health care team is vital.

Unfortunately, the open climate necessary for effective and supportive interchanges is more the exception than the rule in institutional settings. The resultant communication problems are reinforced by the hierarchy of power characteristic of our health care delivery system (see Chapter 14). Profound effects on the experiences of dying patients and their families are likely to be made by lower echelon members of this hierarchy. These are the very individuals who encounter the most obstacles in communicating with physicians, although their information and suggestions may be quite relevant and useful. The resultant atmosphere of tension and resentment is likely to affect negatively the management of the dying.

Closed communication channels among health care team members seriously detract from optimal care by restricting the flow of data to those whose performance could benefit from ready exchange of information. The resulting deficiencies in care clearly make things worse for patients and families in an immediate sense. In addition, long-standing resentment of the medical profession in general that further clouds the picture is likely to arise. The emotional climate that results when clinicians' strong feelings remain unspoken generally is sensed on some level by patients and families. This is likely to cause them to feel increased uneasiness in an already alien and threatening environment.

Burnout

A considerable decrease in energy or sheer exhaustion often result from working in a tense atmosphere. This leaves health care team members less able to deliver the warm, human contact and support that patients and families so desperately need.

The word *"burnout"* probably derives from space program terminology used to describe what happens to the booster rockets that are disengaged from space vehicles and discarded as empty hulks once their fuel is spent. This analogy holds well for individuals working in high stress settings without adequate provisions for emotional nurturance. Many statistics reflect that the highest turnover rates within institutions are found among those who care for the dying and for the critically ill.

Those who choose to work in these settings require special personality traits, training, motivation, and experience to perform optimally. Partly as a consequence of burnout, crucial roles may be filled increasingly by inexperienced personnel. An inadequate terminal care situation is thus perpetuated, and the seeds are sown for the next round of burnout. Burnout is not an inevitable phenomenon, nor does it take a specific form. Rather, it is one of a number of symptomatic expressions of a late-stage emotional crisis that is usually preventable by supportive interventions.

We believe that the responsibility resides with the institution to safeguard an optimal environment for terminal and critical care. Emotional support, facilitation of communication, variation of tasks, and sufficient motivational incentives should be available to those working in these highly stressful settings.

Burnout *is a common result of problems in terminal or intensive care settings.*

Institutions bear the responsibility to provide support for terminal care staff.

Graceless Dying and Its Sequelae

Introduction

Graceless *dying is characterized by feelings of abandonment, desperation, humiliation, rage, and dehumanization.*

In modern settings, the terminally ill often undergo a dying process that might best be characterized as *graceless.* It is a sad commentary on our culture that so many of us leave the world feeling desperate, abandoned, humiliated, enraged, helpless, and even dehumanized.

Graceless dea'h frequently is the product of poorly managed terminal care. We have already discussed a number of the more immediate consequences of these problems. Frequently, however, of even greater importance are longer term phenomena, the *ripple effect* of a graceless death.

Ripple Effect of Negative Experiences

Because everyone focuses on the dying patient, the nature of the death will affect profoundly all involved.

We begin with a metaphor taken from wave motion. A stone cast into a still pond will disturb the surface in expanding wave-fronts whose exact shapes become difficult to predict as they encounter more and more surface irregularities. Similarly, the profoundly moving experience of facing death will have sequelae that extend throughout a person's life, and may echo down years and generations. Dying patients, who are at the center of those expanding ripples, are the pivotal figures in the entire drama. Because these individuals generally are the focus of all concerned, the quality of their death will have a critical effect on everyone involved. The greater removed a particular after-effect of a pathological encounter with death, the more convoluted a pathway one must follow to understand and deal with it. The earlier clinicians recognize and address problems that may arise surrounding death and dying, the simpler the coping tasks will be for all involved.

The following material is quoted with thanks from a personal communication by David Spiegel.

CASE ILLUSTRATION

The importance of grief work is illustrated by the history of a family that sought psychiatric help 10 years after the death by cancer of a maternal grandmother. The presenting problem was a serious school phobia in one of her granddaughters. This bright child was so severely impaired that she had undergone psychiatric hospitalization for a year before she was finally able to resume normal activities. During the course of therapy it was ascertained that the grandmother's terminal year had been one of terrible stress for the family. This was related at least in part to their strict adherence to a physician's advice not to discuss the grandmother's diagnosis with her. The daughters had taken turns spending a day a week in vigil with their mother, all the while unable to discuss with her the seriousness of her condition. This painful year was an experience from which the patient's mother had never fully recovered. The mother's unresolved grief about the grandmother's death was revealed as a major contributing factor in the granddaughter's school phobia. As it turned out, the mother was covertly requesting that the child not leave her at home alone because she found the sense of isolation unbearable. Thus, in this family, incorrect management of the terminal illness contributed to their inability to do the necessary grief work. The result was a serious psychiatric disability for a surviving daughter, as well as for her child who was not even born when the death took place.

This case demonstrates the profound effect that an all too common, although well meant, defect in the management of terminal illness can produce. Its aftereffects are seen immediately, in the longer term, and even in generations to come.

Bowen (1978) discusses over a quarter century of experience in intergenerational family studies, and points out nearly universal serious effects upon survivors of the death of a significant family member. He labels the concept the *emotional shock wave*, and describes it as "a network of underground aftershocks" of serious life events. He notes that aftershocks occur even years after the precipitating event, which is often a death.

Emotional shock wave sequences are related, rather than separate, events. (6)

Immediate Effects of Graceless Dying

One of the direct consequences of a graceless dying is the immediate emotional trauma for survivors of helplessly observing the pain and degradation of someone close. This accentuates their personal loss, which already is potentially devastating in its own right. The sense of frustration that arises may lead to feelings and expressions of guilt and anger that families find confusing and inappropriate.

The unfortunate individuals who are experiencing a graceless death are bound to express negative feelings in their interactions with those around them. Most patients tend to identify health care personnel with their illness and with the frustrations inherent in institutional care. Clinicians constitute handy targets for whatever resentments patients may feel even in the most optimal of terminal care settings.

Another relatively immediate effect of a graceless dying process is interference with resolution of unfinished emotional business. If there can be any advantage to death by a chronic disease, perhaps it is that foreknowledge of impending final separation can motivate loved ones to undertake important communications they may have avoided for years. No matter how well adjusted a family is, they are bound to have some unfinished emotional business, or at least it is likely to arise in reaction to an impending loss. The period between the realization that an illness will prove fatal and the actual death can be a crucial time in which families have maximal motivation to make important communications. Pattison (1978) provides an interesting conceptual framework of a *living–dying interval* that sheds light on this issue.

Graceless death tends to interfere with resolution of unfinished emotional business.

We have observed a number of families in which there were unresolved issues that had caused untold hurt for many years. In a surprising number of cases, these old problems finally were addressed when an impending death made discussion of them more pressing. We urge readers to think back on any final moments they may have had with loved ones, and to ponder the influence of these few instants on their subsequent lives.

It is clear that a few sentences of emotional communication before a death may resolve issues which would require many hours of skilled therapy later. Health care professionals should try to support these end of life transactions. Unfortunately, when dying is graceless, the climate of resentment and despair is anything but conducive to the intimate communication required to achieve emotional resolutions. One prominent way clinicians can help is by promoting an appropriate death as much as possible.

Effects on Attitudes About Death

The quality of the process of dying is vital in shaping the way in which the bereaved approach the whole subject of death. The terminal illness of a loved one is one of the very few contexts in which most Americans have prolonged contact with the reality of death. Sadly, families most often are exposed to the graceless death common in modern institutional settings. As a result, their attitudes toward death are apt to be negatively influenced. Such adverse experiences reinforce the cultural message that death is an obscenity which people should avoid at any cost until they must inevitably confront it. Given that adaptive coping mechanisms for dealing with loss are more likely to fail in such a climate, dying is unlikely to be dignified. Thus, the very discomfort that prevails in our culture surrounding death is bound to be reinforced in all observers because of higher probability that their future encounters with death will be even more disturbing.

Poorly managed terminal disease adversely affects family attitudes about death. (17)

Another long-term effect of a poorly managed terminal illness is that families may develop a negative attitude toward the health care system in general. Observing traumatic experiences of loved ones suffering graceless deaths serves directly to promote the association of medicine with degradation, dehumanization, and pain. Health care professionals easily can appear as perpetrators of these indignities, often regardless of the reality of their behavior or intentions. The negative effect of such attitudes on cooperation between professional and family care providers in the difficult task of management of terminal illness is clear.

Family attitudes toward medical care may also be poisoned by a graceless death. (14)

Families' negative attitudes about the health care field and those who work in it have disturbing long-term consequences. For example, those who have observed some of the more unfortunate aspects of the health care system may be less willing to seek help for themselves. When confronted with a disturbing sign or symptom, even if they suspect a serious cause, they often feel that the benefits of involvement with doctors and hospitals are unlikely to outweigh the drawbacks they have witnessed. Further, when such persons do seek medical care, their resentment often surfaces in passive or uncooperative behavior.

Interference with the Grief Process

Graceless death often interferes with the resolution of grief.

Detrimental results of poorly managed terminal illness also may affect the grief process. We have discussed the nature of bereavement and principles of its management in Chapters 1 and 9. Here, we will examine specific ways in which ordinary healing mechanisms can be derailed. Given the common lack of cultural support, families' mechanisms for healthy coping with loss and grief are likely to meet snags even in the most appropriate of deaths. When clinicians manage terminal illness poorly and death is graceless, successful resolution of bereavement by survivors is further threatened. Indeed, family members may be so traumatized by their immediate experiences that they are unable to focus on their loss and process it in a healthy manner.

Clinically significant depression is a common manifestation of unresolved grief.

One of the most prominent manifestations of unresolved grief is a clinically significant depression. This has been recently documented in a study by Zisook and DeVaul (1983). *Clinical depression* is to be distinguished from the *depressed mood* that is the common and appropriate acute reaction to a loss. We presented criteria for making this distinction in Chapter 9. Depression itself tends to be self-reinforcing, in that it may further isolate and alienate someone who is already having problems coping with the loss of an important relationship. Depressed persons tend to become demoralized and to lose the distinction between their actual loss and the unconscious loss of self-esteem they are feeling. They often feel as though they are less than whole functioning persons, and this symptom is useful in distinguishing normal grief from depression.

For those experiencing reactive depression, inability to reenter the mainstream of life is likely to have profound consequences. As was shown in our case illustration of the child with the school phobia, the influence of such problems is not limited to the depressed individual alone. In fact, the chronic psychosocial morbidity of unresolved grief may well have a measurable effect on the health and economics of the nation, in addition to its incalculable emotional cost to individuals and families.

Unresolved grief often is associated with an increase in medical problems for the bereaved.

Another particularly prominent manifestation of unresolved grief is an increase in medical problems in the bereaved. In Chapter 9 we discuss studies of the health of widows and widowers that clearly document a striking increase in visits to physicians, morbidity, and mortality during the year after their losses compared to age- and health-matched populations. Physicians often encounter patients whose health problems are associated with the chronic stress resulting from grief pathology. Systematic investigations of the relationship of such problems to unresolved grief are in their infancy, but preliminary findings tend to be confirmatory. Certainly, case study material and our own and our colleagues' clinical experiences add to our strong impression that there is a relationship between health problems and grief pathology.

It has been shown clearly that death of a broken heart is more than a popular myth (see Chapter 9). We generally assume that people are endowed with the necessary equipment to resolve the inevitable emotional traumas of loss; grief-related medical problems indicate some breakdown in healthy mechanisms. As of yet, the role of graceless dying in the genesis of medical problems complicating the grief process has not been delineated clearly. It is safe to say, however, that witnessing a poorly managed death is unlikely to have a salubrious effect on anyone.

References

Bowen M. 1978. *Family Therapy in Clinical Process.* New York: Jason Aronson, Inc.

Glaser, B. G., and Strauss, A. L. 1965. *Awareness of Dying.* Chicago: Aldine Publishing Company.

Pattison, E. M. The living-dying process. In Garfield, C. A. ed. 1978. *Psychosocial Care of the Dying Patient.* New York: McGraw-Hill Books, Inc.

Weisman, A. D. 1972. *On Dying and Denying.* New York: Behavioral Publications, Inc.

An outstanding scholarly study of the pivotal role of the process of denial during the final stages of life. The text is replete with cogent and practical clinical illustrations. It is probably most valuable for those involved in understanding and treating untoward psychological reactions during terminal care.

Yalom, I. 1980. *Existential Psychotherapy.* New York: Basic Books, Inc., Publishers.

Zisook, S. and DeVaul, R. A. 1983. Grief, unresolved grief, and depression. *Psychosomatics.* 24:247–256.

Principal Psychosocial and Environmental Influences on Care of the Dying

14

Brief Contents

Overview

In this chapter we consider first the life experiences of health care team members that are likely to influence care of the dying. We examine ways in which patients' expectations contribute to the atmosphere surrounding their own terminal care. The emphasis here is placed on factors that are most likely to result in treatment problems and that tend to make dying a poorer experience for all concerned than it needs to be. Finally, we look at the influence of health care environments on experiences associated with death. We specifically examine functional and interpersonal elements in the modern health care system that have important effects on the dying and their loved ones. Again, emphasis is placed on the attitudes and milieus that can lead to suboptimal management of terminal illness.

Individual Experiences of Health Care Professionals

Early Experiences with Separation and Loss

Reactions to death are profoundly affected by early experiences with separation and loss.

The manner in which we react throughout our lives to issues surrounding death and dying is influenced profoundly by early personal experiences with loss and separation. Adult responses to existential concerns about death are affected strongly by such universal phenomena as birth, weaning, and separation from parents. We discussed developmental issues relevant to the psychology of death in Chapter 1. Clearly, those providing health care are unlikely to be exempt from developmental and cultural influences simply because they are professionally familiar with death.

Our culture encourages a stoic reaction to separation.

In mainstream American culture, there are certain common messages regarding appropriate behavior when confronted with loss. Role modeling by authority figures allows children to learn socially acceptable responses. Perhaps the most fundamental of these is that the optimal emotional expression in such situations is a stoic one, if any at all. From earliest childhood most of us are encouraged to be *brave* when we express fear or sadness about a separation. Public demonstration of vulnerability is regarded as an embarrassing lapse, and generally causes discomfort in observers.

Related to this is the cultural tendency to exclude from funerals those children not old enough to *control themselves*. This prohibition is nominally intended to spare the child a traumatic experience. In fact, it may be designed more to protect uncomfortable adults from confronting the uncensored emotions of those not yet schooled in *appro-*

priate behavior. Further, when adults discuss death with children, they usually couch the issue in euphemisms. This reinforces not only the avoidance of direct expression of feelings, but also the viewpoint that death and its attendant emotions are awesome matters which are better forgotten.

Many clinicians choose their field in response to a personal experience with loss. (16)

Our personal experience with colleagues, as well as a study by Livingston and Zinet (1965), demonstrates that a significant fraction of health care professionals choose their field in response to some personally traumatic experience with loss. This reaction probably constitutes their attempt to regain some sense of control over phenomena that make them feel powerless. Because of this background, health care personnel may be even more likely than the lay public to harbor strong, unresolved emotions surrounding issues of loss and death. Terminal care settings are almost bound to evoke these feelings. Hence, it is critical for those who care for the dying to examine their own profound existential concerns surrounding mortality. Successful exploration and resolution of these issues will facilitate optimal caretaking in the setting of terminal illness.

Resolution of concerns around one's own mortality is important for those engaged in terminal care.

Medical Student Selection

In addition to partaking in the general conditioning that most Americans receive, health care personnel fall heir to a number of occupation-specific influences on attitudes toward death. Some of these involve the professional school admission process and subsequent educational programs. Others are related to cultural attitudes and expectations surrounding the caring professions, and the structure of the modern health care system. We begin with a look at some experiences specific to physicians that strongly influence their management of terminal disease.

Medical school selection criteria are strongly biased toward analytical and technical orientations.

A good starting place is the rigorous selection process by which most aspiring doctors are chosen for their medical training. Clearly, the criteria on which selection is based significantly affects the characteristics of those beginning training. The sheer bulk of the applicant pool requires admissions screening measures that have at least some claim to objectivity. The chief initial qualifying criteria are high undergraduate grade point averages and scores on national standardized tests. Both reflect a strong emphasis on mathematics and science. Applicants have to rank high in these two areas in order to reach the stage of the admissions process where more personal and humanistic values would come into play.

A remarkable competitive fervor is generated among undergraduates by the knowledge that even relatively bright, analytically focused students have only a marginal chance of admission to medical school.

The medical school admissions process emphasizes technical traits above humanistic ones.

This atmosphere of cutthroat competition for a prestigious goal spawns another self-selection criterion. We question whether the most successful competitors for grades necessarily also make the most sensitive clinical practitioners, regardless of their intellectual or technical capacities. To be sure, this orientation proves remarkable in promoting the development of medical technologists. We suspect that, unfortunately, it has quite the opposite effect with regard to medical humanists. It is in terminal care, perhaps more than in any other aspect of medicine, where technical and analytical concerns must take a secondary role to human and emotional issues.

Analytical and technical biases are reinforced throughout medical training.

The analytical, competitive, and technical biases that are characteristic of the medical school admissions criteria persist throughout medical education. Indoctrination has only begun when students have negotiated the competitive rigors of premedical education and the admissions gauntlet.

Initial Contact with a Corpse

The anatomy laboratory experience can reinforce maintenance of emotional distance from death.

Among the factors influencing physician reactions to death and dying is the initial professional contact that most of them have with the human body—the anatomy laboratory. Our culture offers few opportunities for direct experience with death during childhood and early adulthood. Many medical students have never seen or touched a corpse before beginning their gross anatomy class. Further, a detailed grasp of the way in which the human body is put together is rightly considered to be fundamental to much of the remainder of medical education. Thus, most physicians have this initial awesome encounter early in their training, often on the very first day of medical school. Unfortunately, few medical schools make any special effort to deal with the psychological impact of this encounter, such as providing a forum for addressing concerns or reactions that may arise. The implicit message is that one is not *supposed* to react strongly to such issues. Students are often left with the feeling that whatever reactions they might have should not be expressed or should be worked through privately.

Medical Education

During the next several years, students encounter an overwhelmingly large and complex body of information and techniques. These are mainly oriented toward the production of language and thought patterns useful in understanding and managing human pathology. The task is so enormous that virtually no one could be expected to emerge with a solid sense of mastery of everything encountered. The tendency in such circumstances is for students to shift their focus toward learning that which can be defined and tested with least ambiguity.

For example, knowledge of differential diagnosis, recognition of symptom complexes, or performance of technical procedures all may be readily assessed. In contrast, concepts dealing with thoughts, feelings, and actions, recognition of behavioral syndromes, and appropriate responses to patients' everyday emotional concerns may be much more difficult to evaluate. It is not surprising that students tend to invest the bulk of their energy in mastery of those tasks in which they can assess their progress more clearly. The net effect is a strong reinforcement of unfamiliarity and discomfort with the emotional concerns that are most relevant to the care of the terminally ill and bereaved.

Physician Role Models

Clinical role models strongly influence student acquisition of interpersonal skills.

A particularly telling influence on interpersonal clinical skills derives from role models encountered during professional training. Although the various tasks to be performed are determined primarily by the situation at hand, the style in which they are best carried out is seldom so clearly defined. All students look to their teachers in clinical practice for clues as to specific behaviors and techniques that constitute an acceptable bedside manner.

Clinical detachment can work against the provision of optimal terminal care. (12, 16, 17)

Physicians who act as role models quite appropriately assume a posture of emotional detachment in certain clinical settings. They also tend to take such a stance when they feel uneasy, as, for example, when they experience anxieties about issues surrounding terminal disease. Thus, physicians often display an air of *clinical detachment* when confronted with death and dying. However, any sense of emotional isolation of the dying and their families from their physician contributes even further to feelings of alienation generated by hospital settings as well as by confrontation with death.

In anxiety-provoking situations, uncertain trainees tend to rely unquestioningly on behaviors of authority figures they have observed in similar circumstances. Additionally, medical students and house staff often are overtly counseled to maintain an air of clinical detachment. The result can be a rote perpetuation of an inappropriate sense of distance that serves the true needs of no one. These patterns may be difficult even to call into question because of the emotional uneasiness of those involved.

Stress and Exhaustion

Exhausted and stressed physicians are not likely to provide optimal terminal care. (17)

The long hours and high levels of stress that characterize the clinical training and practice of most physicians have profound influences on patient-physician relationships. Historically, most medical schools and teaching hospitals have incorporated pressure and sleeplessness as prominent features in their training programs. Consider the effect of this on health care personnel and their patients. In our experience, a physician working under stress is less likely to perform optimally in most settings than a relaxed colleague of similar abilities. Similar reasoning applies to the exhausted physician.

One particular effect of working in such circumstances is the tendency to do as little as necessary with each patient, in order to move on to the next task. The pressured atmosphere that results may be deadly to any kind of emotional exchange, particularly surrounding issues that are likely to be highly charged for everyone involved. Once again we see that the organization of medical training and practice can work against the development of the interpersonal skills most vital in terminal care settings. This is often simply because of physicians' lack of time and energy to address such issues. Indeed, if any relevant skills are likely to emerge they may be directed more toward fending off emotional concerns than toward encouraging patient–physician communication.

Physicians' Life-Cycle Tasks

Life-cycle tasks of early- and mid-adulthood reinforce behaviors antithetical to compassionate terminal care.

How do the particular life-cycle tasks faced by physicians influence their care of the dying? During early adulthood, physicians strive to establish professional identity and to achieve a sense of mastery in their work. These tasks tend to reinforce earlier emphases on technology, competition, clinical detachment, hard work, and long hours. As Feifel et al. (1967) have observed, physicians' concern about death and fear of dying become even more intense during this time than the death anxiety of medical students and laypersons. These factors further reinforce behavior antithetical to compassionate terminal care.

For those who successfully negotiate the tasks of early adulthood, death anxieties begin to take a back seat to worries about meaninglessness. In middle age (40 to 65 years), physicians often become concerned about the possibility of dying without having been a worthwhile person. There is a conscious refocusing away from oneself and toward compassion and concern for the rest of humanity.

Expected Attributes of Primary Care Physicians

Introduction

The idealized family doctor is a wise paternal advisor, and a warrior against disease. (8)

Consider the influence of patients' expectation of their primary care physician. Whether or not the traditionally described role of the family physician ever actually existed, it is the source of many of the cultural expectations placed upon doctors. The specific attributes of this ideal-ized family doctor that are most relevant here include those of *possessor of special knowledge, warrior against disease,* and *source of paternal advice.*

Possessor of Mystique

Professional use of unfamiliar technical language increases medical mystique and patient helplessness.

The doctor's fluency in an unfamiliar technical language contributes heavily to patient expectations that physicians possess a special mys-tique accessible only to initiates. It is easy to imagine the emotions that would arise were one placed in jeopardy while traveling alone in a country whose language was foreign. The insecure and helpless feelings one might experience approximate those of patients as they overhear discussions that may be of crucial import for their lives, but are unable to decipher the vocabulary.

Given this fundamental language barrier, it is not surprising that many people attribute a certain mystique to health care professionals. This is enhanced when the emotional stakes are increased, as in set-tings surrounding life-threatening illness. In terminal care, the effect on patients and families of conversation studded with unfamiliar tech-nical terms must become a vital concern for the caregiver.

Medical technology also is likely to intimidate many patients.

People have become more accustomed in general to mechanization over the same years that there has been a significant growth in medical technology. Thus, it is difficult to say whether patients are more or less intimidated by medical procedures at present than they have been historically. The indignity and pain associated from earliest childhood with many medical procedures may contribute as much to this intim-idation as the perceived complexity of the procedures themselves. In any case, this dynamic adds to the alienation felt by many patients in medical settings and to the evolution of negative attitudes toward health care professionals.

The process of diagnosis is likely to enhance the doctor's mystique.

A third factor suggesting that physicians possess mystique is their ability to use signs poorly perceived by patients to reach awesome conclusions. The complaints that prompt patients to seek medical attention often are not well defined by those suffering them. Many patients find themselves answering a battery of questions that do not seem to fit into any understandable framework. Then they are often probed and examined in undignified ways to elicit signs that are equally mysterious. Finally, intimidating and often painful tests are performed by instrumentation, the results of which are often poorly understood by most patients. From these data, physicians draw conclusions that may have earthshaking ramifications for their patients' lives. Yet this diagnostic information is often either not communicated to or poorly comprehended by the majority of patients. Thus, the medical mys-tique is further enhanced.

Warrior Against Disease

Another major expected attribute of physicians that bears upon the management of the terminally ill concerns the doctor's role as a warrior against disease. Most of us regard disease and death as frightening and implacable enemies. Confrontation with these villains in ourselves or our loved ones is bound to be deeply disturbing. This attitude prevails among health care professionals as well as their patients, and has several ramifications.

For many patients, the act of seeking medical help constitutes an admission of helplessness in the face of the problem at hand. Patients often regard physicians as *champions* whom they designate to represent them in battle against an overwhelming foe. If medical intervention is successful (or if the patient improves in spite of it), the physician becomes identified as a valiant rescuer and advocate of life and health. Everyone then can retire from the field of battle in a comfortable glow of achievement and relief until the next opponent rears its ugly head.

Physicians who are identified primarily as warriors against disease are bound to lose at last in every case.

The problem arises because in such a model a whole line of enemies is always on the march. The only outcome for all patients—and their champions—is eventual defeat. If patients and health personnel succumb to this characterization of medical care, patients will feel let down, and clinicians will feel like failures. There is no area of medical practice in which such dynamics come more sharply into play than that of terminal care.

Source of Paternal Advice

The physician traditionally has been regarded as an authority figure who can provide wise counsel to individuals and families confronted with overwhelming problems. In days past, a long-term patient–physician relationship and intimacy with several generations of any given family tended to be more common. The knowledge and acceptance that often emerged over a span of years provided a sound foundation for the successful realization of a paternally advising role. This was particularly important in crisis situations such as those involving death. At such times, the knowledge that one may turn to an authority with whom there is a solid personal relationship can be of enormous benefit in coping with feelings of alienation. Given the growing prevalence of specialization and the greatly increased mobility of most families, relationships of this variety are currently more the exception than the rule. However, the expectation that modern physicians should fulfill a paternal advisor's role is still often present.

Patients traditionally expected their doctors to shepherd them through life's crises from cradle to grave.

Further promoting the view of the physician as a fatherly authority was the disparity in education and exposure to the world that often existed in small-town America between doctors and their patients. Two generations ago, a college educated person (let alone the holder of a post-graduate degree) was much rarer than is the case today. This was particularly true in the small communities where a much larger fraction of the population then resided. Travel opportunities and exposure to mass media also were more limited. Persons who had spent as much as a decade in metropolitan settings were likely to have a much broader experience of the world than the average citizen. Hence, doctors were distinguished from their patients by a larger margin than at present because of their education and relative cosmopolitan sophistication. Such a disparity could only enhance the tendency to defer to physicians as authority figures even in contexts beyond those related to health care.

Doctors are still expected to be able counselors.

Traditionally, medical practitioners also were assumed to possess particular expertise concerning human and emotional issues. Families would turn to their doctors for advice and counsel when confronted with overwhelming concerns. Family counseling usually took place without assistance from any other professionals, except ministers. The expectation that doctors should be effective counselors survives today to varying degrees, regardless of whether or not they possess the necessary skills and sensitivities.

Structure of the Modern Health Care System

Historical Perspective

Although the traditional image of the family doctor may live on in the hearts and minds of many Americans, realities have changed. The growth of specialization among health care professionals working in modern medical settings has altered patient care drastically. There are several aspects of this system that have influenced strongly the experiences of patients and their families with respect to terminal illness and grief. The evolution of *compartmentalized* medical care, for example, results in frequent loss of contact with one's primary physician during the course of a terminal illness. The development of intensive care techniques and life support systems and the predominance of institutional death raise new ethical questions. The increase in litigation has led to the unfortunate prevalence of the practice of *defensive medicine*. Finally, evolving roles and changing relationships among health care professionals have significantly altered the reality of medical care. We now examine some patterns and problems emerging from each of these concerns as they are related to the management of life-threatening disease.

Growth of Compartmentalized Medical Care

The concept of *compartmentalization* of medical care is a model wherein each of an individual's various health care needs is addressed by a different specialist. Although the percentage of family physicians appears to be on the rise, most medical care currently is delivered by other specialists. These may be either primary care specialists (such as pediatricians and general internists), or members of specialties and subspecialties other than primary care. In either case, compartmentalization of medical care seems to be the rule today, rather than the exception.

Vertical compartmentalization *is the successive transfer of care to various doctors over time.*

The term *"vertical compartmentalization"* describes the partitioning of medical care tasks to various primary care specialists over time throughout our lives. Thus, for the first nine months or so during and immediately following gestation, the obstetrician is the person in charge of monitoring and optimizing our health. Once we enter the less comfortable and decidedly more complex extrauterine environment, the pediatrician takes over for the next decade or two. Somewhere along the painful transition into adulthood, we enter the care of the internist. In our later years, many of us turn to geriatricians for advice and comfort in coping with diminishing health. At last, although we may never have the honor of establishing a personal acquaintance, many of us are relegated to the tender mercies of the pathologist. Thus, during the course of a healthy life without any major illness before death, it is quite possible to have members of five medical specialties concerned with one's life, well being, and mortality.

Horizontal compartmentalization *is the division of care among specialists at a given time.* (7)

The term *"horizontal compartmentalization"* signifies the division of medical care at a given time among professionals with special expertise, often associated with specific organ systems or tasks. This division can occur in the absence of disease, but impinges most strongly on patients and families when they are confronted with an illness. Women who are well may at any given time have standing relationships with a primary physician and a gynecologist, at a minimum. In coping with minor ill health, ophthalmologists and dermatologists may enter the picture. Major trauma or serious disease may involve the recruitment of surgeons, radiologists, and subspecialists such as neurologists, oncologists, or psychiatrists. In short, the patient with a health problem may encounter a bewildering array of medical specialists just when some sense of continuity and security becomes most important.

The reliance on subspecialists in the presence of life-threatening disease is understandable considering the expertise required to manage complex medical problems. It is often difficult for a primary care generalist to be certain that appropriate therapeutic choices are being made without the advice of a consultant. At the same time, patients confronting terminal disease probably need more than ever the sense of continuity provided by an established relationship with their physicians. The quandary is apparent.

The need to involve specialists, at least on a consulting basis, is legitimate in many aspects of terminal care. There may be situations where the interests of patients are served better by a transfer of primary responsibility to, say, the oncologist. However, even in such cases there usually is no good reason for the original family physician to lose contact with the patient (issues of territoriality notwithstanding).

Compartmentalized care can cause problems in terminal care by breaking contact with the primary physician. (6)

Unfortunately, in our experience patients often are transferred in a *lateral pass* to a new and unfamiliar doctor. In such cases, they may feel abandoned by the physician with whom they have developed a sense of trust and familiarity. We wonder how much this phenomenon reflects a genuine judgment that patient interests are better served by the doctor's withdrawal. Relinquishment may be done with a sigh of relief from a clinician who may feel guilty, discouraged, and frustrated. Further, there may be a strong desire to avoid dealing with the difficult personal issues presented by taking on the terminal care management of the patient in question. As a result, even a semblance of the *womb-to-tomb* relationship with physicians that was possible for many of our ancestors is much more the exception than the rule in modern medicine.

Intensive Care Techniques and Life Support

Capability for indefinite extension of life has a major impact on the reality of modern terminal care. (20)

A second phenomenon that profoundly affects the management of terminal disease has been the development of a highly effective life-support and intensive care technology. During a recent conference on ethics and terminal care, a director of a major university intensive care facility stated that with currently available techniques he could keep almost any patient alive for a minimum of a few weeks. The definition of life implicit in this statement will be examined below, but we have no reason to question the informational accuracy of his statement. This potential for the indefinite extension of quasilife has a far-reaching influence on the experience of many terminal patients and their families. This is equally true for clinicians who are called upon to make decisions taking these new factors into account.

Complex technology is introduced into many deaths without full consideration of the consequences.

Unless there is a very clear understanding to the contrary among health care professionals, life-support measures are almost certain to be instituted when someone presents in a moribund state. This is reasonable in view of the urgency of such situations and of the stakes for all involved in an inappropriate decision not to resuscitate. However, the existence of such life-support capability also means that high level technology is introduced into a large number of terminal situations. Further, this often takes place regardless of ethical or moral

Life support and intensive care create difficult ethical, legal, and economic questions.

considerations. Aside from possible catastrophic effects of inappropriate resuscitation for patients, we must take into account the overwhelming nature of such situations for involved bystanders. The addition of the intimidating paraphernalia of life-support is likely to make the emotional climate even more stressful on loved ones who are present.

A number of difficult ethical questions arise for patients, families, and health care professionals in the context of life-support and intensive care. For example, the initiation of life-support creates some very knotty problems around the issue of its discontinuance. There are many cases in which brain death is not present, but where it is clear that patients are incapable of surviving without life support systems. In such situations, there usually is much torment on many levels for patients, family, and clinicians. It is no wonder that intensive care units often are remembered with distaste by those who have passed through them in any capacity.

Another very sensitive issue that arises in such settings is an economic one. The current cost of intensive care often exceeds two thousand dollars per day. Even moderately well off families who have exhausted their insurance coverage and fail to qualify for state aid may become bankrupt in a few weeks. Given that the terminally ill are likely to be older, this often means that surviving spouses are left with small fixed incomes after losing whatever assets they may have accumulated over a lifetime. When one looks critically at the quality of life that is purchased for a short time at such a price, it becomes difficult to justify this practice with the terminally ill. And yet, how many of us feel comfortable placing an economic limit or value on human life?

As long as patients are conscious and mentally competent, the issue of institution or withdrawal of life-support usually can be reasonably clarified and resolved. Once mental status becomes questionable or unconsciousness ensues, health care professionals and family members are left with difficult decisions in pursuing the best interests of the patient. Natural Death Acts (Chapters 5 and 7) have arisen partly as an attempt to deal with ethical and legal concerns stemming from the increased capability to support life in the absence of consciousness. With the evolution of these directives, patients' own views of their best interest can be effected more readily past the point where direct inquiry is reliable. Even when patients have signed *Living Wills*, however, the situations still are not devoid of ethical and legal complexity.

Predominance of Institutional Death

Another relevant aspect of our modern health care system is the prevalence of institutional death. We will detail some statistical specifics of

Most Americans now die in institutions.

this phenomenon in Chapter 17. Suffice it to say that within mainstream American culture it is by far more common to die in an institution than at home. This is particularly true when one eliminates deaths that are sudden and unexpected, and focuses solely on deaths associated with chronic illness. This fact has some important ramifications, among which is a strong association of hospitals with death in the minds of many patients. This tendency may both reflect and reinforce the cultural reluctance to confront death directly.

As institutional death becomes more common, health care professionals are being cast in increasingly major roles in the final dramas of most of our lives. Although professionals generally are well qualified in many respects to act in behalf of their patients, important problems still arise. Many of those thrust into these crucial roles have had little preparation in sharpening the interpersonal skills required in terminal care situations. Further, the organizational context of an acute care hospital may be diametrically opposed to the needs of the dying patient. The major goal in general hospital settings is to save lives. Thus, a death is experienced as a *failure* by the health care team. In turn, this attitude is transmitted to patients, whose emotional needs may be left unmet. Indeed, the physical surroundings are seldom conducive to the close interpersonal exchanges helpful in promoting a more appropriate death.

Hospitals are mainly designed to save lives rather than to promote a more appropriate death. (16)

One prominent result of the prevalence of institutional death is a sense of dehumanization in the minds of most people as they look toward their own encounter with death. Conversation with the dying reveals that while the idea of death is terrifying in its own right, even more frightening are the prospects of abandonment, loss of control, and loss of human dignity. Perhaps these issues were less of a problem when terminal care was provided at home by loving and familiar hands. All too often, the setting is now an institution, and loved ones are replaced by professionals who may reflect their discomfort by their distant behavior. In such situations, abandonment and loss of control become disturbingly real possibilities.

Institutional settings may compromise human dignity. (5)

Many of the most brutal aspects of terminal disease in any setting are related to loss of dignity. Most current institutional settings are unlikely to enhance a person's sense of human dignity or individual importance. This is in stark contrast to the manner of death promulgated in the *Ars Moriendi* tracts of the middle ages, which bears a striking resemblance to scenes described even today in rural Latin America. Dying often assumes a particular dignity in these situations. The family is gathered around and deeply involved, and the self-esteem of the dying person is protected elaborately. To be sure, it is naive to suppose that the values and practices of such traditional cultures readily could be transplanted into the complexity of modern settings. However, even in modern America it still must be possible to facilitate the experience of more dignified dying.

Increase in Litigation and Defensive Medicine

Persistence in heroic measures during terminal care usually is questionable. (13)

A growing facet of modern medical practice that affects management of life-threatening illness concerns litigation and defensive medicine. As a more aggressively consumer-oriented climate has evolved, health care professionals are more subject to questioning and even cross-examination regarding their practices. Given the size of financial judgments likely to be awarded by juries dealing with highly charged emotional issues, it is not surprising that clinicians have developed a defensive stance surrounding measures they take with the dying. Their tendency is to perform procedures primarily to protect themselves against charges of negligence. This can result in heroic measures to preserve life even when the quality of the time thereby gained is miserable at best. Ethically, such practices are highly questionable.

Wise physicians have long known that death was their colleague after a certain point in the process of dying. It used to be a common clinical pearl that pneumonia, for example, could indeed be "the old man's friend." Increasingly, physicians tend to go to great lengths to avoid the slightest appearance of culpability even in the final stages of an illness. Often, uneasy clinicians intervene when the doctrine of *benign neglect* would be much more appropriately applied. An absurd extension of problematic interventions can be found, for example, in the following legend among house staff. There is reputed to be an unofficial standard at a prominent teaching hospital that everyone who dies should do so with all electrolyte levels within normal limits, and all cultures negative. Although it is thought-provoking that the parameters of this standard are entirely technical, we find such a concept profoundly disturbing. One shudders at the agonies to which patients and families may be subjected in order to remove even the slightest hint of technically imperfect management. The additional economic implications of such an attitude we leave to the reader.

Evolving Roles Among Professionals

Addressing Human and Emotional Needs

Professional roles strongly influence terminal care.

Roles and relationships among professionals are another aspect of our modern health care system that vitally influences the nature of terminal care. Clearly, they are principal determinants of the emotional atmosphere of the treatment setting.

In Western civilization, the profession of physician has been defined in some manner for millenia. During most of that period, those caretaking tasks not performed by doctors generally were left to families. Coincident with the evolution of modern industrialized society came a growth of medical science and technology. Concurrently, a radical shift away from the extended family structure has taken place in developed countries. While doctors focused more on their technical offerings, relatives became less available to fulfill the caretaking needs of ill family members. Thus, the task of addressing the human and emotional needs of the dying was relinquished to some degree by both physicians and families. The job of meeting these needs gradually has been assumed by nonphysician health care professionals for whom analytical and technical bias is far less of a problem than it is among physicians.

Selection and training of nonphysician health care professionals reflects less of an analytical bias.

The selection and training of nonphysician health care professionals generally reflects a more humanistic and less analytical or technical orientation than does that of physicians. In particular, nurses, psychologists, clinical social workers, and chaplains generally receive an education directed strongly toward caring for the human needs of those whom they serve. We do not imply that specific technical training is less than a primary focus during their professional education. Rather, balanced education in these fields speaks more to the nature of the issues currently addressed by each of these professions.

Division of Caretaking Tasks

We have noted increasing specialization and compartmentalization of care among physicians. A similar division of caring tasks has developed among the various other professionals involved in terminal care. Thus, certain duties are carried out by various nursing personnel such as nurse's aides, licensed vocational nurses, and registered nurses; other tasks belong to pharmacists; some to inhalation therapists, physical therapists, or various other specialized technicians; some to medical social workers or clinical psychologists, and so on through a long list of specialized personnel.

Caretaking tasks are divided between various health care professionals as well.

Many physicians do not recognize the fairly strict demarcation of duties in effect for these various health care professionals. Crossing these lines, even in descending hierarchy, often incurs the wrath of those upon whom one has tread. The tensions created by physicians or others on the health care team who fail to take this complex system into account can certainly have an adverse effect on dying patients and their families.

The Nurse–Physician Relationship

Two key figures in most medical settings are the physician and the nurse. The traditional hierarchical nurse–physician relationship was based historically on major differences in education, skills, socioeco-

Conventional nurse-physician relationships are likely to create problems in terminal care settings.

nomic status, and power. Symbolic of the extreme nature of this hierarchy is an injunction that prevailed in most nursing schools in this country as little as twenty years ago. At that time, student nurses still were instructed to stand when a physician entered the room, despite contrary cultural gender roles. Such highly conventional authority relationships between doctor and nurse often created obstacles to optimal health care management.

This particularly applies to terminal care settings, at that stage when the expertise of nursing personnel is likely to become more crucial to quality of life than that of physicians. As medical science begins to offer less and less to the dying, issues of personal dignity, comfort, companionship, and emotional support assume primary importance. Nurses not only may be more vital to the quality of care received by terminally ill patients, but also may be more likely than physicians to possess the expertise to be authoritative. The potential for conflict becomes only too apparent.

Fortunately for all involved, the physician–nurse hierarchy is becoming somewhat less sharply defined. The major reasons for this are better education, clearer definition of roles, and higher standards of practice. In part, however, this is because of the evolution of the *primary nurse* concept. In this model, nurses are regarded less as employees under orders of physicians and more as coprofessionals.

Redefinition of the nursing role can improve terminal care.

This redefinition of the nursing role to enable nurses to assume appropriate control over welfare of patients in certain aspects of care stands to benefit the terminally ill and their families. Improvement in care is achieved by increasing the power of those best qualified to exercise it in the best interests of patients. Ideally, the result will be a more relaxed atmosphere in terminal care settings, and an improvement in patient care.

Another important role in terminal care is served by the public health nurse, who often provides vital services in the patient's home. The cornerstone of this role is the home visit, and the expertise of the nurse is applied to evolving practical solutions to problems arising in the home context as well as providing family-focused care.

Redefining Roles of Other Health Professionals

There are other health care professionals who significantly influence the experiences of those facing life-threatening illness. Prominent among these adjunctive professionals are medical and psychiatric social workers, discharge planning coordinators, and chaplains. It also should be emphasized that trained volunteers have an increasingly vital influence on terminal care throughout the country (see Chapter 12).

Social workers are key contributors to optimal terminal care because they mobilize societal resources. (16)

Social work is yet another caretaking profession that is redefining its roles to be more fulfilling to its members and to better serve the needs of its clients. As chronic illness is likely to be extremely taxing on social and economic as well as on emotional levels, the role of social workers in this setting is apparent. The social worker has the expertise to mobilize societal resources such as homemaking services and visiting nurses to soften this problem, and thereby to improve the experience of patients and families.

Further, social work personnel are receiving increased graduate training in the theories and skills of psychological counseling. Doctors and nurses are often too uncomfortable or busy to deal with such issues, and many patients resist psychiatric or psychological referral. Hence, the role of social workers as primary emotional supporters of the dying and their families is growing. These health care professionals are rapidly becoming equipped to act as skilled patient advocates concerning both environmental and emotional problems.

Discharge planning coordinators represent a new health care profession that is rapidly becoming indispensible in many hospital settings. Most of those in this field have nursing or social work backgrounds, and their tasks fall somewhere between these two professions. They are able to facilitate appropriate placement and services to optimize quality of life for patients and families. As such, they play key roles in providing high quality, ongoing care.

Chaplains often have more to offer in terminal care settings than any other professionals. (16)

Another professional group that has great importance in terminal care settings is the *chaplaincy*. The appropriateness of chaplains as central figures in this context is obvious considering the existential questions naturally emerging for those confronted with the transience of human life. Further, chaplains are also increasingly well versed in providing nonsectarian psychological and emotional counseling as well as fulfilling their more traditional role as spiritual advisors. Some hospital chaplaincy services even have developed programs to assist other professionals in addressing ethical and moral issues emerging around death and dying. This demonstrated expertise and active willingness to confront these central concerns has resulted in requests for consultation from the health care staff even when overtly religious issues are not at stake. In terminal care, the intervention of a skilled chaplain may be of far greater importance to patients and families than any particular item on the medical agenda.

References

Barton, D. 1972. The need for including instruction on death and dying in the medical curriculum. *J. Med. Ed.* 47:169–175.

Feifel, H., Hanson, S., Jones, R. and Edwards, L. 1967. Physicians consider death. *Proceedings of the 75th Annual Convention of the American Psychological Association.* 2:201–202.

Illich, I. 1977. *Medical Nemesis: The Expropriation of Health.* New York: Bantam Books, Inc.

The author tears apart our current medical care system, blaming most of humankind's current ills on the physician-based health care system—on iatrogenesis. His thesis is that the system produces damages outweighing potential benefits, obscures political conditions that render society unhealthy, and takes from the individual the power for self-healing and environmental change. His criticisms of the system are based on facts, but his rhetoric regarding causes and effects is specious. In addition to containing a historical chapter on death by Borreman, the book is valuable as a reminder that modern medicine often overemphasizes technique to the exclusion of a humane approach to people.

Livingston, P. B., and Zinet, C. N. 1965. Death anxiety, authoritarianism, and choice of specialty in medical students. *J. Nervous and Mental Disorders.* 140:222–230.

Sudnow, D. 1967. 'Passing On: the Social Organization of Dying.' Englewood Cliffs, New Jersey: Prentice-Hall, Inc.

A brief, well written volume highlighting the findings of a sociological study of death in a county hospital. A novel view of the management of death is provided. This book takes an important look at less well publicized practices of those who care for the dying and near-dead in an institutional setting.

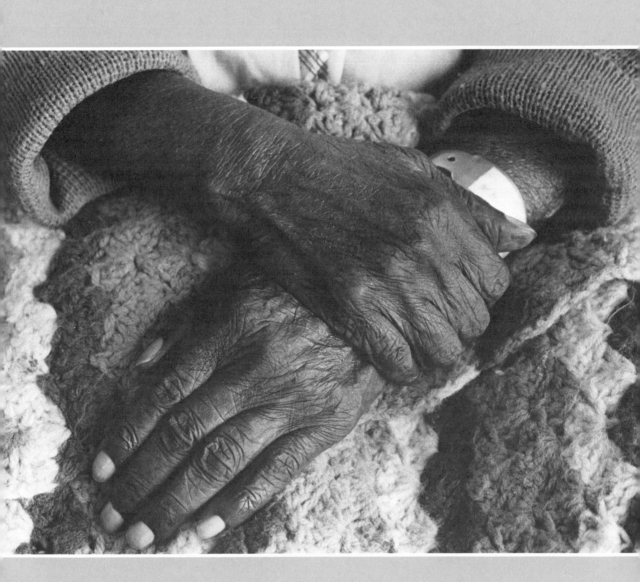

PART 6

Facts and Patterns Surrounding Death in America

In this section, we turn to more specific factual material relevant to the establishment of an effective model for terminal care. This reflects our conviction that there is value in a balanced understanding of the lay of the land. Those who manage life-threatening disease should find that this information contributes to a comprehensive orientation toward care of the dying.

15 Some Basic Parameters Concerning Death

Overview

We begin our examination of the basic parameters concerning death by noting the data that indicate that little change in life expectancy may be realistically expected from now on. Thus, quality of life considerations will assume greater importance. Next, we define death and proceed to categorize the manner in which Americans die. The major influence of our life-style upon the manner in which we die is striking. We end with a survey of the stressfully high monetary costs of dying in America.

Duration of Life

Eternal Youth

Much like modern disciples of Ponce de Leon, Americans are intensely preoccupied with the maintenance of perpetual youth. Supermarket checkstands frequently sport newsprint tabloids proclaiming the revelation by "prominent scientists" of new research promising eternal youth for everyone. We certainly do not expect our readers to be influenced by this *junk food* of the publishing industry. We suspect, however, that few of us are immune to the attractiveness of the vision of a vanquished Death slinking forever from the field of human affairs. This hope has significant influence on encounters between health care professionals and their patients, for someone must be defeated if Death is victorious.

We will first examine the effect of medical science on life expectancy. This issue has been cogently addressed by Fries and Crapo (1981), and much of what follows derives from their writings.

Changes in the Past Century

We begin by comparing the years of life expectancy for a 75-year-old person in 1900 with those for persons of the same age today (Figure 15-1). Hopes for a longer lifespan often are based on the belief that modern medicine can push back the age at which the body becomes inherently incapable of maintaining homeostasis even in the absence of major illnesses. If this were true, the curve of expected years of survival for the very elderly should reflect the rapid rise in life expectancy from birth during the same period. Instead, Figure 15-1 shows an almost flat line; a 75-year-old person in 1900 had an expected average survival of about 8 years, as compared to the current average of 11 years. This reveals an average increase of around 0.04 years of life expectancy for each year of this century.

Projected life expectancy by the mid-twenty-first century is about 85 years.

Further light is shed on this issue by projecting past trends to their point of convergence (Figure 15-1). The increasing curves intersect at an expected mean length of life of about 85 years, attained by the year 2045. Thus, if medicine continues to advance at the current rate, a theoretical limit of lifespan should be reached within 60 years. Of course, these projections would be invalidated by some fundamental breakthrough, such as the discovery of a method of resetting a genetically programmed "aging clock."

If we postulate that 85 years constitutes a mean theoretical limit for human life expectancy, a measure of the progress in this century can be made. In 1900, the average person perished 38 years "prematurely," in 1950 the average age at death was only 17 years before this limit, and in 1980 white women died on the average ónly 7 years "early." In that the commonly accepted margin of error is about 5 years, it is apparent that the limit is being steadily approached. Given that violent deaths account for about 3 years of the shortfall at present, it is clear that the medical tasks of eliminating premature death are largely complete.

Approach to a Genetic Limit

There are other approaches to the estimation of an inherent limit to the human lifespan that reinforce the validity of the life expectancy derived above. For example, suppose it were possible for humans routinely to live longer than a century, and that we were approaching this achievement with improvements in public health and medical science. More people would now be living exceptionally long lives than in the past. At least a few individuals worldwide should have lived well into their hundreds.

Records do not support claims of exceptional longevity in various regions.

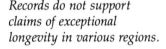

The lack of careful record keeping in many societies until the middle of the last century has been a barrier to investigations of this sort,

Figure 15-1   Trends, limits, and convergences in life expectancy in the United States

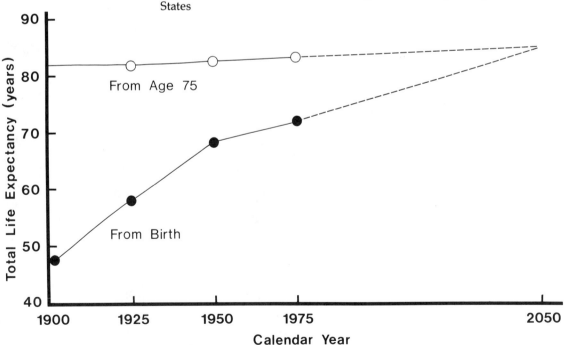

From Life Tables, United States Bureau of Vital Statistics, 1977.

but a few conclusions are now available. Adequate data have been recorded in England, Sweden, Japan, and the United States for about 150 years. Despite the giant steps made in changing average life expectancy during this period, there has been no significant growth in the proportion of people living past the age of 100 years, or in the maximum ages of persons dying in a given year. There are a few isolated areas in the world that are claimed to contain unusual numbers of centenarians, but the veracity of these reports is highly questionable (see Fries and Crapo, 1981, for documentation of the following statements). For example, newly uncovered records have established that residents of small Andean communities where longevity is highly valued routinely credit themselves with the passage of 1.3 years for each year they achieve past the age of 70. Information from the defected Soviet demographer Medvedev has now cast considerable doubt on the correctness of the claims of residents of isolated communities in the Caucasus that they routinely achieve 120 years of life. *The Guinness Book of World Records* (1980) has noted a correlation of 0.83 between claimed density of centenarians and illiteracy in a given region. Further, according to Guinness, there has never been an acceptably documented lifespan of greater than 117 years anywhere in the world. If longer life were within the realm of possibility, then it would seem reasonable that at least one person would have done so in the last century and a half in the areas where reliable records are kept.

There is no well documented lifespan of over 117 years.

A number of other lines of reasoning support a limit on mean life expectancy of 80 to 90 years. For example, several authors have argued that human cells *in vitro* seem to be limited to a finite number (around 50) of doublings before they fail to reproduce and eventually die. This limit appears species-specific, with cells of longer lived species having a higher limit on number of doublings than those of the shorter lived. These data speak to the existence of some sort of *genetic aging clock*, or programmed senescence. On a medical level, if one plots aortic fibrosis, intracellular water content, renal plasma flow, maximum breathing capacity, nerve conduction velocity, and cardiac output against age, some interesting results emerge. In most of these measures of general and specific organ system function, the capacity in young adulthood is four to ten times that necessary to maintain life. With advancing age, each of these values shows a relatively linear decline, and all of them approach limits necessary to maintain normal homeostasis at average ages of about 80 to 90 years. Thus, even in the absence of specific disease, simple degeneration results in progressive diminution of the organism's ability to maintain itself, until the slightest challenge can result in death. The conclusion is inescapable: whatever we might wish, we probably will die before we reach the age of 90 years.

Current biological data also support a limit of about 85 years on human life expectancy. (20)

This picture may seem rather gloomy to those who fancy at least a shot at eternal life. However, as Fries and Crapo (1981) point out, medical technology coupled with preventive medicine and a more

Postponement of morbidity and emphasis on quality over quantity of life are appropriate goals.

ideal sociopolitical environment can indeed offer the majority of Americans increased years of fruitful and enjoyable life. For even if morbidity and mortality cannot be avoided forever, there is good evidence that they can be postponed until very late in the lifespan. Treatments for many of the diseases that currently kill Americans before they reach their potential duration of life are being improved by medical science. Similar progress can be anticipated with many of the nonterminal degenerative conditions (such as osteoarthritis) that currently reduce the quality of life of the elderly. Thus, the goal is the *compression of morbidity* into the very last years of each person's lifespan. Current evidence suggesting that *disuse*, rather than *overuse*, of a given faculty causes problems leads Fries and Crapo (1981) to contend that the body tends to "rust out, rather than to wear out." Thus, *use it or lose it*, and *run, not rest*, rather than *lie down until the urge to exercise passes* are becoming the watchwords of those who care for the aging in this country.

Definition of Death

Historical Developments

Standards for the definition of death have evolved from lung- to heart- to brain-related functions.

That the development of medical technology has strongly affected terminal care is reflected in the very definition of death. For millenia, there was very little controversy concerning whether or not someone had died. This probably was largely due to peoples' inability to alter the natural course of most ailments. The criterion most commonly employed to determine if someone was alive was the most macroscopic one: *breathing*. The fundamental nature of this pulmonary definition of death is clearly apparent in common phrases such as "he drew his last breath," "last gasp," or even "the patient has expired." In fact, a great concern developed in the eighteenth and nineteenth centuries over the possibility of premature burial. Many people had elaborate precautions placed in their wills requiring that their bodies be observed for a specified period while a mirror was placed below their nostrils, or a feather rested on their lips.

In an historical sense, the *cardiac* definition of death is virtually as fundamental as the pulmonary definition. It is hardly more difficult to assess the presence of a pulse than it is to observe condensation on a mirror. Further, awareness of the physiological necessity of cardiac function is quite ancient, and with the evolution of the stethoscope the emphasis shifted to auscultation of the heart as the final arbiter of the presence or absence of life. Predominance of the cardiac definition of death increased with development of resuscitation techniques allowing mechanical support of breathing in the presence of cardiac function. Further, the invention of the electrocardiogram removed even the need for acute skill at auscultation to establish the certainty of death. The flat electrocardiogram became the gold standard for determination of death.

As medicine became more adept at resuscitation, more cases emerged where lost cardiac function could be restored. This often happened in spite of a period of cardiopulmonary failure sufficient to result in permanent loss of varying degrees of brain function. In many cases, enough brainstem capacity remained to permit spontaneous respiration as well, in spite of the clear absence of higher cortical function or consciousness. Development of the electroencephalograph allowed a further reduction in uncertainty in cases where the absence of cortical function was suspected.

Shifts in definition of death have reflected evolution of better diagnostic and therapeutic tools.

The final impetus for a widespread acceptance of the absence of brain function as the definition of death came from surgeons. In particular, the pragmatic need for it arose out of the development of practically feasible heart transplantation in the 1960s. The issue was brought to a head when a noted cardiovascular surgeon was questioned by a rigorous medical examiner who objected to the transportation of a brain-dead accident victim across a county line before the heart was removed for transplantation. The surgeon asserted that the victim's heart was beating and that therefore he was not technically dead. The medical examiner then demanded to know of what cause the man had died. The resultant squabbles made it apparent that the prevailing legal codes were inadequate in light of the technological realities of modern medicine. Clearly, changes were necessary lest famous surgeons be charged with murder. Although certain of their colleagues might not have been unhappy about such an eventuality, it was averted by the evolution and adoption of new legal definitions of death based on status of brain function.

Technological realities of transplant surgery motivated the update of the definition of death.

Current Definition

One of the earliest models for a more realistic definition of brain death emerged from the *Harvard Ad Hoc Committee* (1968). They evolved the following set of criteria for irreversible coma:

1. Unreceptivity and unresponsiveness even to intensely painful stimuli

2. No movement or spontaneous respiration for three minutes off of a respirator

3. Complete absence of reflexes, both deep tendon and central

4. Flat electroencephalogram for at least ten minutes of technically adequate recording, without response to noise or painful stimulus

5. All of the above tests repeated in 24 hours with no change

6. No evidence of history of hypothermia or central nervous system depressants before onset of coma

These criteria and the many similar sets adopted by most states have doubtless served to eliminate many legal uncertainties stemming from previous cardiopulmonary definitions of death. The latter, however, still serve important practical and legal functions and remain on the books in parallel with definitions of brain death.

The *Uniform Determination of Death Act* states that, "an individual who has sustained either (a) irreversible cessation of circulatory and respiratory functions, or (b) cessation of function of the entire brain, including the brain-stem, is dead. A determination of death must be made in accordance with acceptable medical standards." Current guidelines for such standards are outlined by a Presidential Commission (1981). Though this represents an important step beyond the Harvard Criteria, the Commission Report is by no means the final word.

Standards of practice pioneered at Stanford University include the designation of *who* shall make the determination of brain death when organ transplantation is involved. Such decisions are wisely left to impartial neurologists or neurosurgeons and the physician of the potential donor. Members of the transplant team and physicians of potential recipients are specifically excluded from making the diagnosis of death in such cases.

hical, moral, legal, and
ancial dilemmas associated
th the concept of brain
ath still persist.

Ethical and legal dilemmas that arise surrounding decisions as to when a coma has become irreversible are still unresolved. For example, a person in whom neocortical function had been obliterated while sparing brainstem functions would not be defined as having an irreversible coma by these criteria. This is in spite of the fact that consciousness, personality, and all of the behavioral attributes previously associated with that individual would be irretrievably lost. Thus, further refinement of definitions of brain death based on a more precise estimate of neocortical function is needed. Such revision probably will take place as society examines the enormous costs of maintaining "life" in patients who have no chance of recovering more than vegetative function.

Categorization of Manner of Death

Illness

atural causes account for
er 90% of deaths.

Generally, anyone who dies as a result of an illness is considered to have undergone death by natural causes. If we separate out deaths by accident, suicide, and homicide, 92% of those who died in 1979 did so by a natural cause (see Table 15-1). We note that the proportion of the time and space allotted to the coverage of deaths in the news media probably is about the inverse of these percentages.

A striking aspect of the list of leading causes of death in Table 15-1 is the nature of the diseases represented. At least 75% are degenerative or neoplastic. Further, the population that is likely to succumb to the more acute infections is sharply skewed toward the elderly and debilitated. We will examine age-related statistics in Chapter 16. Here, we emphasize that death in modern America is likely to result from gradual diminution of the capacity to maintain homeostasis, rather than the assault of some invading organism. This reasoning applies to malignancies as well, if one accepts that survival of a neoplastic cell is partly contingent on the failure of normal immune surveillance mechanisms.

Modern life-styles are closely related to the most common causes of death.

A further correlation exists between each of the nine leading causes of death and certain elements of modern life-styles. Tobacco and alcohol abuse, stress, increasing environmental levels of carcinogenic chemicals and ionizing radiation, obesity, noncompliance with antihypertensive regimens, lack of exercise, improper diet, inadequate fire safety measures, as well as our national love affairs with firearms and

Table 15-1   Provisional Mortality Rates for the United States general population, 1979*

Cause of Death	Death Rate per 100,000	Percent of total
All Causes	866.2	100
Major cardiovascular diseases	431.6	49.8
Malignant neoplasms	183.5	21.2
Accidents and adverse effects	47.0	5.4
Chronic obstructive pulmonary disease	22.7	2.6
Pneumonia and influenza	20.0	2.3
Diabetes mellitus	15.0	1.7
Chronic liver disease and cirrhosis	13.5	1.6
Suicide	11.7	1.4
Homicide	10.0	1.2
All others	132.9	15.3

*From the Statistical Bulletin of the Metropolitan Life Insurance Company, April, 1980.

the automobile are all linked with at least one of the major causes of death. Humans have begun to master many of the environmental factors that previously contributed significantly to the death rate. In modern America, however, nonhuman causes of death are being replaced by the one aspect of the world we have the most difficulty controlling—ourselves. Thus, the host and the disease become inextricably bound up with each other.

Over 60% of deaths result from gradual failure of homeostatic mechanisms.

Chronicity emerges as a significant factor in Table 15-1. Ischemic heart disease, cerebrovascular disease, pneumonia, influenza, accidents, suicide, and homicide lead to relatively acute death in most cases. These factors cause about 45% of total deaths, probably a somewhat high estimate of death by acute cause—an indeterminate proportion of deaths by ischemic heart and cerebrovascular diseases actually occur in a setting of chronic illness. Thus, a rough estimate is that at least 60% of those who died in 1979 did so as a result of chronic conditions. The magnitude of this figure reinforces the necessity that clinicians become sensitive to issues involving terminal care and chronic disease.

Accidents

Accidents are the third leading cause of death in the United States, accounting for over 100,000 deaths per annum.

Accidents are the third leading cause of death in America, accounting for over 100,000 deaths per year in the United States. According to *The Statistical Bulletin of the Metropolitan Life Insurance Company* (July, 1978), accidents were responsible for 5.5% of American deaths in 1975. There are a number of revealing points regarding accidental deaths. First, motor vehicle accidents accounted for 47% of accidental deaths in men, and for 41% in women. Pedestrian accidents made up roughly 15% of the total motor vehicle accidents for both men and women. The remaining causes of accidental death (percentage of total in parentheses) in descending order were: (a) falls (10% in men, 23% in women), (b) drowning (7% in men, 4% in women), (c) fires (5% in men, 8% in women), (d) poisoning (4% in men, 5% in women), and (e) firearms (3% in men).

There are striking gender differences in accidental death rates, some of which are not surprising in view of common cultural sex roles. Seven percent of men die by accidents, whereas only 4% of women do so. Accidents with firearms are not ranked among the top causes of death in women. Death by inhalation of food, on the other hand, accounts for over 4% of accidental deaths among women yet is not a significant cause of accidental death in men.

There are also strong age correlations in the statistics of death by accident. Accidents account for over 50% of the deaths of males under 30 years of age, and for roughly 35% of female deaths in that age group. Death by fire is common among children under 4 years (17% of the total for boys, 21% for girls), and among the elderly (8% for men, 7% for women). This is consistent with the fact that these groups are less likely to escape from a burning structure. Falls are the most common cause of accidental death among the elderly (35% among men, 52% among women), but accidents are responsible for only 2% of total deaths among elderly men and women. Motor vehicle accidents account for 60% of the accidental deaths and 40% of the total deaths among teenage boys, and for about 80% of the accidental deaths and about 30% of the total deaths among teenage girls. On the other end of the scale, car accidents ranked lowest in percentage of the totals at any age group among those over 65 years (28% for men, 19% for women).

Suicide

The 25,000 suicides reportedly annually are probably only 20% to 50% of the actual number of self-murders.

We have dealt at length with the eighth-ranked cause of death, suicide, in Chapter 11. Here we shall restrict our comments to its incidence. As we noted in Chapter 11, suicide accounts for around 25,000 deaths annually in the United States. However, this is probably only the tip of the actual suicide iceberg. In fact, this figure has been estimated by various authors as two to five times lower than the actual number of persons who willfully take their own lives.

The discrepancy between reported and actual suicides is attributable in part to the social and religious stigmata attached to this act. An additional factor is likely to be the difficulty in assessing the presence or absence of intent following an apparently accidental death. For example, some degree of suicidal motivation is suspected in as high as one-third of single car accidents resulting in death. This is virtually impossible to prove when the victim does not leave a note or other obvious expression of intent. It would be conservative to assume an error of only a factor of three between reported suicides and actual self-murders. In that case, suicide would rank as the fourth leading cause of death, immediately behind accidents.

Homicide

The current homicide rate in the United States is the highest in our history.

The ninth-ranked cause of death in America in 1979 was homicide. During that year, more than 22,000 persons were intentionally killed by other people, accounting for 1.2% of the total deaths. Let us examine homicide rates in this century. In 1900, Americans killed each other about a tenth as frequently per capita as is currently the case. That rate persisted until about 1905, when there began a steady climb which climaxed in 1933 with a rate of 9.7 homicides per 100,000 population. Then began a gradual decline, which reached a nadir at 4.5 per 100,000 in 1957. Since that time, the homicide rate has steadily risen to the current value of about 10 per 100,000, which is the highest in history for the United States.

Our homicide rate is much higher than that in the rest of the industrial world.

Some contrast to homicides in the rest of the world can be drawn from a 1970 World Health Organization report comparing homicide rates and methods between selected countries worldwide, including the United States. Of the 17 countries for which data were available, the rate in the United States was exceeded only by that of Venezuela. Further, when compared to other nations of similar industrial development, the rates in this country were between two and ten times those reported elsewhere.

Equally disturbing were American trends between 1960 and 1970, during which decade no other country reported a substantial increase. In stark contrast, our own total homicides rose by about 50% during that period. Further, the homicide rate in this country has continued to grow at an alarming rate since 1970.

There has been a particularly striking increase in homicides in urban areas. For example, between 1959 and 1979 in New York City, during a slight decline in overall population, the annual homicide total increased from 390 to 1747, or from a daily average of about one to almost five murders. We will not attempt to evaluate the reasons for these increases; we suspect that the reader will find them as disturbing as we do.

Firearms account for about 65% of murders in the United States, and that percentage is steadily increasing.

A final point regarding homicide in America concerns the methods by which people kill each other. In 1950, about one-half of all murders were accomplished by firearms, 25% by stabbing, and 18% by battery. By 1970, the percentages changed somewhat, with about 65% of killings accomplished by guns, 18% by stabbing, and 17% by battery. This trend parallels that observed among suicides, and has been postulated to reflect the increasing availability and prevalence of handguns. One particularly chilling statistic remains concerning death by firearms: in over three-quarters of cases of gun-related killings, the assailant is known to the victim.

Monetary Costs of Dying

Possibility of Exploitation

The final parameter we will consider here concerns the cost of dying in the United States. We limit our discussion to immediate monetary expenses involved in managing the terminal illness and disposing of

The cost of dying in the United States represents a possible exploitation of the most vulnerable. (8)

the body. American values and practices in these areas have been called sharply into question on the basis of potential for exploitation of the vulnerable and defenseless. Indeed, there is probably no situation in which there is more likely to be a lapse in the consumer awareness that is a prerequisite for the fair operation of a free market. Those caring for the terminally ill often can be of assistance to patients and their families by being aware of the specific costs likely to be incurred.

Costs Before Death

It is not easy to arrive at accurate figures for the costs of medical care to terminal patients in this country. However, by a variety of more or less indirect comparisons of data from various sources, it is possible to make some estimates. As far as national figures are concerned, the best recent source available is the Spring 1980 edition of The Health Care Financing Review, from which we derive the following data for persons over 65 years. Slightly more than 2 billion dollars were spent in 1978 for health care of this population group. Of this, about 1.3 billion dollars was provided by federal or state agencies. The 8% of those over 65 who died during that year were the beneficiaries of almost 21% of the total expenditures.

Rough estimates of the percentages of the $3400 per deceased individual spent on various services indicate 43% was dedicated to hospitalization, 26% to nursing homes, 18% to physicians' services, and 7% to drugs and sundries. We emphasize that these figures apply to all who died during that period, and that costs for those suffering from chronic diseases were likely to be many times these average figures. Clearly, it can be an expensive proposition to die in this country, especially if one suffers from a chronic debilitating disease.

Illness expenses during the last year of life are likely to be very high.

There are some less direct ways of estimating the costs of death in this country, particularly insofar as inhospital costs of illnesses ending in death are concerned. Schroeder et al. (1981) examined the survival of high cost patients from nine acute care hospitals in the San Francisco Bay Area. They defined high cost patients as those accruing bills of $4000 or greater. This group comprised about 13% of the total patient population while accounting for 39% of the total charges made by these hospitals. There were a number of factors significantly associated with death in this group (over 34% of whom had died within two years of admission). These included diagnosis of cancer (62% died), age greater than 65 years (44% died), discharge from a medical rather than surgical service (42% died), and total hospital bill over $10,000 (48% died).

A recent survey of cancer deaths in particular was conducted by Blue Cross and Blue Shield (Hines, 1983). It predicted that the average American who dies of cancer in 1983 will incur more than $22,000 in illness-related expenses during his or her final year of life. The last six months of life for the average cancer patient were projected to include 38 days spent in the hospital (15 during the last month), accounting for 78% of the total last-year-of-life medical expenses. The study also showed that hospice care was roughly one-third as expensive as conventional care. We conclude that a large portion of medical dollars are spent on persons whose prognosis is questionable at best.

Costs After Death

Professionals can be of use to patients and families by being aware of funeral practices and expenses.

It is much easier to arrive at reliable estimates for funeral and burial costs in the United States than it is to estimate the costs of terminal illness. This is partly because services after death generally are provided by a single industry, one that has been scrutinized more carefully than the health care establishment. This is particularly true in the two decades since the publication of Mitford's (1963) scathing critique of the funeral industry. Factual information about the funeral industry is relevant for health care professionals involved in terminal care for two reasons. First, it provides an estimate of the financial stresses that survivors may encounter. Second, health care professionals are people from whom survivors are likely to seek advice following a death (see Chapter 8).

A Federal Trade Commission Report (1978) established average costs and ranges for 1976, based on information from a number of sources both within and without the funeral industry. To those figures we apply the inflation estimate from the National Funeral Director's Association (quoted at 8.5% per annum in the 1978 report) to arrive at cost estimates applicable to 1983 (Table 15-2).

We begin with the traditional funeral service, which consists of a ground burial in a casket following services performed in a funeral home or church. A basic service includes pickup of the body at a hospital, morgue, or other place of death; transportation to the funeral home; arrangement for necessary certification of death; publication of obituary notices; preparation of the body (usually including embalming); purchase of a container; rental of a room for display purposes; rental of a chapel for services; provision of a fee for the clergyperson; and transportation of the body and family members to the grave site.

An average estimated cost of a funeral and burial in 1983 is about $4300.

Cemetery costs include: purchase of a grave site; a fee for opening and closing the grave; purchase of a grave liner (required by most cemeteries to prevent grave subsidence and allow maintenance with automatic mowers); and purchase and installation of a grave marker.

Table 15-2   Estimated Funeral and Burial Costs for 1983

Item	Cost (dollars)
Funeral home charges	2400
Vault (grave liner)	300
Obituary notices	30
Clergy	60
Death certification	20
Grave purchase	480
Opening and closing	240
Monument	350
Monument installation	180
Flowers (by family only)	250
Total	4310

Funeral homes are required to itemize their costs on request, but need not do so if not asked.

In addition, there may be a fee for care of the grave site. The estimates of these costs for 1983 may be found in Table 15-2.

It should be noted that these are average costs for the entire country. Costs in rural areas tend to be lower, whereas costs in urban areas can range as much as three times the amount for an average funeral. Additional charges not listed above which often are incurred by families include about $400 in one lump sum for perpetual care of the grave site, or about $50 per annum if care is not purchased perpetually. Included in the funeral home charge is an average cost of $800 for a casket, about $125 for embalming, about $60 for burial clothing, and about $100 for limousines and hearses. Funeral homes are required to itemize their costs on request, but need not do so if not asked.

The range on a number of these values is quite large. For example, caskets may cost from about $150 for a simple cloth-covered wood container to over $1200 for a hardwood casket to as much as $5000 or more for a copper or bronze model. Vaults can range between $100 for a simple concrete box and $1500 for an airtight steel and asphalt container designed to resist near-miss nuclear bombardment. The costs of crypt or mausoleum burial can vary from about $600 to amounts that exceed the total health care budget of a developing country. The average amount of money spent on flowers by all who contribute them is about $650. In short, a death in the family can be, and frequently is, very expensive.

Alternatives to Burial

Growing numbers of Americans are turning to alternatives to traditional ground burial. (6)

Growing numbers of Americans are turning to alternatives to the traditional ground burial. The most common of these is cremation. Use of this alternative has increased from 4.3% of dispositions in 1968 to 7% in 1976 to an estimated 10% in 1982. The cost of a direct cremation without embalming or services ranges between $255 (which happens to be the current Social Security Death Benefit) and about $500, with an average cost of $400. The cost of cremation after a regular funeral service (usually conducted with a rented casket) comes to a total of about $1200, not including disposition. Costs for disposition of cremated remains (dubbed "cremains" by the funeral industry) may vary widely. They range from nothing if the ashes are scattered privately to between $50 and $500 for an urn, plus an additional $50 to $1750 for a niche or burial. Commercial scattering firms may charge as much as $250 for their services. Finally, there are generally no costs associated with donation of bodies for medical or scientific purposes.

Reasons for Professionals to Stay Informed

A knowledge of some of the monetary issues immediately associated with death in America provides an important perspective for health care personnel. The strain that costs such as these often add into an already highly stressful situation can adversely influence patients and families in terminal care settings. Awareness of the magnitude of these costs may prove helpful by helping professionals to accept behaviors on the part of their patients and families that may be motivated by financial stress. Further, such knowledge can better prepare them to inform properly those who seek their advice.

References

Consumer Reports. 1977. *Funerals: Consumers' Last Rights*. Mount Vernon, New York: Consumers' Union.

The Consumers' Union is well known for objective counsel on consumer goods, services, and the expenditure of family income. This is their straightforward and well documented practical report on conventional funerals and burial, as well as some alternatives. Its content is more inclusive and up-to-date than that found in Mitford's classic.

Federal Trade Commision Report. 1978. *Funeral Industry Practices*. 16CFR, Part 453.

Fries, J. and Crapo, L. 1981. Vitality and Aging. San Francisco: W. H. Freeman & Co. Publishers.

The authors put forth the thesis that (a) the human life span is fixed, (b) the age at first infirmity will increase, and therefore (c) the duration of infirmity will decrease. They present convincing evidence that the appearance of chronic diseases will be postponed until near death, and that people will remain healthy until close to that event. These arguments should be in the ken of all who are interested in death and dying.

Harvard ad hoc committee. 1968. A definition of irreversible coma. *JAMA* 205:337–340.

Hines, W. February 9, 1983. *Chicago Sun-Times*. p. 72.

McWhirter, N. 1980. *Guinness Book of World Records*. 17th ed. New York: Bantam Books, Inc.

Mitford, J. 1963. *The American Way of Death*. New York: Simon & Schuster.

An earlier, hard hitting account of the practices of the American funeral industry. The author's keen journalistic style no doubt was a factor in leading the way to an ongoing critical review of funeral practices.

Presidential Commission for the Study of Ethical Problems in Medicine and Biomedical and Behavioral Research. 1981. Guidelines for the determination of death. *JAMA*. 246:2184–2186.

Schroeder, S. A., Showstack, J. A. and Schwartz, J. 1981. Survival of adult high cost patients. *JAMA* 245:1446–1449.

Statistical Bulletin of the Metropolitan Life Insurance Company. July 1978 and April, 1980.

———. 1970–1971. *World Health Statistics Annual*. Geneva: World Health Organization. p. 306–315.

———. *Health Care Financing Review*, Spring, 1980. p. 81.

16 Influence of Modern Life on Mortality

Overview

In the preceding chapter we surveyed a number of basic parameters concerning death. Now we will more specifically examine the influence of modern life on causes of death in the United States, and the implications for those who care for the terminally ill.

Public Health Measures

Life Expectancy

Life expectancy in the United States has increased strikingly since Colonial days.

Table 16-1 presents data regarding life expectancy since the turn of the century. These data demonstrate a radical change during this century in the age at which one might reasonably expect to die. Even more striking are estimates of life expectancy stretching back into history (Lerner, 1970). Various sources have posited an average duration of life of about 18 years for prehistoric man, with rare individuals reaching the age of 40 years. Life expectancy in ancient Rome has been estimated at about 22 years, and increased in Medieval England to about 33 years. In Colonial America, one-half of all liveborn people were dead by about the age of 35, and by the late nineteenth century a person living in England could expect to live about 41 years.

Cause of Death

Although these figures clearly document a striking change in average life expectancy, they shed no light on the reasons for these changes. In order to make some guesses in that direction, we turn to causes of death, which are presented for the year 1900 and the year 1979 in Table 16-2 (from the United States Bureau of Vital Statistics).

Table 16-1   Expectation of Life at Birth[†]

Year	Total	White Male	White Female	Nonwhite Male	Nonwhite Female
1977	73.2	70.0	77.7	64.6	73.1
1970	70.7	67.9	75.5	61.0	69.0
1960	69.9	67.6	74.2	61.5	66.5
1950	67.8	65*	70*	*	*
1940	63.4	61*	66*	*	*
1930	59.2	57*	60*	*	*
1901	49.2	48.2	51.1	32.5	35.0

[†]*From* the Life Tables for 1977 of the United States Bureau of Vital Statistics.
*approximate figures for whites and non-whites combined

Table 16-2   Leading Causes of Death in the United States*

A. 1900 Cause of Death	Death Rate (per 100,000)	Percent of total
All Causes	1,719.1	100
Influenza and pneumonia	202.2	11.8
Tuberculosis	194.4	11.3
Gastroenteritis	142.7	8.3
Heart disease	137.4	8.0
Strokes	106.9	6.2
Chronic nephritis	81.0	4.7
Accidents	72.3	4.2
Cancer	64.0	3.7
Infant's diseases	62.6	3.6
Diphtheria	40.3	2.3
All others	615.3	35.9
B. 1979 Cause of Death	**Death Rate (per 100,000)**	**Percent of total**
All Causes	866.2	100
Heart disease	330.4	38.1
Cancer	183.5	21.2
Stroke and vascular disease	101.2	11.7
Accidents	47.0	5.4
Chronic lung disease	22.7	2.6
Influenza and pneumonia	20.0	2.3
Diabetes mellitus	15.0	1.7
Cirrhosis of the liver	13.5	1.6
Suicide	11.7	1.4
Homicide	10.0	1.2
All others	132.9	15.3

*From the Life Tables of the United States Bureau of Vital Statistics, 1979.

In 1900, over one-third of reported deaths did not result from one of the top ten causes. By 1979, however, only about 15% of the reported deaths were not caused by one of the ten major killers. In part, this difference probably reflects improvements during this century in the understanding of human pathology. The designation of "death by natural causes" was considerably more likely to appear on a death certificate at the turn of the century than it is today. We suspect, however, that another phenomenon also is reflected in this difference. In 1979, the top five causes of death listed accounted for nearly 80% of the total deaths, whereas in 1900 the top five causes were responsible for less than 50% of the total. The explanation for this change is likely to be found in the nature of the diseases in question.

In contrast to the preceding millenia, death in modern America is more likely to result from wear and tear than from an acute attack.

In 1900, people were most likely to die of communicable or infectious diseases, whereas today the degenerative diseases seem to be the great killers. Advances in public health have resulted in the virtual elimination of the epidemics of cholera, typhoid, diphtheria, and other bacterial infections that periodically have plagued humankind since the beginning of history. Bacterial pneumonia and tuberculosis used to slay millions each year in Europe and the United States. Now they are fatal mainly among the elderly, immune compromised, or otherwise profoundly debilitated. Diseases of infancy, also relatively acute, no longer rank among the top ten killers.

Given that life expectancy has increased more than 20 years since the turn of the century, certain changes in cause of death are not surprising. For example, insufficiencies of the cardiovascular system—which is particularly susceptible to age and stress—account for fully one-half of all deaths at present. At the turn of the century, cardiovascular dysfunction was responsible for only 14% of deaths. In 1983, death is much more likely to result from chronic wear and tear or abuse of the body than from an acute attack on an uncompromised host by an outside invader.

Other Factors Influencing Mortality

Medical Science

Medical science and technology have greatly influenced the changes in primary cause of death since 1900.

Another profound influence on the differences between the primary causes of death in 1900 and those at present lies in the realm of medical science and technology. Immunization alone has been responsible for the reduction of diphtheria, the tenth leading cause of death at the turn of the century, to a quite rare disease. Smallpox was once a scourge that periodically annihilated large percentages of urban populations worldwide. It has now been officially declared extinct, and survives only in a few carefully sealed laboratory containers. The development of renal transplant techniques and of hemodialysis has resulted in elimination of kidney disease as a leading cause of death. Modern antibiotic therapy has reduced infectious diseases of the lungs to slayers of the debilitated, and virtually has eliminated syphilis as a significant cause of death in this country.

Elimination of the top five causes of death in 1970 would add only 16 years to the mean life expectancy in that year.

The following data are computed for the years 1969 to 1971 and are taken from the Life Tables of the Bureau of Vital Statistics. If all cardiovascular disease was eliminated as a cause of death, for example, an estimated 11.76 years would be added to the average life span. If all malignant neoplasms were treated successfully, the average individual would live about 2.47 years longer. If all accidents were prevented, an additional 1.33 years of life would result. If chronic lung diseases were vanquished, life expectancy would be increased by less than .36 years. Thus, in 1970, elimination of the top five causes of death, which accounted for about 75% of all deaths that year, would have resulted in a net increase of about 16 years of life on the average, to yield a total life expectancy of 86 years. The lion's share of that increase would result from eradicating cardiovascular disorders. These actually may be as much attributable to simple wear and tear and decline in vascular elasticity as to any actual disease.

Gender

In 1977, males of all ages died at an average rate 180% that of females.

In 1977, the average life expectancy for women was 77.7 years, a full 7.7 years greater than that for men. This difference has been demonstrated consistently throughout this century. In fact, it has been in evidence since large reductions in female mortality associated with childbirth were accomplished in the last century. *The Statistical Bulletin of the Metropolitan Life Insurance Company* (May, 1980) plots the ratio of male-to-female mortality in various age groups since 1900, and some surprising figures emerge. Over all ages, in 1977 males died at a rate 180% that of females. In that year, the mortality of males aged 15 to 24 years was 285% that of females, the highest differential during the entire period. Gender differences by cause of death also showed the highest differential mortality in 1977 to be in the 15- to 24-year-old age group perishing via suicide. Males in this cohort died 416% more often than female contemporaries. The second highest ratio was for 25 to 44 year old people whose deaths were caused by accidents, with the men's rate 379% that of women. The only instance in which the female death rate significantly exceeded that of men was for mortality by cancer at ages 25 to 44 years, wherein men died only 87% as often as women. Although the differential decreases somewhat in inverse proportion to age, in no age category does male mortality fall below 140% of females for all causes combined.

Gender differences in life-style account for much of the mortality differential between men and women.

The reasons for these gender differences in mortality statistics may be inferred from various data. We begin with the following combinations of statistics. Males under 45 years have the highest mortality from what might be termed "external" sources such as accidents, suicide, or homicide, rather than from disease. Between the ages of 45 and 64 years, the main difference between men and women arises in death due to diseases of the heart. In contrast, among persons aged 65 years and over, malignant neoplasms contributed most strongly.

In the cases of those under 65 years, cultural differences in life-style between men and women probably account for much of the disparity. There may be an additional effect from whatever protection female hormones may afford against cardiovascular disease. In the one group where women exceed men in mortality, cancers of the breast and reproductive organs account entirely for the difference. If one accepts the Surgeon General's opinion regarding smoking and lung cancer (the largest killer of men among the neoplasms), the long-standing masculine predominance in smoking introduces the issue of life-style into the picture for people over 65 years as well. As women begin to smoke as much as men, the difference in incidence of lung cancer between the sexes is diminishing rapidly.

One striking result of these gender differentials is the current surplus of widows over widowers. According to *The Statistical Bulletin of the Metropolitan Life Insurance Company* (September, 1977), in 1976 12.5% of all American women were widows, whereas less than 2% of all men were widowers. Further, the number of widows compared to widowers by age group ranged from 760% for women aged 35 to 44 years to 490% for those 75 years and over.

Infant Mortality

Infant mortality has dropped six-fold in the past 75 years.

At the beginning of this century, infant mortality was one of the prominent causes of death among Americans, ranking ninth among the top causes. Indeed, the striking and relatively steady decline in the death of infants (generally designated as anyone under one year of age) is one of the success stories of modern medicine and public health. From a mortality rate of 95.7 per 100,000 live births in 1915 to 1919, the Bureau of Vital Statistics (1977) documents a steady decline to 15.7 in 1975. Infant mortality generally is divided into neonatal (birth to one month of life) mortality and infant (one month to one year of life) mortality. There have been relatively parallel declines in both of these figures over this century, the rate being generally higher for neonates (for example, 11.2 per 1,000 for neonates as opposed to 4.5 for infants in 1975).

Diagnostic and technical advances account for the changes in infant mortality during this century.

The mortality for neonates less than one day old stayed constant at about 1600 deaths per 100,000 live births until 1938, when it began a steady decline. The significance of these general figures may be inferred from data regarding specific causes of infant death. Since 1951, steady declines have occurred in deaths by congenital malformation, birth injury, and immaturity. Most other cause of death diagnoses have declined intermittently and slightly over each ten year span. These trends probably reflect the development of better prenatal care as well as more sophisticated obstetrical diagnostic and delivery techniques. Improvements in life-support systems and corrective surgical techniques for neonates also may have enhanced survival rates. Postnatal asphyxia and nutritional maladjustment, however, have increased substantially. This may be related to the increasing survival of low birth weight infants, who are more likely to have problems due to inadequate respiratory and gastrointestinal development. Finally, strong and disturbing correlations between race, socioeconomic status, and infant mortality will be examined later in this chapter.

Mortality After Infancy

We present Table 16-3 to remind health care professionals that being old is by no means equivalent to being dead. Note that 75-year-old people are likely to live for an average of at least another decade. There is a tendency in mainstream American culture to discount or ignore the remaining years of life for the aged. We often assume that a retired person has chosen to exit from the realm of normal living. Elderly people may tend less to consider long-range goals, and hence may end up being unpleasantly surprised. We are reminded of an older

Table 16-3   Expectations of life at various ages in 1977*

		Age (years)							
	Birth	**5**	**15**	**25**	**35**	**45**	**55**	**65**	**75**
Males	69.3	65.6	55.9	46.8	37.6	28.7	20.6	13.9	8.7
Females	77.1	73.2	63.4	53.8	44.2	34.9	26.2	18.3	11.6
Difference	7.8	7.6	7.5	7.0	6.6	6.2	5.6	4.4	2.9

From the Statistical Bulletin of the Metropolitan Life Insurance Company, May, 1980.

colleague of ours who stated ruefully, "If I had known I was going to last this long, I would have taken better care of myself."

For example, how many 75-year-old people make financial plans for at least an additional decade of life? Despite the dictum of "Use it or lose it!" regarding many types of function, how many of our elderly consciously plan to engage regularly in function-maintaining activities over a long span? Health care professionals can make a profound difference in the lives of their elderly patients if they are able to communicate and emphasize properly the importance of long-term planning.

Professionals should encourage the elderly to engage in function-maintaining activities.

One intriguing way to look at death and aging is taken from *The Statistical Bulletin of the Metropolitan Life Insurance Company* (November, 1978). In Table 16-4, we present their data on chances of survival through specific life events.

Table 16-4   Chances of Surviving Through Specified Life Periods (1976)

From: Age	Event	To: Age	Event	Percent Surviving
Male				
0	Birth	5	School enrollment	98
5	School enrollment	18	Entry into labor force	99
18	Entry into labor force	23	Marriage	99
		65	Retirement	70
23	Marriage	55	Marriage of last child	86
55	Marriage of last child	65	Retirement	81
65	Retirement	75	Ten years past retirement	63
Female				
0	Birth	5	School enrollment	98
5	School enrollment	18	Entry into labor force	99
21	Marriage	30	Birth of last child	99
		61	Husband's retirement	88
23	Birth of first child	53	Marriage of last child	94
30	Birth of last child	61	Husband's retirement	88
61	Husband's retirement	71	Ten years after	85

From Statistical Bulletin of the Metropolitan Life Insurance Co. October-December 1978.

It should be noted that the bias concerning sex roles reflected in the categories chosen for Table 16-4 does not originate from us. In any case, these figures serve to illustrate graphically the portions of the life cycle in which death is more likely to be encountered by men, women, and children. They provide rough estimates of the probability that persons will encounter death during a given period of their lives. Note that the differential mortality between men and women is once again highlighted.

We will review briefly the correlation between age and principle causes of death. In Table 16-5 we reproduce figures taken from *The Statistical Bulletin of the Metropolitan Life Insurance Company* (May, 1980) describing the top five causes of death in each age group for males and females of white and nonwhite groups in the United States during 1977.

Accidents represent the leading cause of death for those below 45 years old, and remain among the top five causes for all age groups. Motor vehicle accidents account for about one-half of all accidental fatalities. Given our cultural shock at untimely death, it is surprising that we are so resistant to traffic safety measures.

Table 16-5 Mortality From Leading Causes of Death in 1977

Age (years)	Cause of Death	Death Rate per 100,000 Population White		Nonwhite	
		Male	Female	Male	Female
1–4	All causes	69.7	55.0	108.1	87.1
	Accidents	29.4	20.8	42.9	30.7
	Congenital anomalies	8.6	8.5	9.7	10.4
	Malignant neoplasms	6.2	4.5	4.6	4.5
	Influenza & pneumonia	2.9	2.3	6.0	4.8
	Homicide	1.9	1.6	8.2	6.3
5–14	All causes	40.6	25.3	52.8	31.0
	Accidents	21.7	10.9	30.8	12.4
	Malignant neoplasms	5.8	3.9	4.8	3.7
	Congenital anomalies	1.9	1.7	1.9	2.2
	Homicide	0.9	0.9	2.9	2.4
	Influenza & Pneumonia	0.9	0.9	1.1	1.2

Table 16-5   (Continued)

| Age (years) | Cause of Death | Death Rate per 100,000 Population | | | |
| | | White | | Nonwhite | |
		Male	Female	Male	Female
15–24	All causes	167.3	57.2	205.1	80.1
	Accidents	101.1	28.3	76.6	20.6
	Suicide	22.9	5.5	15.5	4.0
	Homicide	11.5	3.9	65.5	16.9
	Malignant neoplasms	8.4	4.8	6.4	5.8
	Heart Disease	2.6	1.5	6.5	4.1
25–44	All causes	211.6	104.0	508.9	221.5
	Accidents	62.5	16.5	99.2	20.6
	Heart Disease	35.0	9.8	66.8	30.7
	Malignant neoplasms	26.3	30.3	37.7	39.9
	Homicide	14.2	3.9	109.1	19.7
	Suicide	25.9	10.1	21.7	6.1
45–64	All causes	1259.0	646.6	1956.8	1103.5
	Heart disease	526.9	161.7	623.3	331.3
	Malignant neoplasms	324.7	262.3	487.0	307.4
	Accidents	60.2	22.9	110.8	32.7
	Cerebrovascular disease	50.5	39.1	134.8	103.8
	Cirrhosis of the liver	50.9	23.0	88.1	40.5
65+	All causes	6545.4	4447.0	6218.8	4435.8
	Heart disease	2894.8	1999.9	2331.4	1851.0
	Malignant neoplasms	1330.0	752.1	1414.0	707.6
	Cerebrovascular disease	647.5	655.5	729.4	706.1
	Influenza & pneumonia	214.3	142.3	211.3	108.2
	Accidents	129.6	83.9	146.0	72.3

From the Statistical Bulletin of the Metropolitan Life Insurance Company, April–June 1980.

Table 16-5 emphasizes the prominence of suicide and homicide among the relatively young. It is not until the age of 45 years that neither suicide nor homicide appear in the top five causes of death. We are disturbed to note that homicide is the fifth leading cause of death among children aged one to four years. The cultural implications of this finding are complex and uncertain. It provides strong testimony to the overwhelming stresses encountered by a considerable fraction of those who undertake parenthood. The fact that this statistic is so seldom publicized speaks clearly of the extent to which our society ignores this ugly reality.

Homicide is the fifth leading cause of death among children aged one to four years.

Socioeconomic Status

Introduction

The last issue we will consider concerns the relationship between socioeconomic status and death. Unquestionably, the social and ethnic realities of their lives have a profound influence on both the way Americans live and the way they die.

Specific Instances of Death

A recent example of the effect of socioeconomic status on manner of death among Americans occurred in the summer of 1980 in a broad region crossing the southern United States. Record breaking heat dominated the newscasts for weeks at a time during that summer, and a surprising number of individuals, perhaps over 1000, perished as a consequence of the high temperatures. *Time* magazine (September 1, 1980) quoted figures from the Center for Disease Control showing a total death count of 148 in Kansas City alone. Seventy-two percent of these deaths were among those over 65 years of age, with a median of 73 years of age. Further, when the division of deaths in Kansas City was posted strictly along socioeconomic levels, the death rate was 9.6 per 10,000 in low income districts, as opposed to less than 0.1 per 10,000 in relatively affluent areas.

Rates and Causes of Death

There is an equally striking connection between socioeconomic status and mortality on a much more general level. Data from the Life Tables for 1977 of the National Bureau of Vital Statistics reveal some interesting correlations during this century between race (which is clearly related to socioeconomic status) and mortality. For example, in 1900 the total life expectancy of white men and women was 48.23 and 51.08

years respectively, whereas among nonwhite Americans the expectancies were 32.54 years for men and 35.04 years for women. In 1977, white men could expect to live 70.0 years, and white women survived for 77.7 years on the average. The life expectancy from birth among nonwhites in that year was 64.6 years for men and 73.1 years for women. Although the differences between races in life expectancy have become less prominent during this century, it is still clearly to one's advantage with respect to longevity to be born white.

Citizens of wealthier states live longer than those of poorer ones.

Similar differences persist when we eliminate the issue of race and look strictly at *per capita* income. Lerner and Stutz (1977) examined this question in some detail in their study of mortality in 1960 and 1970. One simple way in which they addressed the issue of the advantages of being wealthier was to look at life expectancies in the ten poorest versus the ten richest states, defined by per capita income, during those years. In 1960, residents of the ten states with the highest per capita income had a mean life expectancy of 70.13 years, as opposed to 68.71 years for those inhabiting the ten poorest states (by this measure). In 1970, the figures were 71.00 years for the highest income states versus 69.39 for those with the lowest per capita income. Further, although everyone's life expectancy increased during that decade, that in the wealthier states increased more than that in the poorer states, further widening the gap with the passage of time.

The relationship between socioeconomic status and mortality is highlighted by the specific causes of death by age as a function of race. We will point out a few of the more arresting differences derived from Table 16-5, in which death rates were shown by causes among various age groups also separated by sex and race.

In 1977, nonwhites aged 25 to 44 years died over twice as frequently as whites of the same ages, and were murdered eight times as often.

We note that only at ages over 65 years did mortality of the white population exceed that of the nonwhite. This figure probably is an artifact of the selective effect of high death rates among nonwhites in all younger age groups. The maximum differential among males occurred in the 25 to 44 year age group; whites died at a rate of 211.6 per 100,000, whereas nonwhites perished at a rate of 508.9 per 100,000. The most striking difference in cause of death for men of this age was in homicide; whites were killed at a rate of 14.2 per 100,000 as compared with a rate of 109.1 per 100,000 for nonwhites. Similar prominent differentials in the homicide rate occurred for both sexes at all ages. If one considers deaths by accident, at every age (excepting women over 65 years), the mortality rates for nonwhites exceeded those among whites. Among deaths caused by diseases, only in the malignant neoplasms did whites exceed the mortality rate for nonwhites, and this applies only to those under 25 years of age. However, the suicide rate was greater among whites of both sexes than it was among nonwhites at every age reported.

Infant and Maternal Mortality

From *The Statistical Bulletin of the Metropolitan Life Insurance Company* (August, 1978), we have the following figures. In 1975, the mortality for white neonates was 10.0 per 1000 live births, and 3.7 per 1000 for white infants. In the same year, the corresponding figures among nonwhites were 16.5 for those under 1 month of age, and 7.3 for those aged 1 month to 1 year. In 1965, white children died at a rate of 15.8 per 1000 and 5.2 per 1000 for those under 1 month and 1 year respectively, compared to 25.1 and 14.4 per 1000 respectively for nonwhites. Thus, death rates decreased 37% for white, as opposed to 34% for nonwhite, neonates; and 29% contrasted with 49% for white versus nonwhite infants, respectively. Here, at least, the advances seem to be roughly parallel.

Maternal mortality rates reflect the influence of race on mortality perhaps as much as any figures we have examined. The Life Tables of the United States Bureau of Vital Statistics for 1961 highlight figures divided according to race from 1915 to 1961, and we reproduce some of their data in what follows. In 1915, white women died by causes related to childbirth at a rate of 700.3 per 100,000, as opposed to a rate of 1253.3 for nonwhites. By 1961, these rates had declined to 24.9 per 100,000 for whites, and 101.3 per 100,000 for nonwhites. Thus, nonwhite maternal mortality rates during World War I were less than twice that of whites. In contrast, by 1960 the nonwhite maternal death rate was over four times that of whites. These figures negate rather sharply the notion that the gaps in health care and mortality between those of higher socioeconomic status and those of lower are closing on every front.

References

Lerner, M. 1970. When, why, and where people die. In Schneidman, E. S. ed. *Death: Current Perspectives*. Palo Alto: Mayfield Publishing Co. p 87–106.

Lerner, M. and Stutz, R. 1977. Have we narrowed the gaps between the poor and the nonpoor? *Medical Care*, 15:620–625.

McKeown, T. 1965. *Medicine in Modern Society*. London: George Allen and Unwin.

The first third of this book is suggested primarily for those interested in a more comprehensive historical analysis of the causes and consequences of past improvements in health. Although the statistics deal with a British population, the conclusions are broadly applicable in the United States.

Statistical Bulletins of the Metropolitan Life Insurance Company. September, 1977, August and November, 1978, and May, 1980.

"Victims of Heat." *Time*, September 1, 1980, p. 55.

United States Bureau of Vital Statistics Life Tables. 1961, 1969-1971, 1977, and 1979.

17 Cultural Considerations Surrounding Death

Brief Contents

Overview

We now turn to a brief survey of some sociocultural issues concerning death in America. First, we look at current mainstream cultural patterns affecting the dying. Then we will review major subcultural variants on these patterns. Our aim in this chapter is to round out our presentation of various ways in which society contributes to the context of terminal care.

Mainstream Cultural Patterns

Reinforcement of Denial

Denial often seems to be our culture's major tactic for coping with death, and may be tacit, overt, or anywhere between these extremes. We begin by examining common manifestations of this phenomenon.

Sequestration of the aged, ill, and dying reinforces the denial of death.

An important and obvious sociocultural reinforcement of the denial of death may be found in the sequestration of the aging, ill, and dying. The decline of the extended family has paralleled a decrease in the amount of contact that children, for example, usually have with aged or dying family members. Although visits with grandparents are anticipated gleefully by all involved, youngsters often are isolated from the day-to-day realities of aging and infirmity. There has been an increasing movement toward the establishment of elaborate retirement communities whose residents are limited to the elderly. Finally, there is a rising prevalence of reliance on institutional as opposed to familial care for those who are acutely moribund or disabled by their advancing age.

The net result of these developments is an effective isolation of the aged from the rest of the population. This undoubtedly contributes to our cultural discomfort with age, infirmity, and illness. We suspect that it also reflects the basic tendency of American society to turn a blind eye toward the reminders of inescapable demise that come with daily contact with the aged and dying. For, as we have experienced directly in the course of our work in terminal care settings, it is hard to work closely with the terminally ill and avoid entirely the reality of one's own death.

American culture reinforces denial of death by emphasizing maintenance of at least the appearance of youth. (3)

Another rather obvious manifestation of the pervasive cultural denial of death is apparent in our scrupulous efforts to avoid as much as possible the appearance of deterioration. Products and services advertised in the various media highlight the emphasis on maintenance of an appearance of youth quite literally at any cost. The amount of money spent by Americans on cosmetic preparations and devices, specialized clothing, and even elaborate and painful cosmetic surgery surely extends well into the billions of dollars. This contrasts sharply with more traditional societies in which age is associated with honor rather than shame, and is less likely to be concealed.

Religious beliefs about death are often misused in support of maintaining denial.

Although religion often affords a comforting and constructive bulwark against death anxiety, societal discomfort with death is also apparent in the misuse of religious beliefs regarding death. An example is the telling of pseudoreligious stories to children when they inquire about death. Most commonly, adults display a much greater certainty than they actually feel in describing the ways in which the dead person or pet is not really dead at all. Nominally, this sort of story telling is intended to comfort children and to spare them anxiety or nightmares. We suspect that its real motivation lies often in a sort of "whistling past the churchyard" on the part of the adult. Children generally will sense the grownup's underlying uncertainty and anxiety surrounding the topic. Simple explanations that clearly do not even satisfy the individual offering them are likely to engender confusion and mistrust. The topic thereby becomes further shrouded in mystery and ambiguity, and the child is tacitly encouraged to perpetuate the denial. If the dead person isn't really dead after all, then why is everyone so upset?

Funeral customs often support the denial of death as well.

Some of the specifics of mainstream American funeral customs seem particularly aimed at the denial of death. Professional jargon and techniques common throughout the funeral industry stand as evidence for this phenomenon. The corpse is assiduously prepared to look as lifelike as is technically possible, often with results that border on the ludicrous. Whatever she looked like for most her life, when in her coffin she is likely to appear well groomed and in the pink of smiling good health. Further, before her funeral her body is likely to undergo a period of "repose" in a well appointed "slumber room." The possibilities for parody are almost endless, as demonstrated by Waugh (1948) in *The Loved One.* Funeral practices appear dedicated to the preservation of the deception that death is not really death at all. Surely Death can be defeated—at least in appearance—by the miracles of modern cosmetology.

Cultural emphasis on material rather than humanistic or spiritual values reinforces the denial of death.

The rather striking focus of American culture on material as opposed to human or spiritual values is subtly related to the denial of death. Intense concentration on appearances and material acquisition might be interpreted as the construction of an elaborate rampart between each individual and the cold reality of worldly transience. The frenetic intensity with which we go about amassing material wealth speaks rather strongly to the fundamental nature of the drives underlying it. Conversely, patients who accept impending death often turn away from mundane preoccupations to focus on interpersonal and spiritual concerns.

Negative Reactions to Acute Grief

The manner in which the adaptation to a loss is facilitated by a society is often a direct indication of its basic attitude toward death. Clearly, current mainstream American cultural tendencies surrounding grief and mourning have a profound bearing on terminal care. Some have a negative effect and others assist in the tasks of assimilating a death.

Many professionals expect, but fail to support, expression of strong feelings by the acutely bereaved. (14)

Most Americans seem to expect strong expression of intense feelings by the acutely bereaved. Relatively few, however, seem to know how to provide human comfort while still supporting the emotional process. The personal uneasiness reflected in this common sense of inadequacy extends to health care professionals, whose role is particularly crucial given the increasing prevalence of death in institutional settings. One sadly common reaction of health care team members faced with powerful expressions of the emotions of acute grief is evidenced by the following case illustration.

CASE ILLUSTRATION

There occurred at a prominent Northeastern hospital a particularly tragic death of a young man. The new widow began to clutch at the body of her dead husband and to cry quite loudly, both of which constitute common and expected acute reactions in such a setting. An older nurse approached the scene with a loaded syringe held behind her back, and asked the obviously nonplussed intern at the bedside for permission to sedate the grieving woman. After some argument among the staff, the woman was indeed sedated and the decorum of the ward safely restored.

In assessing appropriate interventions in cases such as this, clinicians must weigh potential effects on other patients against those on the bereaved (see Chapter 8). Perhaps too often, as in this example, it is the bereaved who are not allowed a helpful catharsis, albeit to relieve the temporary discomfort of others. As a consequence, the acutely grieving may not receive the fundamental support that clinicians can provide by close contact and empathic reflection of their loss and the feelings generated by it. Instead, the bereaved frequently are greeted by reactions that mirror the discomfort of their companions. They may be encouraged not to cry, to pull themselves together, and to be brave and keep a *stiff upper lip*. Well meaning onlookers may attempt to provide consolation with religiously based reassurances that the dead person is not really lost at all, but only awaits them in Heaven. Frequently, such interventions interfere with the vital grieving process. Given the painful nature of that undertaking and the common resistance to engaging in it, we suspect that such diversions actually may lead to long-term pathology in some instances.

Uneven Support for Grief and Mourning

Grieving is assisted by congregation of the support community around the bereaved.

On the other hand, a number of phenomena that support the grieving process take place in mainstream American society immediately following a death. One of these is the congregation of extended family and friends around the immediate family. If anyone doubts the truly social nature of human beings, this reaction of a sociological unit to the loss of one of its members should help to dispel such notions. When we are painfully confronted with our relative finitude and fragility, we tend most often to seek solace in congregation with those who are meaningful to us. It is as if we need to reassure ourselves of a sense of communal continuity in spite of the loss.

Gifts of food are very often brought by those who gather around in such times, in what may reflect a modern translation of very archaic symbols of life and regeneration. Children frequently are excluded from such gatherings on the grounds that this will protect them in some way. This is unfortunate in that their presence often can provide both youngsters and oldsters with solace. Once again, this probably is related to a fundamental reassurance that in spite of the acute loss, the species will persist. In any case, this gathering of a support community is likely to persist from the time of death to a few days after the funeral has taken place.

One potentially untoward consequence of this usually supportive social reaction to a recent death is related to the bereaved persons' frequent inclination to provide generous hospitality. If those who gather around are not sensitive to the need to grieve, the bereaved may occupy themselves totally in caring for their guests. We have had a number of patients who actually felt relieved when the funeral was over, the flood of visitors had gone, and the condolences had diminished. Then they could get on with their own emotional processes. To be sure, such chores sometimes provide a welcome distraction from the painful work of grieving. All too often, however, they clutter a critical period with relative trivialities.

Cultural tolerance of grief is exhausted rapidly.

Within a week or so of a death, in the majority of American families all but the closest relatives have returned to their usual lives. The chief mourners are left relatively alone with their grief. Our cultural tolerance of the grieving process is rapidly exhausted, and a rather sharp reduction in support from its initial level generally takes place.

Although there may exist a degree of acceptance of the persistence of overt evidences of mourning among close family members for a few weeks, this too tends to subside after the first month. Beyond this period, the bereaved tend to encounter ever more messages that the time has arrived for them to *get on with living*. Failure to heed these messages can result in the withdrawal of those who were formerly close. This, in turn, tends further to reinforce the sense of abandonment and isolation that is common among mourners.

Lack of a Defined Mourning Period

The lack of a clearly defined mourning period hinders the completion of this process.

Many of these problems may reflect the lack of any clearly defined, acceptable grieving period in our polymorphous culture. This, combined with the pervasive societal denial of death, encourages mourners to withdraw from bereavement as soon as possible after the customary immediate rituals. We may begin to avoid those who continue to display evidences of their grief for longer than a month, although we may feel uneasy about doing so. This avoidance is often an attempt to escape unpleasant feelings aroused in us by the mourner.

Our culture clearly possesses mechanisms for dealing with the death of its members in the short term, but these patterns lose definition within a few weeks. In support of the view of mainstream American culture as primarily death-denying, little structure is provided for longer-term coping with death. Almost as though in response to direct cultural pressures, the majority of us are most comfortable to get on with the business of consumption and acquisition as soon as possible. We make as hasty an exit from the field as we can, perhaps in hopes that the dead will bury themselves (at least psychologically).

Shift to Institutional Death

Significant changes in the location of death have taken place since the turn of the century, and clearly have important implications for those who care for the terminally ill. Indeed, the location in which a given individual dies is bound to have a profound impact on the experience of everyone concerned. Reliable data for recent years concerning this topic are difficult to obtain. In part this is because compilers of national mortality statistics apparently do not recognize the importance of these figures in guiding health policy.

In 1900, only 20% of deaths took place in institutions, whereas today nearly 80% do. (5, 13)

In 1900, over 80% of deaths took place at home. Although national data are not available for the period since 1959, some local data are. Specifically, in New York City the mortality records for the period from 1955 to 1967 show a steady change from about 30% of deaths at home and 66% in institutions in 1955 to under 25% of deaths in the home and over 73% in institutions in 1967 (Lerner, 1970). As regards the national picture, these figures are undoubtedly skewed (for example, in 1959 69% of deaths in New York City took place in institutions, as opposed to around 61% nationally). However, they probably reflect the national trend over that period rather well. Thus, we estimate that between 70% and 80% of all current deaths in this country occur in institutional settings.

The percent of deaths in American institutions in 1958 for each of the top ten causes of death as reported by Lerner (1970) allow us to infer a number of issues relevant to terminal care. First, it is notable that a high percentage of deaths from the chronic diseases, which now account for most American deaths, occurred in institutions. Second, we emphasize the relationship of the reversal of the location of death from homes to institutions during this century to widespread cultural attitudes toward death. Lack of routine exposure to any aspect of life is likely to contribute to a general discomfort with it. The shift of the place in which people die from private homes to institutions probably has contributed significantly to the separation of death and the dying from the mainstream of life. It is unclear whether this change is a causal factor in or a reflection of our cultural discomfort with death. In either case, the close relationship of the two phenomena is unquestionable.

The shift from dying at home to dying in an institution has often adversely affected terminal care. (16)

Further, this relocation of death into unusual and intimidating settings promotes a general attitude that death itself is something alien and terrifying. Additional reinforcement of peoples' inability to deal gracefully with death is nearly inevitable. Also, if hospitals and chronic health care insitutions are the places where most people go to die, then for many these places and those who work in them become identified with the anxiety-provoking spectre of death. As a result, death-related tension can have a negative effect on willingness to seek medical care or to involve oneself with the health care system even when terminal illness is not in question (see Chapter 9).

The reasons for this shift toward death in institutions are difficult to ascertain with certainty. Prominent among them must rank the dissolution during this century of the traditional extended family. Even the nuclear family is becoming rarer as divorce rates continue to climb. Further, rapidly increasing mobility within our culture has made it considerably less likely that many members of a given family will even reside in the same state, let alone under the same roof. Finally, the current move toward work outside the home for the majority of American women who traditionally have been the caretakers for those family members requiring care at home also contributes to this equation.

Relatively few families have the personal or financial resources to support aging or terminally ill members in their homes. As long as these trends continue to predominate, it is likely that the majority of deaths will take place in institutional settings. Thus, the task for those involved in the management of terminal illness is to search for ways to optimize the experience of patients and family members within the less than ideal environments prevailing in most institutions.

Major Subcultural Practices

Introduction

There is a striking lack of scientific literature on American subcultural practices regarding death. A prominent exception is a book by Kalish and Reynolds (1976). In this work, they report the results of field surveys of over 400 individuals, including about 100 each of Black Americans, Mexican Americans, Japanese Americans, and White Americans. The sample population was evenly divided between male and female. Subjects were relatively evenly distributed between the ages of 20 and 70 years (mean age was 47 years). All subjects resided in the Los Angeles area. Careful attempts were made to compensate for socioeconomic status while still maintaining representativeness within each group.

In what follows, we will review findings from this and other sources regarding Black Americans, Mexican Americans, and other less numerous groups including Jewish Americans and Native Americans. Finally, we will mention briefly some religious groups whose attitudes or practices surrounding medical care or death differ significantly from those of the mainstream population.

Black Americans

Most black families have been on this continent longer than the average white family.

Black Americans are a people whose roots lie in the soil of a different continent, and yet who most often have been in this country for more generations than the average white. Cultural anthropologists have developed two schools of thought regarding the relevance of African attitudes to an understanding of American Blacks. One faction notes the brutal and systematic way in which families and tribal groups were dispersed upon transport of slaves to this continent, as well as during the centuries of residence in this country for many black families. They conclude that African cultures are much less relevant than patterns that developed in America. The other side contends that in spite of the above adversity, African culture still pervades black consciousness at profound levels. They hold that these roots have persisted across the generations to influence strongly current black attitudes and beliefs.

African cultural patterns around death are strikingly diverse.

We will make no effort to take sides in this argument, recognizing full well when we are out of our depth. However, a practical issue enters the picture at this point. A probe of the anthropologic literature for pan-African patterns regarding death reveals a striking diversity in attitudes between both different geographic divisions and different tribes within a given region. We do not doubt that African roots may profoundly influence the attitudes of individual Black Americans toward death. We have, however, found no clearly African-based patterns that are broad enough to warrant presentation here. Thus, we will concentrate primarily on events since the arrival of blacks on this continent.

For slaves, death could be a liberator.

The first clear influence on the experience of blacks in America is their initial role as slaves. For a slave, death can come to be equated with freedom, as the lines of an old spiritual reflect: ". . . and before I'll be a slave, I'll be buried in my grave, and go down to the Lord and be free." Thus, to some extent, death was not simply an intruder, but had the potential to be a liberator.

Blacks are more likely to have encountered death than their white counterparts.

A related factor, the high prevalence of violence and sudden death, has been present for Black Americans for many generations (see Chapter 15). Not only have the causes of their deaths been slanted toward violence and acute infections for many years, but blacks have had shorter lives than whites in this country. Thus, as the Kalish study reflects, Black Americans are more likely to have encountered death than their white counterparts. This may have led to blacks' realization that death is a concrete possibility for any given individual at any particular moment. In turn, the result may have been their more graceful adjustment to death as a result of a greater familiarity.

The correlation of poverty with inferior medical care and higher levels of violent crime also make death a more common occurrence among the poor. Figures from the United States Census Bureau make it clear that Black Americans are indeed at a socioeconomic disadvantage to whites, both in income and education. Poverty must affect black attitudes toward death, but its specific role is difficult to distinguish.

Blacks find more comfort in religion, fear death less, want more to know if they are dying, and grieve more openly than mainstream whites.

Kalish and Reynolds (1976) observed a number of fairly prevalent attitudes among their black population. They found that the blacks in their sample were significantly more religious than their white counterparts. Further, blacks also rated themselves as significantly more likely to find comfort in their religion in the face of death. Religious rituals surrounding death were considerably more elaborate in the black community than among whites, and were regarded as important and helpful by those who engaged in them. Further, blacks rated themselves as more likely to turn to religious figures for support and comfort during grief than to rely on family members. This group of Black Americans valued their lives highly, and expected to live a long life regardless of demographic realities. They demonstrated a lower overt fear of death than their white counterparts, and were more likely to regard their own death as unimportant in the grand scheme of things. The blacks in this study quite clearly wanted to know about their impending death if that knowledge was available. Further, they felt that people in general should be told if they were dying. They grieved more openly than whites, and reported getting more comfort from that process.

Hispanic Americans

Another American subculture often encountered by clinicians in many areas of the country is that which speaks Spanish. Whereas Puerto Ricans and Cubans probably constitute the majority of this group on the East Coast and in Florida, throughout the Southwest and West the bulk of the Hispanic population is of Mexican descent. Further, the major portion of our own clinical experience and of the systematic studies we have seen are based primarily in the Mexican American population. Thus, we will focus on that subgroup (which numerically is the most nationally prevalent) in what follows.

Spanish-speaking Americans descend from a diverse group of native cultures, and have disparate attitudes toward death.

A look at the original American roots of Hispanics in this country reveals a large diversity of native cultures from which present day Spanish-speaking Americans are descended. Thus, their attitudes toward death are likely to be fairly disparate. Any generalizations which can be made are approximate, and offer at best a guide for issues about which health care professionals should be sensitive.

Given these disclaimers, there do seem to be some patterns among Hispanic Americans that are significant. First, there is a rather sharp socioeconomic class demarcation regarding attitudes toward death both within Latin American countries and in the United States. The upper classes' attitudes toward death are much like those of most other Americans. They engage in similar levels of denial and avoidance as are practiced in our cultural mainstream. It is only as we move away from the monied classes that the influences of native heritage become more evident. Among lower socioeconomic groups in Latin American countries, as well as among recent immigrants from these groups in this country, there is a strikingly more accepting attitude toward death than there is in the United States mainstream.

Mexican Americans are more accepting of and involved in deaths and mourning.

The Kalish and Reynolds study found a basic acceptance of the reality of death among their Mexican American subjects. This bordered at times on fatalism, which was in contrast to the other groups surveyed. Those Mexican Americans they interviewed had strong feelings about death, and expressed a powerful sense of involvement in the deaths and mourning of those in their community. This cohort had the strongest extended family ties of any of the ethnic groups studied. There was clearly a more pervasive intergenerational influence and continuity. Mexican Americans in this study tended to rely centrally on the Catholic church for ritual reactions to death. For emotional support, however, they were much more likely to turn to family members than to any nonfamilial organizations. They were also relatively comfortable with the inclusion of children under 10 years of age in deathbed gatherings.

Mexican Americans rely on the Catholic Church for ritual, and the family for emotional support.

The Mexican Americans in this study were less likely than any group to want to be told about a terminal illness, and were also unlikely to feel bound to communicate such information to a loved one. However, a significant proportion of this group still wanted to know if they were dying. There was a strong aversion among Mexican Americans toward disturbance of a body after death, and a particularly negative attitude toward autopsies.

Mexican Americans want less to know if they are dying, and do not like autopsies.

There was considerable encouragement for immediate discharge of feelings regarding a death among this population. This may be reflected in our own clinical observations of less grief pathology among Mexican Americans than occurs in the general population. Funerals and mourning seemed to be strong family symbols among this group, and tended to be quite elaborate and well attended.

In summary, the strength of family ties and the vitality of family support seemed to be the most important factor in the Mexican Americans studied by Kalish and Reynolds. It is important for those working in terminal care settings to be aware of this, and to be sensitive to any messages that they may be intruding on an established and effective support system.

Jewish Americans

Jewish funeral practice is specified by religious law.

Jewish Americans have a particularly well developed and specific ritualization of grief and mourning defined by the religious laws of Judaism. These begin with the arrangements after the death itself, and include prohibitions against disturbing the body (unless required by civil law) beyond ritual cleaning and dressing by designated religious groups. Bodies generally are supposed to be buried as soon as possible after death, although there is some flexibility to allow for travel time for close relatives. Open coffins are discouraged in the Talmud, as is cremation or any other disposal of a body except earth burial.

Jewish grief and mourning are bounded by specific rituals during a one year mourning period.

Once the prescribed rituals of death and burial are complete, a seven day period of full mourning termed *"shiva"* is initiated. During this time no activities except those necessary to sustain health are permitted. Visits from friends are strongly encouraged after the first few days, but there are specific recommendations against empty condolences. After the seven days of full mourning, a one month period of partial mourning ensues in which joyous celebration is proscribed, but wherein work and life begin to resume. For a year following a death, specific prayers are said each Sabbath by mourners, and at the end of that year the tombstone is ceremonially unveiled. This unveiling marks the official end of the mourning period, and there are injunctions against continued grief past that point. This ritualization of the process of grief and mourning provides a complete and clearcut structure that is lacking in mainstream American culture.

Native Americans

Great differences in death attitudes and practices exist between various Native American tribes.

Among Native Americans, once again the cultural differences between tribes are great enough to make generalizations hazardous. Some tribes demonstrate the same accepting attitudes toward death as do Latin

Americans. Others are so profoundly uncomfortable with death that they actually abandon a house or building in which a death has taken place (which leads to particular problems regarding, for example, hospitals). When caring for Native Americans in terminal care situations clinicians must be particularly sensitive to the cues they receive from patients and families. Those who are willing to inquire openly when confused are unlikely to go too far astray.

Religious Groups

A principal reason for discussing American religious subgroups here is that certain prominent denominations differ significantly enough from the mainstream that professionals may run into problems if they are not aware of this.

Mormons derive strong support from their church communities, who often discourage active mourning.

One significant population group in which this may be the case consists of the adherents to The Church of Latter Day Saints, or *Mormons*. In our experience, one distinguishing feature of this group is an impressively strong general support community within the church for virtually all of its members. Coupled with this is an expectation that members will turn toward that community for support, rather than toward outside agents such as medical professionals. Further, the belief in an afterlife is so strongly advocated by church members that some Mormons are actively discouraged from mourning, as the deceased person is not regarded as truly lost. Alert clinicians should be aware, however, that Mormon patients or family members may benefit from a private opportunity to ventilate the emotions of grief. Our own observation is that bereaved Mormons who show little, if any, evidence of grief are not particularly prone to grief pathology. This speaks at least in part to the value of a strong support community.

Two other religious groups are mentioned in this context because of particular beliefs they hold about medical care in general. The first of these are members of the *Jehovah's Witness* church, who observe what they interpret to be a strict Biblical prohibition against blood transfusions. The second are the *Christian Scientists*, who have more widespread prohibitions against standard medical interventions. The issues surrounding the right to refuse care are both legally and ethically complex, and we will not attempt to broach them here. Rather, we call the attention of health care professionals to these groups to remind them that special dilemmas may arise when their patients follow these beliefs. In such situations, early communications on the limits of treatment or intervention are particularly vital. This will increase the probability of arriving at some plan of action which is acceptable to all involved.

Need for Cultural Sensitivity

The need for clinicians to be sensitive to cultural predilections regarding death cannot be overemphasized.

An important lesson deriving from our examination of sociocultural issues is that it is often difficult to anticipate how any individual will react when faced with death. Cultural differences between patients and professionals, however, increase the likelihood that the needs of patients and families will differ from the clinician's expectations. The wise professional will avoid assumptions as much as possible, will inquire of patients and families when there is any doubt, and will be as sensitive as possible to the prevailing emotional climate. In this way, the interests of patients, families, and clinicians are likely to be served best.

References

Fox, R. C. ed. 1980. The social meaning of death. *Annals of the American Academy of Political and Social Science* 447:1–101.

Although this book is copyrighted 1980, its contents largely represent the thinking of the 1960s. Nevertheless, it contains an important series of essays by physicians, ethicists, historians, and others who deal with the various sociocultural aspects of the "rediscovery of death." More questions are raised than answered, but it is made clear that attitudes of health care practitioners are changing. We recommend this volume to people interested in terminal care.

Kalish, R. and Reynolds, D. 1976. *Death and Ethnicity.* Los Angeles: University of Southern California Press.

A well designed comparative field survey of death attitudes and practices among Black, Mexican, Japanese, and White Americans residing near Los Angeles. The findings are clearly presented and carefully interpreted. Problems entailed in the research are also well described, making the project a valuable guide for those undertaking similar studies.

Lerner, M. 1970. When, why, and where people die. In Brim, O. G., Freeman, H. E., Levin, S. and Scotch, A. eds. *The Dying Patient.* New York: Russell Sage Foundation.

Riemer, J. 1974. *Jewish Reflections on Death.* New York: Schocken Books, Inc.

An outstanding series of essays focused on death-related traditions and rituals derived from Judaic Law. The value to the bereaved of expressions stemming from ancient rituals is dealt with most sensitively.

Waugh, E. 1948. *The Loved One*. Boston: Little, Brown & Co.

A hilariously satirical caricature of Hollywood funerary customs that highlights the seamy side of the funeral industry. When combined with Mitford's exposé, presents a scathing indictment of American funeral practices.

Epilogue

We began this book with four very personal accounts of experiences with terminal care. We ended with a survey of demographic and cultural patterns relating to death. In between, we presented theoretical concepts, strategies for interpersonal communication, and clinical information basic to the care of the dying and their families.

At this point, we suggest that the reader return to the case studies with which we began. A number of readers have found that they "read" rather differently with the perspective of the entire book behind them. We hope that they help drive home the message of this work. Finally, our greatest hope is that we have provided a practical approach to care that may help make dying a more humane, rich, and graceful experience: a dignified dying.

Afterword

Dying Dignified: The Health Professional's Guide to Care is a highly polished mirror reflecting honestly and accurately the scenes that occur many times each day during the course of terminal illnesses in America. It is written in a helpful, well-balanced, and nonjudgmental manner. It contains many practical suggestions pertaining to the difficult problem of achieving a proper balance between emotionally supportive and medically therapeutic approaches to the treatment of patients stricken with mortal illnesses.

The authors clearly espouse the philosophy of Joseph Fletcher, that in the many ethically complex decisions arising in the course of terminal care, the answers always must aspire toward the most loving solution to whatever therapeutic problems are presented.

The facts and messages of this work are much needed by those who care for dying persons and their families. I have practiced medicine for over forty-five years, and have found that the book already has aided me. I have no doubt that others involved in the care of terminally ill patients will find it extremely useful as well.

Readers of this book will be better prepared to help dying persons to live their final days, weeks, and months as free men and women. Further, those who take these insights to heart should be enabled to aid people confronting death to do so with as much dignity as possible.

Louis Shattuck Baer, M.D.
Professor Emeritus of Internal Medicine
Stanford University School of Medicine
Stanford, California

Name Index

Adams, P., 185, 191
Aisenberg, R., 30, 44ar
Alsop, S., 92ar
American Cancer Society, 168
Anderson, W. E., 203
Anthony, E., 191-192ar
Aries, P., 34, 44
Authier, J., 69, 76ar

Baer, L. S., 109ar, 300
Balint, M., 109ar
Barton, D., 21ar, 249
Bednarski, N., 15
Benjamin, B., 174
Bernal, P., 109
Blank, G., 29
Blank, R., 29
Bloom, V. L., 129
Bok, S., 58ar
Bowen, M., 228, 231
Bowlby, J., 38, 39, 44, 162, 192
Brim, O. G., 298
Brisell, E., 11
Brody, H., 143ar

Note: ar indicates annotated
    reference.

Broughton, P., 2
Brown, B. W., 128
Brown, C. R., 128

Cadden, V., 92ar
California Medical Association,
    206, 212ar
California, State of, 109, 133, 143
Caplan, G., 92ar
Carr, A. C., 129ar, 143ar, 159ar,
    174ar
Castaneda, C., 43, 44
Childers, P., 181, 192
Choron, J., 31, 44
Cohen, K. P., 212ar
Consumers' Union, 269ar
Continental Association of
    Funeral Directors and
    Memorial Societies, 158
Corby, J., 98, 109
Crapo, L., 256, 258, 259, 270ar

Davidson, G. W., 137, 143
De Vaul, R. A., 230, 231
Donne, J., 30
Dorpat, T. L., 197, 203
Durkheim, E., 28, 44

Edwards, L., 249

Fagerhaugh, S., 128ar
Farberow, N. L., 28, 194, 203,
    203ar
Federal Trade Commission, 267,
    269
Feifel, H., 28, 238, 249
Finer, B., 121, 128
Fletcher, J., 300
Forrest, W. H., Jr., 119, 121, 128
Fox, R. C., 297ar
Frederick, C. J., 194, 203
Freeman, H. E., 298
Freud, S., 28, 38, 44ar
Friedel, R. O., 129
Fries, J., 256, 258, 259, 270ar

Gibson, C. D., v-vi
Garfield, C. A., 59ar, 231
Gershon, S., 121, 128
Glaser, B. G., 58, 59, 109ar, 112,
    128, 184, 192, 223, 231
Glick, I. O., 162, 173
Gonda, T. A., 117, 128, 206
Grobstein, R., 192

Subject Index